Date Due

NOV 8 '72			
JAN 2 1973			
FEB 8 1973			
APR 3 1973			
SEP 4 — 1980			
JY 9 '86			
JY 24 '91			
FE 25 '01			
AP 06 '01			
NO 20 '02			
JY 29 '03			
JY 29 '03			
AP 07 '15			
AU 1 0 '21			

W9-AKB-239

921
Mi

10,413

Miller, Robin
Flying nurse

EAU CLAIRE DISTRICT LIBRARY

FLYING NURSE

+
610.73

m

FLYING NURSE

ROBIN MILLER

WITHDRAWN

EAU CLAIRE DISTRICT LIBRARY

TAPLINGER PUBLISHING COMPANY
NEW YORK

Baker and Jayen - 9/26/72 - $5.50

10,413

74860

First published in the United States in 1972 by
TAPLINGER PUBLISHING CO., INC.
New York, New York

Copyright © 1971 by Robin Miller
All rights reserved

No part of this publication may be reproduced or transmitted in any form or by any means, electronic or
mechanical, including photocopy, recording, or any
information storage and retrieval system now known or
to be invented, except by a reviewer who wishes to quote
brief passages in connection with a review written for
inclusion in a magazine, newspaper or broadcast

Library of Congress Catalog Card Number: 70-174244

ISBN 0-8008-2892-5

Printed in Hong Kong

DEDICATED

to

my father, Horrie Miller

a veteran of aviation

and to

the memory of my sister, Juliana

who remains with me in spirit wherever I may fly

CONTENTS

ILLUSTRATIONS

Map showing the areas of Western Australia covered by the author when she was flying to country centres and to outback stations and camps to administer Sabin poliomyelitis vaccine.

KALUMBURU
GIBB RIVER
WYNDHAM
KUNUNURRA
ARGYLE
ORD RIVER
CAPE LEVEQUE
LOMBADINA
BEAGLE BAY
DERBY
GLENROY
BROOME
LEOPOLD DOWNS
HALLS CRK.
NOONKANBAH
FLORA VALLEY
BILLILUNA
BALGO
PORT HEDLAND
MT. GOLDSWORTHY
DAMPIER
ROEBOURNE
MARBLE BAR
ONSLOW
OON'S MOB
WITTENOOM
EXMOUTH
BAY OF REST
MT. TOM PRICE
JIGALONG MISSION
MUNDIWINDI
MINNIE CRK.
CARNARVON
GASCOYNE JN.
DIRK
HARTOG IS.
DENHAM
USELESS LOOP
MEEKATHARRA
WILUNA
MT. MAGNET
GERALDTON
KALGOORLIE
PERTH
RAVENSTHORPE
ALBANY
ESPERANCE

VACCINATION ROUNDS ——— FLYING DOCTOR BASES ‑‑‑‑‑

DERBY (VIC SECTION)
PT. HEDLAND
CARNARVON } (W.A. SECTION)
MEEKATHARRA
KALGOORLIE (EAST GOLDFIELDS SECTION)

1
URGENT MEDICAL FLIGHT

"THERE'S BEEN A BAD SMASH UP AT GERALDTON," SAYS A FAMILIAR voice over the telephone. "Two stretcher cases to be flown down. Can you be in the air within thirty minutes?"

"Yes," I say, and replace the receiver. My two bags are always packed ready to go, one with odds and ends including emergency rations, medical supplies and flares, the other with maps and flight plans made out for almost any airstrip in Western Australia. No need to leave a note for Mum. She's used to my coming and going at all hours and she'd ring the Flying Doctor Service if she wanted to know my whereabouts.

The duck that my young brother raised from a chick, and which now rewards him with eggs, quacks disconsolately as I hurry past her to my car. No time now to turn over flower-pots in search of worms, an occupation which is, from Duck's view-point, my role in life. A minute after receiving the late afternoon emergency call I am backing out of the garden into the sleepy suburban street, past houses that even in my memory have supplanted the virgin bush where we made "cubbies" and gathered wildflowers in the spring.

My father bought our Nedlands block near Perth's Swan River

1

in 1934, when he came to the West from South Australia to open the MacRobertson Miller Air Service in which he was partner. He and Mother were married in 1938 and soon afterwards built the house in which I spent most of my childhood. It kept on growing with the family, as did the garden which Dad, in competition with a neighbouring friend, filled with a quite improbable variety of trees and shrubs. Dad must have won this game but his victory was an expensive one, for from the time the trees grew to maturity a constant succession of plumbers has gleefully demonstrated the drain-blocking habits of their enterprising roots.

As I join the city-bound traffic, one level of my thoughts intent on the road, I speculate on what might lie ahead. That telephone message from headquarters could mean almost anything. The accidents with which the Flying Doctor has to deal today are seldom of the simple outback type of former times—a fall or a kick from a horse, a wound from the horn of an angry bull, the result of an Aboriginal argument with nulla-nullas and spears, the side effects of ritual circumcision carried out with a rusty razor blade or a piece of broken bottle.

Nowadays the majority of cases tends to be more sophisticated. Men's familiarity with the mechanical slaves that exploit the earth's hidden wealth often breeds a disastrous contempt, and many accidents are those in which soft human flesh and brittle bones have tangled with machinery. There are falls from oil-rigs and hands crushed in gears, sometimes terrible burns caused by electrical faults or explosions.

And then, of course, there are the motor accidents—often the worst and somehow the most meaningless. Unlike the mishaps suffered in the course of a day's work, many of these seem to have been incurred almost deliberately, as though men today, in some abstruse test of courage, take to the road like gladiators to the arena.

Western Australia's primary airport is Perth International at Guildford, whence portly jets lumber off to Sydney or Singapore and loudspeakers herd mobs of passengers like yapping dogs manoeuvring sheep. Jandakot, out of which I operate, is a sort of working man's airfield. Many of its several hundred aircraft are engaged on workhorse flights and bread-and-butter missions such as crop dusting, newspaper delivery runs, general charter,

2

special charter for mineral prospecting teams and flight training organisations. At weekends it hums like a beehive with industrious amateurs who fly for fun and with visitors hoping to witness a "crash."

To those associated with flying, each machine comes to assume an almost human character; a combination of its type, colour, name and history, the area it covers, the sort of work it does and the person who flies it. Even human class distinctions apply to these aircraft "types." The veterans and the sleek new models rate as "top drawer," while the rest assume appropriate places down the social scale.

Jandakot feels like home to me, I suppose because I've spent so much time around aerodromes for as long as I can remember. Flying has always been a part of my life. A wartime baby, I was born with the sound of aircraft thundering overhead as American Catalinas came home to roost on the nearby reaches of the river Swan. During the war years Dad, driving a green Chevrolet with a gas producer bulging from the back, used often to take me with my sisters, Patsy and Julie, to the Guildford aerodrome. I knew that he was somehow connected with planes and the god-like young men who flew them. His face, as his eyes scanned the sky for aircraft or watched them landing and taking off, implied that they were "fun things" that must also be taken very seriously. I think I decided, even then, that they must delight and involve me too. And so they have, from that time to this.

On arrival at Jandakot I file the flight plan headed "Urgent Medical," which gives priority to proceed directly through controlled airspace instead of possibly having to divert or wait for other air traffic to pass. This privilege is most important, because delays in the air can be critical at times when every minute counts. A glance at the weather report warns me to expect a strong head wind at any altitude above 3000 feet on the return flight. I reckon that I will have to stay low in any case, as the patients are sure to have head injuries and altitude can cause further complications to damaged brain and eye tissue. I decide, therefore, to run up to Geraldton, a coastal town 240 miles north of Perth, at 7000 feet with a good tail wind, and to return at 1000 feet.

I park the car and walk across to the Royal Flying Doctor

3

Service hangars. The engineers nod cheerfully as they hurry around the Beechcraft Baron, making sure that all is set to go. Some of this team are commercial pilots themselves and often take a turn in the field. They are used to seeing me working around aircraft, hands and face smudged with grease and hydraulic fluid, and battling with the wind for control of my skirt. I rarely wear slacks when flying, mainly, I think, because girls are expected to, as though in deference to their having invaded a "man's world."

Bevan, the chief engineer, has heard a few details of the accident. "Six young blokes in a head-on with a tree," he says. "There's a big noise doctor going along with you. Tell him the resuscitator machine is ready for use if necessary."

By the time I have checked to see that stretchers, blankets, oxygen and other equipment are aboard, the surgeon from Royal Perth Hospital has arrived. Fortunately he has flown with me before, so I am spared that "what-am-I-in-for" look that I often receive from passengers. Nor do I have to retaliate with the special "no-nonsense-from-*you*" look that was part of my nurse's training.

Everyone's concern for the injured men causes the take-off checks and airways clearances to go through with the utmost speed and proficiency. This routine, although casual on the surface, is the result of long experience and rapid communication between Department of Civil Aviation operation centres behind the scenes. Only one thing is always new. That is when a pilot taxies into position for take off; his dials and instruments confronting him expectantly and the runway clear ahead.

"Foxtrot Delta Juliette cleared for take off," announces the control tower. This is the point at which a pilot's mind becomes locked in absolute concentration, and every factor of the situation blends into that moment when man and machine become as one. Not quite yet, as the aircraft rolls forward with increasing speed, and not as the runway blurs past, but *now* as the plane lifts sweetly into the wide embrace of the air.

It is a recurrent miracle in which many things combine, beginning with the complex mechanical wonder of the aircraft herself. Then there is the work of the engineers who keep her running so smoothly, and the skill of the control tower operators who guide her on her way. For me they all contribute to that living experience which I cannot have too often or in too many different ways. The aeroplane is a means of coming to grips with reality, whether in the easy ways of straightforward flights such as this one, or on flights in which human wits and nerves are pitted against mechanical weakness or elemental power.

Many writers have tried to express how men feel about flight. Antoine Saint-Exupery probably has come closest to conveying the experience, but even he confessed to finding words quite inadequate for the task. Certainly it is beyond my powers.

"Two dead, two severely injured, two with comparatively minor injuries," was the curt report the surgeon had received on the accident. The Geraldton doctors, early on the scene, had decided that the survivors should be flown south for urgent specialist treatment.

A St John ambulance, with the two severely injured youths aboard, awaits our arrival in Geraldton. With great care and efficiency they are transferred on to aircraft stretchers and into the plane; snoring slightly under sedation, and a pitiable sight with their deep facial lacerations, black eyes, broken limbs and all the signs of grave internal injuries. The doctor adjusts their blood transfusion and drainage equipment for the flight while their parents stand huddled in shocked silence beside the ambulance.

Within two hours they are in the operating theatre of the Royal Perth, their broken bodies being attended by a deal of devoted skill and fantastically expensive equipment. The two young lives, almost thrown away in a moment of recklessness, are saved. Another emergency flight of the Royal Flying Doctor Service is recorded and filed away.

I drive home, a bubble in the torrent of homeward-bound traffic. Another job done; another wait ahead. In a day or so, or perhaps no more than an hour or two, the telephone will summon me to the next job.

It is a strange way of life, I suppose; being tied to the phone, never venturing on the briefest errand without stating ones whereabouts. But this is the sort of work I always wanted to do, and that far exceeds my early dreams of somehow combining flying with nursing. I find it hard to express the satisfaction I feel in

5

being this particular small cog in a big wheel, taking this little part in the saving of life and limb, being involved with acute nursing problems and at the same time entrusted with $100,000 worth of beautiful aircraft, flying off anywhere, any time. And being paid for it!

I think that I have always had an intense feeling about the wonder of living and the preciousness of every week, day and even hour of life, but since the sudden loss of my younger sister Julie I have felt this more deeply than ever before. She and I were very close in childhood, and though as we grew up we went our different ways we shared the same loved ones, many of the same interests, and a great many memories. It is still incredible to me that from being one minute so vitally concerned with life, so loving and so loved, she was the next withdrawn from us and all her bright young days scattered like leaves on the wind. So, since she was unable to leave any record of her own full and useful life, I feel that I must write, and dedicate to her, my own "rememberings," in many of which she was involved.

2
HOW WOULD
I FACE
THE DEAD?

"THERE'S A BANGING NOISE IN MY AIRCRAFT," I CONFIDED TO
the microphone, keeping my voice as calm as possible. "It sounds
as though it's going to fall apart."

"You haven't fastened your seat belt properly," was the
supercilious comment from the control tower. "The end of it's
sticking out of the door and flapping against the fuselage. You'd
better land and fix it up."

I did so, trying to look as though I was performing some
routine adjustment but knowing that I would hear all about it
from air traffic control staff and other eagle-eyed airfield workers.
As one of only two or three girls learning to fly at that time, I was
the constant butt of their somewhat ponderous humour. "Intersection departures" became "intersexual departures," and when
practising touch-and-go landings the controller would stutter-
ingly clear me for "T-t-touch and go" with the implication that
I was sure to bounce. Whenever there was an accident, it was
inevitably assumed that I must be involved. Luckily, I never was,
but I had my moments.

My first flight with an instructor was memorable for both of
us. The Chipmunk trainer ran into a heavy rain squall; water

poured into the cockpit, soaked me to the skin, and trickled into the throat mike. I was later told that my ladylike enquiries of the instructor sounded like the croaking of a bull frog, and his replies were equally unintelligible. We orbited for quite a time; obviously he was finding it difficult to maintain straight and level flight and to discover the way home with a minimum of instruments. He could not answer the frantic radio enquiries from the control tower, and having been posted "Lost in the training area with a female student" he was as abashed as I was when we squelched out of the cockpits on our return to the airfield.

It had all started a few weeks before, when I was sitting alone in the nurses' lounge at the hospital, mending a pair of grey uniform stockings. Two young men appeared in the doorway and introduced themselves as Dave Munns and Bill Ingham. They asked, with a lack of assurance that was clear proof of their inexperience in this field, whether a couple of nurses might like to go out with them. Taking pity on their embarrassment I asked them to sit down and see whether anyone else turned up. No one else appeared, but before long I had ceased to worry about that. The two boys had just succeeded in obtaining their private flying licences, and I listened spellbound to stories of their hair-raising adventures until the Matron came to turn the lights out and the visitors away.

This meeting changed the whole course of my life. The boys invited me to go flying with them that weekend, and the experience had the same effect on me as a taste of grog on an abstaining alcoholic. The exhilaration I had felt on flights in Dad's little Wackett, and on longer flights in his company's aircraft, returned full force. I realised that the urge to fly was in my blood and was not to be denied.

I discovered that the cost of a flying course was ten dollars an hour—or exactly two dollars more than I was earning per week as a student nurse. However, there was a government subsidy of four dollars an hour for students under twenty-one, so I reckoned that I might be able to afford one lesson a fortnight. Apart from practical flying lessons, the course included the study of navigation, airframes, engines, principles of flight, meteorology, air legislation, and radio. This seemed a formidable programme, especially as I had to study for my nursing exams as well. Since

I was about to start on two months' night duty, however, I thought that I could make a start on flying lessons during the day.

The next two years were the busiest of my life to that time. I had to fit in flying and nursing studies, practical flying and nursing duties, and find transport to get to and from the airport on time. Also I had been elected President of the Student Nurses' Association, which meant a good deal of extra work for part of that period. This office had its compensations, though, because it meant trips as a delegate to other States and to the Twelfth International Congress of Nurses in Melbourne.

My interest in flying did not imply that I was disinterested in nursing. In fact I loved my job and was keenly interested in all aspects of medicine. I only hoped that something would turn up to enable me to combine these two great interests, just as Bill and Dave had turned up to play their part in the shaping of my future. (Strangely enough I was not to see either of them again until ten years later, when we all three found ourselves working together as pilots for the Royal Flying Doctor Service.)

During my latter years at Loreto Convent, Nedlands, I had given serious thought to the matter of a "career," but could never see myself working at some repetitive indoor task. Actually I had wanted to fly for almost as long as I can remember, but Dad had received the suggestion coldly. Flying was an absurdly expensive hobby for a woman, he said, and as for a job! He inferred that a female commercial flier would be as out of place as a ballet dancer in a footy match; a view which I found to be shared by most men when I later obtained my Commercial Licence and started looking for some way of using it.

At the time, however, I supposed Dad must be right, so I turned my thoughts in other directions. A friend who had just completed her nursing training assured me that this career was at least as good as any other, even if not all fun and games. Her stories fascinated me, and whetted my curiosity. Moreover, the idea of a nursing career was approved by my parents. Dad had an "image" of nurses (no doubt dating back to his experiences in the first World War) as gentle angels of mercy, ladies with lamps and so forth. But I still had reservations. Although a member of a big family, and accustomed to a house in which friends and relations are always coming and going, I am to some extent a solitary person and had always hated the idea of sharing a room, even with my sisters. How would I get on in the communal life of a big hospital? I was never lonely, or afraid of being alone, but I was afraid of death—not my own, since of course the young never expect to die, but of having to see others die, and to look at the faces of the dead. How humiliating if I should begin a nurse's training only to find that I couldn't take it!

I was still churning over such questions as these when, as a reward for struggling successfully through my final school examinations, I was whisked off on a trip to Darwin and thence to visit relations in South Australia. While in Darwin I flew on MacRobertson Miller Airways "milk run" in a DC3, visiting the missions and government settlements scattered around the coasts and islands to the north and east of Arnhem Land. I was captivated by the wild beauty and fecundity of the Territory, the meandering tidal creeks, the jungle spilling down to meet the mangroves on the ocean front; by the narrow landing strips carved out between cycads and creeper-enshrouded trees, and by the children—so many, many children, their dark faces aglow with friendly welcome, and often with so pathetically few people to look after them.

At Elcho Island we found that an epidemic of gastro-enteritis had broken out, and that one nursing Sister was coping under almost primitive conditions with dozens of sick people. The pilot was requested to take three of the most severe cases to Darwin Hospital, and since the Mission could not spare anyone I was asked to take charge of them. I was thrilled to be given what seemed to me such an important job, and there was a special satisfaction in delivering the patients safely to hospital. I was delighted next day when asked to fly back to Elcho to look after two more cases. If I became a nurse, I thought, I could do this kind of work all the time. Maybe there was even some way in which I could combine flying and nursing.

By the time I got to Adelaide, my mind was humming with possibilities. But then the mysterious and awful barrier would rise, and I couldn't see any further. Would I ever be able to face the dead?

At last I decided that there was only one thing to do; put myself to the test and see what happened. Quite near to my cousin's home in which I was staying, there was a funeral parlour. As I walked past one day, I saw that the front door was ajar. "Now or never," I thought, and braced myself to step firmly into the sombrely furnished foyer. A middle-aged man, with a pale face set in an expression of perpetual condolence, materialised from somewhere and asked what he could do for me. I looked him straight in the eye and said that I was a registered nurse from Western Australia and was writing a report about mortuaries.

Since I must have looked like the youngest registered nurse on record, and also happened to be carrying a loaf of bread under one arm, he seemed somewhat taken aback. But he pulled himself together and bowed me through to the interior of his grisly establishment. I caught terrifying glimpses of steel sinks and marble slabs as he ushered me into a room lined with refrigerated steel drawers. He reached casually for the handle of one of these and pulled it forward on silent rollers. My knees trembled, and I shut my eyes.

"This is *it*," I thought, and feeling as though I was drawing my last ounce of courage from the bottom of a deep well, forced myself to look.

The drawer was empty, and I stared into it trying to conceal my relief while the undertaker droned on about his business being the best equipped in Australia. "Are you interested in the latest methods of embalming?" he asked.

I told him that I was indeed, but simply couldn't spare any more time just then. He seemed to take this all right, but as I moved towards the foyer I found myself being subtly manoeuvred into a little room, lined with shelves full of model ships in bottles of all shapes and sizes. "You must have a cup of tea before you go . . . it's all ready," he insisted.

As he poured it out he told me that he made the bottled ships himself. "It's a lonely life," he said. "A mortician finds it so hard to make friends—especially with young ladies. I can't understand it. I make a very good living, and what would people do without us?"

His melancholy eyes and monotonous monologue held me hypnotised, and I was not sure whether I would wind up in a bottle, in a refrigerated drawer, or in his bed. Mercifully, the spell was broken by the sound of a car horn. "They're just bringing someone in," he said. "Wait a moment. I'll be right back."

As soon as he was out of sight I made a blind rush for the door and sprinted up the street to my cousin's home. "Where's the bread?" she asked.

"Oh dear," I gasped. "I left it in a funeral parlour."

But I had not fainted, and I decided that even if there had been a body in that drawer I would probably have kept my head—and my feet. To my father's delight, I told the family that I intended to begin training as a nurse.

There are points of similarity between flying and nursing. In both occupations one must be constantly alert, aware, and foresighted, always ready to put an alternative plan into operation, and able to tackle any emergency with whatever equipment comes to hand. Above all, one must never show emotion or alarm; never betray outward feelings of panic even when faced with what seems to be certain disaster. And the strange thing is that if one is resolved not to *show* panic, one can somehow master it.

Unknowingly, Dad had taught me some of these lessons already. I had noticed that his attention to every detail of flying was phenomenal, and that although he is an emotional man, inclined to carry on at length over trifles, he is calm and efficient in emergencies. Once, when I overturned a car in a sandy creekbed miles from anywhere, his neck was dislocated and his spinal cord affected so that he had difficulty in moving, but he remained as steady as a rock and was far more concerned about my distress. than he was about his own condition. Sometimes, in fact, I have suspected that he enjoys being put to the test by perilous emergencies such as he has faced so often during his long flying career.

I was thinking about him when putting on a nurse's uniform for the first time. Whatever I felt inside, I was determined that it wouldn't show on my face.

3

FLOWN HOME
TO DIE

I BECAME FAMILIAR WITH DEATH. NOT USED TO IT, BECAUSE I DOUBT that anyone becomes really used to death no matter how often it is encountered. For those concerned with caring for the sick, death is a defeat; another round lost in an endless battle. Except in cases of the aged or incurable, it is always hard to take and the grief of loving relatives is never easy to face.

At first I was not sure whether I could last the distance after all. The four years of training seemed to stretch endlessly ahead; full of hard and often sordid work, anxious problems and difficult decisions. I found the accident cases the most distressing, and dreaded being assigned to the neurosurgical ward where many of the victims lay sunk in coma only a degree above death, and kept alive—if it could be called alive—by intravenous feeding.

This negative period, however, passed quite soon. Some patients died but many others were restored to health. Emergencies arose but one had the support of a team equipped to conquer them, and I felt a growing sense of fulfilment in learning how to do my job. Even the worst episodes were balanced by the loyal comradeship of fellow workers and the knowledge that we were performing a meaningful and important task.

13

And of course it was not all depressing and grim. Like any other group of young people we enjoyed ourselves whenever possible. The mealtime chatter was more likely to be about fashions, boy friends, holiday fun and the planning of "entertainments" (with the patients as our captive audience) than about sickness and suffering.

The story of my flying background and interests worked around the hospital grapevine, and probably accounted for my sometimes being chosen when a nurse was required to accompany a patient travelling by air.

One of these was an ancient Greek, being returned from hospital to his family in Darwin. He had a brain tumour, and his mental confusion was compounded by the fact that after sixty years in Australia he did not speak a word of English.

As parched and skinny as a mummy, his few remaining teeth stained a dark tobacco brown and eroded almost to the gum, he was able only to totter along at an erratic shuffle and was an unattractive prospect, to say the least.

But for me he was the passport to a flight, and so I jumped at the job. My enthusiasm did not last very long. It was a night flight, and we were assigned two rear seats handy to the toilet. Scarcely were we airborne before I found that, whatever faculties the old man might have lost, his sexual instincts were not amongst them.

I covered him up and had visions of his going to sleep, but he insisted on my feeding him the routine cup of tea which he promptly sneezed into my face and lap. In an effort to avoid his persistently exploring hands I tucked them under the seat belt, at which he gave a wicked cackle and planted a sloppy kiss on my cheek. He soon worked his hands free and continued his advances with a strength and persistence which would have done credit to a man in his prime. My objections became increasingly vocal, causing heads to pop up over the backs of seats, until at last a gallant gentleman across the aisle offered to change places.

I hardly had time to settle down before the patient set up an ominous grunting noise. My kind friend escorted him to the toilet, but after twenty minutes returned him with the news that there had been nothing doing. We sat back again, until I suddenly became conscious of a steady spray of water soaking the front of my dress. With incredible accuracy, the old man was aiming at me across the aisle.

I mopped up the mess, strapped the patient firmly in his seat, and selected a safer part of the cabin. At Port Hedland my faithful friend again escorted the old man to the toilet, where he succeeded in flushing away the cord that had been holding up his trousers. The boarding call had been given and there was no time to look for a replacement, so we had to walk behind him holding up his pants as he tottered across the tarmac.

My helper had to leave the flight at the next stop, so the following few hours were a nightmare. When at last we touched down at Darwin, I steered the old man gingerly down the steps and on to the tarmac, keeping a firm hold on his vital clothing. However, as soon as he saw the relatives lined up to welcome him he thrust me aside, and stepped over the trousers which had fallen around his feet. Almost miraculously his shuffling gait became a brisk and manly stride, and stark naked from the waist down he was received with tears and embraces into the bosom of his clan.

I often contrast this flight with one which I took with another old man, after I had become associated with the Royal Flying Doctor Service. This patient was ninety-six years old and in the terminal stages of cancer, but he was the epitome of quiet dignity and splendid courage. He knew that he had only a very short time to live and wanted desperately to spend his last few days with his family at the old mining town of Mount Magnet.

The doctors thought that he could not survive the 300-mile journey by road, and arranged with the Royal Flying Doctor Service to take him home. I was asked to replace the regular R.F.D.S. pilot, in case any nursing assistance was necessary during the journey, and was glad to agree.

It was mid-winter, and the flight had to be put off several times because of bad weather. The old man's condition deteriorated rapidly, but he held on to life as though determined to make this final journey. At last we were given clearance, and I took off in a Cessna 180 with the patient and his daughter as passengers, the first air journey for them both.

Perth had hardly faded behind us when we ran into real winter weather, and the turbulence sent the little aircraft up and down like a leaf. The sensible thing would have been to put back, but when I glanced round and saw the confident, jaundiced old face looking up from the stretcher I decided to push on.

Clouds and rain whipped past the windscreen and on looking at the ground it seemed that we were hardly moving. When at last the old man could no longer conceal his agony I managed to lean back and gave him an injection of morphine. As it took effect he levered himself up and looked anxiously out of the window.

It took us four hours of flying, through lowering cloud and against a forty-five knot headwind, to travel a distance normally covered in little more than two. As we flew over Mount Magnet I warned my passengers and put the Cessna into a semi-steep turn, so that they could look down on the tiny settlement of a few houses, abandoned mineshafts and poppet heads on the bare red soil. The old man took a long look, then gave me a faint smile and a wink of approval. I will never forget his expression of happiness as he lay back and closed his eyes.

As we circled the airstrip, I glimpsed the windsock lashing in a swirl of wind-driven dust, a group of people huddled in the lee of an old shed, and the rotating red eye of an ambulance. We made a short landing into the stiff breeze, and as we taxied to a halt the waiting family moved forward in a wave. The old man's sons lifted him carefully on the stretcher and carried him from the aircraft.

"We've got a surprise for you, Pop," one of them announced as they slid him into the ambulance. The surprise was a new great-grandson, only a day or so old, awaiting him in the mother's arms.

"Come to take my place, eh, young fella?" the old man murmured as he fondled the little bald head. "I'm just a bit tired now. See you all later on. . . ."

He fell asleep during the rough five-mile journey to the township, and died peacefully during that last happy night in his old home.

A nurse sees so much courage, and so many examples of people working together for the benefit of others without thought of their own feelings, that these things more than compensate for the less happy aspects of her life. One night the Flying Doctor Service received an urgent call from the country town of Narrogin,

120 miles south-east of Perth. A nurse had been seriously injured in a car accident and was in danger of losing both legs, and possibly her life, if she was not flown to Perth for immediate specialist attention.

The only aircraft available was a small R.F.D.S. Cessna 180 that was not properly equipped for night-flying, but there was nothing for it but to declare a mercy flight and hope for the best. Dr Harold Dicks, who was then the President and Supervisor of the Western Australian branch of the R.F.D.S., volunteered to act as pilot. By that time I had had a good deal of contact with the Flying Doctor Service, and I was asked to fly as attendant nurse.

We flew out of Guildford Airport into darkness so thick as to be almost felt, wondering how we were going to locate Narrogin without navigational aids—and how we were going to land when we found it. We knew that the town had two airstrips, both on a farm property; one very rough and the other with a fence running across it. We assumed that some kind of landing guidance would be provided, and flew on with nothing but the glow of the compass to guide us.

We need not have worried. Two large clusters of lights rose over the horizon—one the township itself, the other the head-lights of more than a hundred cars. The townsfolk had organised themselves to provide this lighting for the airstrip, so that it looked more like an international terminal than a bush airfield. One end was indicated by the flashing red light of the ambulance, the other by the headlights of two cars, while the surrounding vehicles had been angled to assure that the pilot was not dazzled by their lights as he landed.

Every detail was organised perfectly. The patient, sustained by an intravenous blood-drip and with her legs splinted and packed in ice, was waiting our arrival. She was in shocking pain and it was obvious that we could not waste a moment if her life was to be saved. Every second that it took to ease her aboard must have seemed like an hour, but she was wonderfully brave and tried to thank everyone for turning out to help her. We learnt that the cars had come in response to an appeal broadcast over the local radio, and the discipline and organisation of the whole manoeuvre was inspiring. None of the motorists left his car, and there was no gaping crowd of people elbowing around. They all stayed quietly in position, waiting for the signal to turn on their lights again for the take-off.

The patient was taken to hospital in record time and although the doctors could save only one leg she made a record recovery and is now back at work. A useful life preserved not only by the skill and devotion of the medical teams but also by scores of anonymous folk who gave their help.

Thus are human beings at their best. It is well to remember such things when encountering them at their worst.

4

"FATE UNKNOWN"

DR HAROLD DICKS, WHO BROUGHT THE INJURED NURSE TO PERTH, was literally a "Flying Doctor." He went to Port Hedland as Government Medical Officer shortly before the second World War, and his duties included those of District Magistrate, Mining Warden, Protector of Aborigines, Quarantine Officer, Chairman of the Pilbara Licensing Court, and "Captain" attached to the Army, Navy and Air Force. He was also required to fly and maintain the Fox Moth and Dragon aircraft used by the Royal Flying Doctor Service. From a salary of £1,000 a year he had to supply his own surgical instruments and car and pay rent on his house. His nearest colleagues were at Broome to the north, Carnarvon to the south and Meekatharra to the east, which meant that he was responsible for 800 miles of coast and hinterland. He was probably the only doctor except Harry Hanrahan of Perth, who relieved him from time to time, to act as official Flying Doctor pilot *and* doctor at the same time. He maintained this position for six years.

When I first encountered Dr Dicks he was in private practice in Perth, and was also medical examiner for the Department of Civil Aviation and Honorary President of the Western Australian branch of the Royal Flying Doctor Service. He encouraged my flying interests, helped me on problems concerning the theory and mechanics of flight, and saw nothing improbable about my ambition to combine flying and nursing as a career.

At first I had looked upon flying with a somewhat romantic eye. From the effortless skill with which pilots appeared to handle their machines, I had assumed that they flew by some sort of instinct—rather like birds. I soon learned, however, that their expertise was firmly based on training, knowledge, experience, practice, and an almost obsessional care of their aircraft.

But I learned such things the hard way. In return for Dr Dicks' assistance I helped him with a monthly clinic which he operated at Ravensthorpe, a farming and coppermining area about two and a half hours' flying time south of Perth. Sometimes he would let me take over and would give me a practice lesson *en route*. During one such flight—this time with a dentist on board— I plunged lightheartedly into a bank of cloud. Almost immediately the aircraft began acting strangely and entered into a spin. I did not then know that when a pilot is in cloud he can lose all sense of balance within a few seconds. Unless he keeps a close eye on his instruments, he doesn't know whether he is going up or down, to port or starboard, and miscorrection of the aircraft can soon develop into a dangerous stall or spin situation. Luckily Dr Dicks was quite prepared for this. He took control at once and quickly established a normal attitude, but I was deeply conscious of my hazardous mistake. My instructor pointed the moral by saying that it had been a good cure for over-confidence, and an indication of my need for more extensive training. The dentist, incidentally, never volunteered to fly with us again.

When I had completed my general nursing and midwifery courses I worked for a time as Dr Dicks' surgery nurse, but before then I had had an even more exciting taste of flying. When spending a day off at the airport, shortly before my midwifery examinations, I happened to meet David Faber, the pilot of a local charter company. He told me that he was leaving for London in three days' time, to fly out an Italian Piaggio which had been purchased for special charter work. "Why not come with us?" he asked. "I'm taking my wife and a friend along, but there are a couple of spare seats if you're interested."

Since I was not due for any leave, and my finals were looming, I felt that I had to turn him down. But when I reported for duty next morning I couldn't resist telling Sister Christina, who was in charge of St Anne's Maternity Wing, about David's offer. I didn't exactly ask permission to go but no doubt I gave her a mighty longing look. "My dear," she said, "if you really want to make the trip, and think that you can be back in time for the exams, I certainly won't stand in your way."

"But this is Monday!" I exclaimed. "They're leaving on Wednesday morning!"

"You'll have a lot to do, then," she said cheerfully. "You'd better go off at once, and I'll work your duty."

I felt as though all my Christmases had come at once, and will never forget the way in which this kindly nun's understanding and unselfishness made a seemingly impossible dream become a reality. After a frantic rush to get ready, the flight to London and three weeks in what felt to me like the beating heart of the world were even more thrilling than I could have imagined. David took delivery of the Piaggio at Luton Airport near London, and our first day's flight on the way back to Australia gave us magnificent vistas of the French countryside, the Alps, and the Riviera. What a contrast to the harsh, bare landscapes over which I had done so much of my previous flying! I became quite dizzy trying to take in every detail of that green, cultivated patchwork of tiny farms and villages, and snow-covered mountain slopes. Next day we hummed over the Mediterranean, all blissfully relaxed and trouble free, and happily recalling the hilarious experiences of our night in Nice. It seemed too good to be true—and it was.

We were over Greece when one of the engines lost power and began emitting an alarming noise followed by the quite unnecessary shriek of a warning siren in the cockpit. It was impossible to maintain height on one engine, and with a range of mountains looming ahead our situation began to look really precarious. David radioed Athens that we were in trouble, but the answer was: "Too busy to deal with emergencies. Go somewhere else."

At this critical stage David spotted a providential airstrip and made a forced landing with one propeller feathered.

It turned out to be a Greek Air Force headquarters, and the moment we touched down we were surrounded by gun-toting

21

airmen and suspicious officers disturbed from their afternoon siesta under the wing of a DC3. They bombarded us with questions which were literally Greek to us, and as they could not understand a word of English we were reduced to a wild pantomime which attempted to signify our country of origin and our reason for landing. This was accompanied by sounds and signs indicating the noise of the failing engine, the warning siren, and the perilous pitch of the aircraft. Our efforts were greatly encouraged by the fact that the suspicious Greeks gradually relaxed to the stage where they were rocking to and fro on their rifles in helpless mirth.

Some Air Force mechanics were allowed to help us uncowl the engine, but the necessary removal of the cylinder heads was impossible without proper facilities. We and the aircraft were searched thoroughly and our passports taken away. After about six hours of fruitless work in the hot sun, we were escorted to the nearest village, Andravdiha, where we spent an uncomfortable twelve hours in a room containing five hard trestle beds still warm from the previous occupants who had been summarily told to vacate the establishment.

Eventually our passports turned up from the town forty miles away, where they had been taken for examination and stamping, and we were allowed to return to our aircraft. David decided to attempt a take off on the one good engine, using what little power the other might produce—a manoeuvre which meant that the passengers and their belongings would have to be left behind. We dragged out every removable item, including our luggage and a collection of souvenirs that sent the Greek airmen into fresh paroxysms of laughter, their most incredulous amusement being provoked by some way-out riding gear which David's wife had bought in London.

But on the take-off run the poor "Pig" was unable to keep straight, let alone gather enough strength to become airborne. We had just decided that we would all have to take the bus for Athens when a sleek little jet fighter alighted on the landing strip. Its pilot was a stunningly handsome young man, who came towards us with hands outstretched and introduced himself in English as Captain Carterus Athanasius. He insisted on escorting us to a private house in the village where he treated us to a strange but splendid meal. As we ate, he apologised quite unnecessarily for the quality of the food, and invited us to his home in Athens to meet his wife and baby son of whom he was immensely proud. He saw us on to the bus for Athens, saying, "I now fly home to my son. It will take me twenty minutes; you, eight hours. I wish you a good journey and expect you to visit me."

In Athens David arranged for an engineer to fly up to the Piaggio with spare parts and tools, after which we contacted Captain Athanasius and were invited to dine at his fine apartment. He greeted us like old friends and we met his sweet young wife and ten-day-old baby son—an enchanting boy with beautiful features and long black hair, dressed in elaborate clothes obviously made for him by loving hands.

Soon a troupe of beaming waiters came in from the street, bearing great platters of sheeps' heads sawn in half and prettied up with garnishings. Proudly, they served us one apiece, and urged us to help ourselves from many other dishes of salads, potatoes, fillets of fish, melons, and ice cream.

Evidently the sheeps' heads, complete with eyes, were considered a great delicacy. The Captain opened the meal by saying grace, then smiled at us happily as he picked out his sheep's eye and munched it with relish. I had always prided myself on having no food fads whatever, but somehow I just couldn't bring myself to eat the eye which regarded me so gloomily from my plate. Nor, I noticed, could any of my more travelled companions. Luckily the Captain's wife was feeding the baby, so as soon as he left to fetch some more wine we forced as much food as possible upon his little dog. My friends quickly piled all the brains from their plates on to mine, and when the Captain returned we were again quietly enjoying our meal.

He entertained us royally and took us sightseeing around Athens while we waited for the arrival of the "Pig". He would not let us repay him in any way, so we said that he must come to Australia where we would return his hospitality. "Not very possible for me," he said. "But perhaps someday my son. . . ."

One morning while Carterus was away in Crete for a few days, we found a book on Australia which we inscribed with an invitation to his boy to visit our country. We called at the Captain's apartment to make the presentation, but we were met in the doorway by a woman dressed in funereal black and from inside we could hear pitiful sounds of mourning. Somehow it was conveyed to us that the little son had been found smothered in his cot.

There seemed to be nothing that we could do, but we left the book anyway and later wrote a letter of sympathy to the parents. It was returned "Address unknown" and we have never heard any more of our hospitable Athenian friends.

After an eight-day hold-up awaiting a new rocker arm, the Piaggio was repaired and flown to Athens. As it touched down here, however, the undercarriage folded up and the aircraft was so extensively damaged that it had to be abandoned. We flew home by jet, not knowing that a brief Reuter's despatch had been cabled to the Perth newspapers to the effect that five Australians had crash-landed in Greece and that their fate was unknown. This meant some anxious hours for our families, as we had not thought it necessary to cable.

When I appeared at the hospital, a few hours after publication of the report, I was greeted as though I had risen from the dead, and embraced with many a "Thanks be to God!" One of the nuns however rather spoilt the effect by saying, "What a waste! We said two Masses for the repose of your soul!"

The outcome of the affair was rather sad. Loss of the Piaggio meant that the charter company lost its contract and soon folded up. David Faber, who was an excellent and polished pilot, became discouraged and abandoned flying, even though the mishaps with the aircraft were due to poor maintenance on the part of the company which sold it. They compensated for the loss, after which David and his wife decided to take up a farm and riding school in the south-west of Western Australia.

It was a bad show for the Fabers, but the experience, which I owe to Sister Christina, taught me a lot and gave me the courage and determination to spread my wings further afield.

5

BROOME
MEMORIES

I PASSED MY MIDWIFERY EXAMS AND HAD COME THROUGH general nursing with the Medical Award for my year. With these things behind me and a private pilot's licence in my pocket I began to wonder where I should go from there. Not being ambitious in the sense of aspiring to a special position or of attaining some rich reward, I was in fact generally rather vague about my "goal," but had at least two quite positive immediate aims. One, since aviation as a mere hobby could never have given me genuine satisfaction, was to put my flying to some definite purpose. The other was to maintain my association with the outback—particularly with the North-West and the Kimberley areas of Western Australia.

These areas had been a part of my life for as long as I could remember, and before that a part of my family heritage. My mother, on her father's side, was descended from an Irish family named Durack which emigrated to New South Wales towards the middle of the last century. They pioneered the Cooper Creek district in western Queensland, and in the 1880s overlanded cattle to open up new country on the Ord River in East Kimberley, where they formed a chain of stations. "Cattle kings," some people called them, to which my great-grandfather Patsy, chafing over the insecurity of tenure and the general lack of official encouragement for their battling enterprise, scornfully replied: "Then we are kings in grass castles that may be blown away upon a puff of wind." It was from this remark that Mum derived the title of her best-selling family saga, *Kings in Grass Castles*.

My grandfather wound up most of his company's interests in Kimberley in 1950. He died in the same year and I did not visit the estate he controlled until considerably later. I had, however, learned a great deal about the stations formerly owned by the Duracks and their partners.

During my early childhood Grandpa, the bearded patriarch, still tall and upright in his eighties, always seemed to be just leaving for or just returning from the Kimberley properties. He was kindly and interested but not really able to penetrate the increasing undergrowth of grandchildren, of which we were only one part. But my grandmother was, as she remains to this time, right in the thick of it; involved in every detail of our upbringing, never forgetting a birthday, never missing a chance to encourage us or to point the homely moral.

"A place for everything and everything in its place," she says, but her home, for all its tidiness, continues to hold a special fascination for us all. Always redolent of roses, floor polish, moth balls and lavender, it is a treasure house of both conventional and curious objects. Along with the cabinets of polished silver and carefully cherished glassware and fine china there are souvenirs of her travels in India and the Far East and a strange assortment of curios from the Kimberleys. These include a fine collection of Aboriginal weapons, ceremonial objects, and carved boab nuts, side by side with the lizards, crocodiles and baby turtles that Gran herself collected and stuffed during her years in the north. Her dressing table set is made from Cambridge Gulf turtleshell; the furniture in her study is upholstered in crocodile hide, and the cabinets are full of specimens which held Grandpa's somewhat premature hopes of a mineral boom.

But that by no means represented my only association with the north. Just after the war Dad, then Managing Director of MacRobertson Miller Airways, had purchased a bungalow in the pearling port of Broome as a convenient half-way house on the north-west air route. Mum was at that time expecting her fourth baby, so Dad suggested that he might take two of us off her hands for a while. Mum was only too pleased to pack Julie and me off on what seemed to us the most exotic of adventures. "Uncle Cyril" Kleinig, who had been with Dad since his flying days in South Australia, and was then Chief Pilot for the company, put us on the DC3 in charge of our favourite air hostess, Kitty O'Neil.

I remember every detail of our flight and arrival in Broome, a 1300 mile journey from Perth, with numerous stops along the way. This took about ten hours in the old DC3, so it was after sundown when we swooped in over the smooth, turquoise waters of Roebuck Bay. As the door was opened a breath of warm tropical air flowed in to greet us and there was Dad placing the aircraft steps in position.

He took us to the hangar where he kept the private Wackett aircraft which he had bought from war disposals, and the blitz waggon, another disposals bargain, in which he lumbered around the north for many years. He pointed out bullet holes in the hangar, made during the Japanese air raid in 1942. It was a savage attack, in which military aircraft on the Broome airstrip were destroyed by machine gun fire, and twelve Dornier flying boats, packed with Dutch refugees from Java, were shot up with great loss of life while they were waiting to take off from Roebuck Bay. But more interesting to us than these historical highlights were the boiled sweets that Dad produced from somewhere with an air of mystery. Later, we discovered that he kept a jar of lollies under the seat of his Wackett, and without appreciating the fact that they were his sole "survival rations" we gradually got down on them. When he found out, I rather lamely suggested that the culprits could have been "mouses," a proposition that he appeared to accept as entirely feasible.

The Broome house, with its wide verandahs and big shutters, could be closed up like a box when the owner was away or if a cyclone or dust storm was in the offing. It had belonged to a pearler named Harry McNee, and in the cupboards we found ships' compasses; boxes lined with green felt for storing pearls; charts and tide tables; a Japanese-English dictionary, and a book on how to speak Malay in ten easy lessons. The big back yard was littered with diving gear, including heavy bronze helmets, canvas diving suits like deflated men, and huge lead-soled boots. The great leafy branches of the poinciana and mango trees made pools of shade in which we set up camp with our treasures and played happily until called to go for a swim, to meet a plane or to fish off the mile-long jetty at the end of town. Few children can have enjoyed such a fascinating playground.

Every day was full of adventures. One of our friends was Archie Maxwell, who drove the little train which brought passengers and freight from the ships into town. He would always stop and treat us to a breathlessly exhilarating ride. And there were the Aboriginal mums who gathered on the beach to fish for their families. Sometimes they would take us miles along the beach to dig for cockles, to search for turtles' eggs at night, or to catch the huge crabs which lived in holes amongst the mangrove roots.

One day Dad, while fishing from the end of the jetty, hooked a fourteen-foot hammerhead shark on a small line. Archie Maxwell sped the train back to the goods shed for a gun, shot the shark, and helped to haul it up on a crane. Julie, typically curious, then had to put her finger into the shark's mouth, which shut on it with a snap. The result was a bad gash, an impressive amount of blood, and enough noise to bring half Broome rushing to the rescue. Archie Maxwell took us by train to the foreshore, where Dad dived into his blitz waggon and produced some field dressings that we'd found in the wreckage of a fighter plane on the rubbish dump.

It seemed that we lived in a paradise of surf and sand, with the big tides ebbing and flowing around rusting relics of the war-shattered pearling industry and wrecks of the aircraft shot up in the bay and scattered over the white salt marsh. We played pirates and Swiss Family Robinson on the beached luggers and "aviators" on the wrecked war planes, myself sitting at the tilted and rusting controls, fingering the mysterious knobs and dials while Julie's shrill voice made "radio communication" from among the crumpled metal.

The Broome pearling industry was at that time just beginning to get on its feet again. New luggers were being built, and their crews—then mostly from Malaya—being reassembled. The town was being tidied up, and its buildings painted dazzling white as they had been in the past. We children, however, were not so much interested in the rehabilitation process as in the great piles of rubbish being dumped on the outskirts of the town. These yielded an endless supply of treasure trove, as they contained everything that had not been snapped up at the military disposals sales. They interested Dad quite as much as ourselves, because the abandoned vehicles provided him with a rich source of spare wire, nuts, bolts, screws and other odds and ends, which we gathered and sorted into separate tins for the shelves of his hangar. Heaven knows how we escaped being poisoned by the tinned food of doubtful date and origin that we gleefully transferred with a selection of battered kitchen gear to our cubby under the poincianas.

Living with my father taught me a few lessons in practical psychology. Julie could never understand that it was no use asking him what he planned to do. Actually Dad seldom made plans for more than an hour in advance and even then he never discussed them. It was therefore necessary to read the signs in order to work out what was afoot. When he changed his sandals for shoes and socks, I knew that he planned a flight in his Wackett. I would sneak out and sit in his blitz waggon and Julie would follow, piping the inevitable questions. Once, Dad turned round and drove home again simply because she wouldn't shut up, but she never seemed to learn.

Starting the Wackett was an adventure in itself. When Julie and I were strapped in the back seat Dad would chock the wheels, plug in an external battery, get into the cockpit to set the switches and controls, climb out again, swing the propeller until the engine fired, jump up to reduce the throttle and richen the mixture, leap out to unplug the battery, drag the battery cart clear, pull away the chocks, and finally swing himself into the cockpit with one hand fastening his flying helmet. This wild burst of activity concluded, we would soar thrillingly above the white houses of the little port, and veer off along the coast, sighting schools of dugong, huge manta rays, turtles, sharks and sometimes even whales. .

Occasionally the spirit of Dad's Western Front days took over and he would begin stunting. I was terrified at first but of course

29

I pretended to enjoy it, and the time soon came when I needed to pretend no longer.

Once we struck a strong cross-wind on coming in to land, and a gust blew the Wackett off centre. We came down at the edge of the strip on a line of white tin markers, one of which ripped the floor from under my seat and went rolling off into the scrub while others were displaced and dinted. Dad carried on unperturbed, and as usual taxied right into the hangar. When I told him about the damage he said only, "Oh well—we needed a new floor anyway. Just nick over and put those markers back in place. Better chuck that dinted one well into the bush."

Broome airfield was uncontrolled in those days. Dad would simply give the air-radio station some idea of his intended direction and flight duration, but would invariably change his mind as soon as he got into the air. Eventually he was forced to install a radio, but this didn't make much difference. He would switch on to the Broome VHF frequency, and while taxi-ing out for take-off would say, "Er—good morning. Are you there, Jack? Horrie here!"

"Alpha India Yankee. This is Broome Radio. Go ahead, please."

"Er, yes, Jack. Looks like a nice day for fishing, eh? Might be good for some salmon down on the jetty, later on. The kids and I are just going to blow the hornets' nests off the old machine. See you on the jetty when the tide turns."

"Roger, Alpha India Yankee. Which area will you be operating in, and for how long?"

"Couldn't say, Jack. We'll just have a general look around, wherever the mood takes us."

By this time Broome Radio would have given up trying to sound official and would say resignedly, "Okay, Horrie. See you later."

Years afterwards I found a little blue book entitled *Radio Procedure* stuck in the Wackett's seat pocket. It had obviously never been opened.

Julie and I had eventually to go back to Perth but Broome was to remain a big part of our family life. It was there we spent all our holidays and, with Mum and the other children, one whole never-to-be-forgotten year. From an adult point of view Broome society is traditionally stratified, but as children we sensed little social or racial distinction and no disharmony. We attended school with a fascinating mixture of children descended from all kinds of cross-marriages between Aboriginals, Asians, and Europeans. It was a valuable lesson in taking people's skin colour for granted and accepting them for what they were. It was also tremendous fun. There was always something being organised for the kids; sports meetings, picnics, barbecues and concerts to which everyone contributed in some way.

Among our special friends was Con Gill, an ex-pearl diver who had drifted to Broome from Jamaica in his youth and who, because of the yarns he span to visiting writers had become quite a famous figure in Australian literature. His gold ear-rings and talking cockatoo have been described by many writers— including my own Mum. We did not realise at the time the extent to which old Con was a walking history of Broome, his memory going back to the rip-roaring boom days when there were three to four hundred vessels in the pearling fleet and Japanese divers and conniving business men played a major part in the industry. Still, we loved his tales of the sea, of luggers, pearling masters, fabulous pearls and miraculous escapes or sudden death from sharks, giant gropers and "cockeye bobs" as they call the cyclonic storms that pounce without warning on that sun-baked coast. For adult ears, it seems that he had different tales to tell of a time when he had been one of those athletic Lotharios who could leap from trees or swarm up ropes into upper bedroom windows. We were surprised, in later years, to learn that he had actually been much sought after by the coloured women of the town, but had somehow managed to go on playing the field without becoming tied down. The only hint he gave of such past prowess when we were around was the knowing twinkle with which he would reply, when asked about his health, "Only middlin' *now*." Mum wrote a ballad about him which we used to recite in the old man's rolling sing-song that we knew so well:

> Sitting in the sun by Roebuck Bay
> Con's only middlin' now but here to stay.
> Plenty men come to this little white town,
> Some gone home and some gone drown.
> Some gone crazy and some stay on
> But nobody stop so long like Con.

31

Nineteen hundred—round 'bout there
I come here first with long, black hair—
Same gold rings in same brown ears—
Carried 'em goin' on eighty years!
The folks here then—old Con can't tell
Which gone heaven and which gone hell.

White man, yellow man, black man, brown—
All together in this little white town.
Luggers lie out on the big, blue tide,
Some pearl honest and some go snide,
White man wink and yellow man nod,
For the pearl is Satan and the pearl is God.

Diver go deep to the cold sea bed
'Til his heart take cramp and his limbs like lead.
Get rich quick and come home soon—
Sail on the tail of the last monsoon!
Push off the saki and the rice from shore
For the souls of the men they don't see no more.

Nooo! Con don't marry, but he got two eyes—
He seen things—ooooh! you be surprise.
But the kids grow fine by the good, jade sea—
Filipino-Chinaman-Abo-Singalee;
And no one go hungry—everybody feast
When the luggers roll home on the big south-east . . .

The land where my mother toil out her days
Gone lost with her boy in the far off haze.
Con only middlin' now, but folks say—"Oooh!
There goes a good man, *a man we knooow!*"
The white birds tell me—those birds don't lie:
"This the town where Con goin' die."

Con attributed some of his hairbreadth escapes to the inter-
vention of Christian saints, and others to the voodoo spells and
charms of his West Indian heritage. One night, when Mum and
Dad were at a party across the road, our kerosene refrigerator
blew up. Flames fanned by a strong breeze roared from the
kitchen area towards the main building where we children were
sleeping. Everyone came rushing to the scene and dragged us out

32

but all efforts at firefighting seemed hopeless. Then along came old Con, and solved the problem by snatching off the "miraculous medal" which he wore around his neck and flinging it into the fire. The wind turned almost immediately, and although the kitchen was burned to the ground the main house was saved. When the ashes cooled, Con fished around and retrieved his medal. Charred but intact, it was ready for the next emergency.

6

INITIATION

THE DAYS OF FUN FLYING AND COMPARATIVELY SLAP-HAPPY conditions disappeared with the introduction of larger aircraft and stricter rules for outback air services. They had to come, of course, but I'm glad I remember something of the way it used to be.

During holidays spent in and about Broome we often went off on what were called "milk runs" around the chain of stations and outposts scattered through that vast empty land. It was a never failing thrill to see an isolated homestead, "buzzed" by a Lockheed or an old Anson, spring to life—waving figures running from the Aboriginal camps while a vehicle with a great plume of dust rising behind came speeding to meet us. Everyone knew the aircraft crews, who brought a welcome breath of the outside world to the lonely hinterland. They would unload mail and freight, pass on the latest news from other stations and along the coast, and exchange friendly banter and "in" jokes as they partook of cool drinks, sandwiches, thermos tea and cakes, brought from the homestead to the rough bough shelter near the airstrip.

Then as we flew off again over the rough, red-brown country

with its sparse timber and dry creek beds we would spot herds of wild camels and brumby horses, scattered sheep and cattle, sometimes a family of sprinting emus or bounding kangaroos. The noise of our passing would disturb great flocks of white cockatoos, black crows or grey and pink galahs, while sometimes brolgas and eagle hawks would appear to challenge our huge bird to a contest in manoeuvring.

Owing to the vast distances travelled between stations, sometimes to drop no more than a single bag of mail, the "station run" which was operated at a considerable loss on a government subsidy was given over to charter operators in 1968. Julie, at that time senior checking hostess for the company, went along on the last scheduled station flight, and with pilots Kevin Yelland and Lindsay Allen made sure that it was a send off in traditional style. On her return she entertained us with an account of the old DC3, coloured balloons floating from the cockpit windows and toilet paper streaming from the fuselage as the station homesteads were "buzzed" for the last time. She said it was the saddest, but one of the most thrilling flights she had ever made. It was also one of her last.

But in those happy, childhood days in Broome it never occurred to me that things were ever likely to be much different, certainly not that we were, in a sense, living in history. If I was around when Dad was called out on an emergency, I always went along with him, never asking if I could go, or whether there was room, but simply finding a place in the blitz waggon, helping him to get the aircraft ready for take-off, and slipping quietly into the back seat. Dad just took it for granted, and treated me like one of his mates on the job, expecting me to know the names and uses of the various tools, and where to find them if required.

Once an Anson made a belly-landing at Noonkanbah Station, near Derby, and we went off in the Wackett to make running repairs and get it in the air again. No one had been injured, and Dad and an engineer soon completed the job and took off for Broome again while I returned with the pilot in the somewhat battered Anson. All went well, but I had missed the regular flight which was to have got me home in time for the first day of the school year.

The next best thing was a DC3 freighter that was flying a

roundabout trip from Derby to Hall's Creek, then south via Jigalong Mission and Meekatharra. "Robs will be your hostie," Dad told the two pilots as he shoved me aboard. I took the job very seriously although the commissariat consisted of no more than a loaf of stale bread, a packet of Kraft cheese, two tomatoes, and a tin of meat. There was no tin-opener or equipment of any kind, but I managed to make sandwiches of a sort with the aid of a pocket-knife borrowed from one of the pilots.

By the time we reached Hall's Creek, weather was blowing up. We dumped the freight in a hurry and headed south for Jigalong, with the storm following and at last enveloping us. It was my first experience of a really rough trip. There were no passenger seats, so I stood between the pilots and tried not to look scared as rain and wind battered the windows and the aircraft bucked wildly through a dazzling blaze of lightning and a continuous crashing of thunder that almost drowned the engine noise.

From snatches of cockpit conversation, I gathered that the pilots were trying vainly to locate Jigalong through an occasional break in the turbulent masses of black cloud. After circling for nearly an hour, they decided to go down below cloud level— which meant almost skimming the treetops. The risk was rewarded by the sight of smoke from a fire which had been lit between showers to indicate the airstrip.

We splashed down on the sodden strip, the object being to pick up two Aboriginal children who were to attend a camp school near Perth. They had been delayed by an overflowing creek, and during our wait one of the pilots got out to put locks on the flapping ailerons. No sooner had he touched the glistening wet alclad of the wing than there was a great hissing crackle of lightning and he fell to the ground as though he had been shot. For an instant I thought he was dead, but he jumped up again with a grin and shook his fist at the heavens.

The two children arrived at last, wet through and shivering, but the pilots, assuring them that they could change in the aircraft, pushed us in and started up without delay. Taking-off, however, was no easy matter as the airstrip had become a swamp and all hands had to turn to laying down clumps of spinifex grass for the wheels to "bite" on. This done, the dogged DC3, most robust and versatile of all workhorse aircraft, was coaxed into

A typical scene on a night emergency flight in 1970. Accident victims from Marble Bar being transferred from a Flying Doctor aircraft flown by the author (in photo) to an ambulance at Port Hedland airfield

the air, but ran into the stormy weather again almost as soon as we got off the ground.

It was impossible for us three youngsters to keep our feet and we had to cling to some empty gas cylinders to prevent ourselves from being thrown around. One moment the aircraft would be flung upwards like an insane lift, the next the deck would drop away beneath us as she plummetted down again, tipping and shuddering wildly from side to side. As soon as he could leave the cockpit for a minute one of the pilots came aft, found some rope, sat us down, and tied us to the side of the cabin. He seemed quite unperturbed. I knew that bad weather was all in the day's work for aircraft crews, so despite my fears I had no doubt that we would get down all right. But for the two Aboriginal children, it was obviously a nightmare. There was no hope of changing their clothes, so they just had to sit there shaking with cold and fright, their eyes enormous in faces which had changed to a peculiar shade of grey. I had heard of people dying of fear, and became desperately anxious—not so much on account of the poor children, but because I was afraid that I might find myself tied up to two small corpses.

This possibility galvanised me into action. I began telling them stories, then singing to them, and finally making cat's cradles, but they just stared into space and shuddered convulsively. When we reached Perth at last they had to be carried out of the plane— two limp, shivering bundles of miserable humanity. I often wonder whether the camp school made up for the horrors of that flight, and whether they have ever been game to board an aircraft again.

For my part, such adventures seemed essential to the business of flying. I had a steady admiration for the pilots and air hostesses I knew, and envied them not only their way of life but their constant association with what I had come to regard as "my country." Later, when the chance I had been looking for came along, I was quite surprised to be warned about the dangers of flying in the north-west. "Don't worry," I said. "It's my home."

In the deepest sense, I felt that it *was* home, and no more expected to come to harm in it than the average person would expect to encounter danger in his suburban garden. That lonely land with its enormous plains, and majestic ranges deeply gorged

The author while she was a nurse at Royal Perth Hospital

by mysterious rivers, was *mine* and it was the place where I most wanted to be.

But first of all I had to find some way of working there. To have become a nurse with the Australian Inland Mission would have limited me to an outpost job and given me no chance to fly. I thought of joining the Royal Flying Doctor Service, but learnt that nurses in this organisation were mostly "grounded" at one or another of the base hospitals.

My desire to find some way of combining two interesting professions made me realise that it would be necessary to gain my Commercial Pilot's Licence. This would, I hoped, prove to be a passport into the world of practical, everyday flying—a world which, in Australia at least, was the exclusive preserve of men.

7

A SNAKE
IN THE
COCKPIT

A COMMERCIAL LICENCE MEANS THAT A PILOT CAN OFFER HIMSELF for hire or reward, and it obviously requires training at a much higher level than that needed for a private pilot. After all, anyone flying with a commercial pilot is likely to have paid for the privilege, and has a right to feel that he has invested his money in someone who knows what he—or she—is doing at any time and under any conditions. The training course, therefore, includes instrument flying, night flying, complex navigational work, and a multitude of written exams designed to ensure that a pilot is infinitely more capable of controlling an aircraft than the average driver is of controlling his car. Flight tests simulate every conceivable emergency, and if the pilot fails to perform the correct remedial actions efficiently he could possibly lose his licence. The Department of Civil Aviation has only one consideration: the safety of those who may fly with these pilots.

I could not have undertaken the course had I not received a Commonwealth scholarship for study and practical training; one of six granted at the time to fifty or sixty applicants in Western Australia. Flying lessons for the course cost eighteen dollars an hour, of which the Government paid two-thirds.

39

Before being given the scholarship I had to pass several written commercial examinations, and to be interviewed by a board of experts from such organisations as the Department of Civil Aviation, the Aero Club, and airline companies. The examiners asked a number of practical questions about aircraft, the handling of various emergencies, my flying experience, and my reason for wanting a commercial licence. They appeared to be interested in my idea of combining a nursing and flying career and asked whether I saw any outlets for this ambition. I told them that there were, for example, mining camps being opened all over the north-west as part of the frantic search for minerals, and that few of these had any medical facilities. I was not certain what I was going to do about it, but felt fairly confident that a trained nurse with a commercial licence should be able to find some kind of niche in the aerial network.

At that time I was working as a surgery nurse, which was not so demanding as a hospital job, but when I began the commercial pilot's course I was busier than a mother with twins. I had to travel twenty miles to night school each evening after work, and attend flight training every weekend or whenever I could snatch an hour off. In summertime I often fitted in a flight between six and seven a.m., so no matter how late I got home there could be no lying in bed.

The commercial pilot's class consisted of thirty men and one girl, who was me. A number of my fellow-students of that time are now airline or charter pilots in other parts of the world. It is fun to run into them in unusual places and to talk shop over a meal or a hurried drink, while now and again we risk the censure of the D.C.A. and exchange radio greetings if we happen to pass in mid-air.

One such happy encounter occurred on a trans-Pacific ferry flight with a new Beech Baron for the Royal Flying Doctor Service. My fellow pilot and I had been twelve hours in the air, trying to dodge a series of menacing thunderstorms between Honolulu and Tarawa Atoll. At about twelve degrees north of the equator we ran into a particularly bad line of storms, and suspected that our trailing radio aerial had been struck by lightning. We had missed several routine hourly position reports, an important safety measure, and I had been calling "all stations" every fifteen minutes or so and giving our estimated position. For over three hours the reply was nothing but deafening static, then through the hideous crackle came a welcome voice: "Hey! That dame with the Aussie accent! This is Fiji Airways, flight 201. Come in again, please."

Relieved at having got through at last I repeated our estimated latitude and longitude, said we had some radio problems, and asked if the receiver would kindly relay the information to Nandi Airport on Fiji. The pilot complied, then came back to ask where we were bound.

"To Perth, Western Australia, with a new aircraft for the R.F.D.S.," I replied.

"Good God! Is that *you*, Robin?" the voice said. "We were in the same navigation class. Then I joined M.M.A. and was flying with your sisters Patsy and Julie. I was one of the pilots they retrenched in 1968 and I'm now with Fiji Airways."

He gave his name but I couldn't catch it, and never sorted out exactly who he was. I gathered, however, that he was one of the First Officers who lost their jobs when M.M.A. amalgamated with Ansett Airlines, and most of the old DC3s were replaced by the Friendship and Fellowship jets that required fewer pilots. Anyway, that friendly chat in the middle of the horizonless Pacific did more than I can say to relieve the tension of the long weary flight.

Among a number of instructors during my commercial training was a Texan named Irwin. On our first cross-country navigation exercise, Irwin told me to practise steep turns and low flying over a lonely area, and then calmly directed me to practise a forced landing into a quarry which seemed most unsuitable for the purpose. But I did as instructed, and simulated a landing into the quarry without mishap. It was not long before I discovered that Irwin was more interested in drilling for oil than in teaching flying, and had decided that it would be a good idea to combine prospecting with instructing. Parts of the south-west reminded him of oil-bearing country in Texas, so the low flying and forced landing practices gave him a good look at it. Luckily I didn't take up much room in the cockpit, because he insisted on wearing a ten-gallon hat and cowboy boots. His pockets bulged with oil samples in plastic containers, and he had a habit of spreading out a huge map of his home state showing thousands of oil leases. Sometimes I was lucky to get a glimpse of the dashboard.

During one of our cross-country exercises he decided we should drop in to visit friends on a property about 100 miles from Perth. As I made a low run over the farm airstrip Irwin spotted a large snake basking in the sun about a third of the way along, and excitedly took over the controls. He brought the Cessna down to a perfect skid landing right on top of the snake, and we then climbed out to greet his friends. I winked at the farmer, and said that Irwin's precision landing had secured us a delicious meal. The farmer entered into the joke, and produced a sack into which I dropped the limp reptile while Irwin made noises of incredulous disgust. "I'm going to take it home and cook it," I told him. "Nothing nicer than baked snake."

I tossed the sack on to the hatrack behind the aircraft seats and we went along to the farm for a cup of tea. When we returned to the Cessna, Irwin dropped his navigation bag on top of the snake, and we took off. About fifteen minutes later a thump from the hatrack caused Irwin to glance round. He let out a terrified yell, for the snake had recovered and was writhing about in the sack only a few inches from his neck. The farmer had muttered to me that the creature was a harmless rock python, but I wasn't going to put Irwin's mind at rest on that score. "Surely it's only a baby to the snakes in Texas," I said.

He wasn't amused, and tried to persuade me to let him take over the flying while I threw out the writhing sack. "No fear," I told him. "It's ages since I had a good feed of snake."

For the rest of the flight, poor Irwin sat huddled on the edge of the seat between the instrument panel and the rudder pedals, hypnotised by the contortions of the sack. As soon as we landed he darted across to the Aero Club to gather witnesses to the fact that he'd flown 100 miles in a Cessna 150 in company with a dangerous snake.

I couldn't give the joke away yet, so dropped the sack in the boot of my car and promised the boys that I'd bring them all a share of the delicacy on the following day. Actually I intended donating the creature to a snake-loving friend, but on reaching home I found that I was wanted urgently to assist at an emergency operation. I hurried into the city and didn't give the snake another thought until the job was finished. It was dark by the time I opened the car boot to give it some air, but it was too late. It had died and was starting to smell, so I laid it out on top of a row of rubbish bins in an alley between the hospital and an office block.

In next morning's *West Australian* I saw the headline: LARGE SNAKE FOUND IN ST GEORGE'S TERRACE. Fascinated, I read that an office cleaner about to empty some rubbish had found an eight-foot python guarding the bin. She had nearly passed out from fright and had called the police to deal with the intruder. It was not known how the snake could have got there.

Incidentally, it appeared that Irwin had been looking for backers to put up $12,000 to drill for oil on a "promising site" in Texas. He was confident that this well would provide the necessary finance to continue exploration in the vicinity of Perth. When we last met he told me that he had raised the money and was off to carry out his plan.

8

WORKING FOR
THE GOVERNMENT

"DO YOU THINK YOU CAN DO IT?" ASKED DR DAVIDSON, THE
Commissioner for Health in Western Australia.

"I *think* I can."

"All by yourself, or will you need an assistant?"

"I'd prefer to try it out alone. If I can't manage I'll let you
know."

"Well, go ahead and start organising. Report to me on what
you've planned and leave me several copies of your itinerary.
Work towards being ready to start in three weeks' time."

As I left the Commissioner's office I had a sudden mental
picture of the sprawling sunbaked hinterland and lonely cyclonic
coastline of the north. I saw the widely scattered stations, the
panting little inland towns and ports with the sun beating down
on their galvanised iron roofs, the busy mining centres with their
multi-racial, mostly masculine, communities. I saw the Aboriginal
camps, the isolated missions and settlements dotted about
between the coast and the desert's rim. In a moment of hesitation
I wondered what I had let myself in for but I soon pulled myself
around. After all, wasn't this just the opportunity I had been
seeking for so long?

Seven years previously Western Australia had suffered a bad epidemic of poliomyelitis. Naturally the majority of cases had occurred around Perth, but many had also emanated from the north-west and Kimberley areas. Having nursed a number of victims who were still in hospital after three and five years, some possibly to remain there for life, I was fully aware of all the heart-breaking aspects of the disease. Salk vaccine had been available, and thousands of people had been immunised by a series of three injections at set intervals, but the problem of administering this treatment to a population of 30,000 scattered over half a million square miles in the north of the State had proved insuperable. A great many had not been vaccinated, and now, after some seven years during which hardly any cases had been notified, the health authorities were worried by finding that the virus was beginning to show up again. In case the State should be on the brink of another epidemic, they realised that it was imperative to re-immunise the population as soon as possible.

By that time, the new vaccine known as "Sabin" was available. This could be administered by mouth, and did not involve such a critical time between doses. The more settled southern areas, with their good roads, already were being covered by mobile teams using cars and caravans. The main problem was the north which could obviously only be covered by air. That was where I came in.

Not long before, I had written to Dr Davidson, the Commissioner, and asked for an appointment. I had gained my Commercial Pilot's Licence, and was seeking some way of putting it to use. A half-serious attempt to obtain a job as pilot with MacRobertson Miller Airways had met with a courteous but obviously somewhat apprehensive reply, to the effect that piloting a passenger aircraft was hardly a female vocation, that there would be problems of accommodation, and that the work would be too heavy for a woman.

I had replied that women were flying commercial aircraft in Europe and the United States and that since accommodation could be found for air hostesses why not for a woman pilot? I added that it was doubtful whether the average airline pilot worked as hard manually as I had done as a nurse—especially on Flying Doctor jobs when I had to heave open ponderous hangar doors, help to refuel aircraft, and manhandle stretchers heavy with patients.

But I did not persist too far in that particular fight for women's rights, as I was already following up the half-formed idea I had suggested to the Civil Aviation examiners. Mineral development in the north-west had continued its explosive growth, and almost every week new prospects were opening up. With them came new mining camps, destined perhaps to become the ghost towns of tomorrow but at the moment vigorously alive. Their populations needed routine medical care of the kind which put a considerable strain on the resources of the R.F.D.S.—such things as first aid for fractures, removal of foreign bodies from eyes, supervision of dressings, attention to cuts and sprains, minor suturing jobs, burns and so forth. There was an almost endless catalogue of minor complaints which while not justifying the flying in of a doctor could become more serious without some kind of skilled attention.

I envisioned the establishment of a series of small clinics run by nurses, with a special aircraft to fly patients out in emergency, and with this in mind had gone into the economics of buying a private aircraft. I reckoned that with a guarantee of 30,000 miles per year at twenty cents a mile I should be able to pay off a small machine within three years, and it was with this proposition that I had confronted the Commissioner for Health.

Somewhat to my surprise Dr Davidson listened to my spiel with interest. When I had finished he said that owing to the current polio immunisation campaign I had come at an opportune time. The job wasn't quite what I had had in mind but it was obviously an important one requiring immediate action. I therefore agreed to take it on with the idea that I could later proceed with my original plan.

But even before I had completed the immunisation job the mining situation in the north had changed from being mainly concerned with mineral exploration and pilot projects to the big "go ahead," in which camps were transformed into towns and ore into dollars. My idea was then no longer practical as these new towns needed not merely first aid centres but well-equipped hospitals. Moreover the population of these larger centres quickly changed from being almost completely masculine to more normal family units.

For the time being, however, I had enough to do planning my immediate schedule. I had already gained a lot of navigational and bush flying experience while working as surgery nurse for Dr Dicks, because I had naturally become closely associated with R.F.D.S. activities through his involvement with the Service. On numerous R.F.D.S. flights, mainly in Cessna 180s, I had learned a good deal about the spur-of-the-moment way in which some outback emergencies had to be tackled. Most of the flying, however, had been in company with one or two other pilots of R.F.D.S. personnel, and I realised it was going to be rather different setting out on a big job alone. Having convinced Dr Davidson that I could plan and execute a single-handed campaign for immunising 30,000 people against polio, I now had to convince myself.

My first move was to visit the aerodrome and look over the range of second-hand aircraft on sale. There was not much choice at the time, but I finally settled for a Cessna 182, VH-CKP, which cost $12,500. I wasn't entirely happy about her, but knew she could do the job. She was a pretty little aircraft, and roomy inside, but had been used for sheep and cattle mustering and felt a bit loose in the joints.

The R.F.D.S. engineers were kind enough to do her over and put her into good shape so my remaining problems were now mostly financial. I managed to raise a loan for the machine itself but still had to pay out for air navigation charges, insurance and radio licence, and to equip myself with a comprehensive set of spare parts, tools and emergency gear. By the time I had fixed all these items I was utterly broke and up to my neck in debt but the happiest girl in the world.

The next move was to visit the Immunisation Centre in Perth and find out all there was to know about Sabin vaccine. I learned that it was completely safe and the process of administration quite straightforward. The main problem was going to be that of keeping the vaccine at a temperature below forty degrees during flights from one centre to the next.

I found out from the staff just what equipment they took away with them on their caravan clinics to the south of the State. From

47

the Health Department stores I gathered up kidney dishes, bowls, disinfectant, numbers of white huckaback towels, four fifty-two pound boxes of sugar lumps on which to administer the vaccine doses, eight boxes of plastic spoons, ten pounds of boiled lollies for the native children, and a huge supply of record cards and pamphlets.

When estimating the boxes of sugar lumps required, by adding up the population of each place to be visited, I realised the enormity of the task to which I had committed myself. But like Caesar conquering Gaul I decided that the only way to tackle it was bit by bit.

I divided the area into two parts, the north-west and the Kimberleys, to be covered in that order. I then divided each area into sections based on its main centres of population, whether they happened to be mining camps, townships or stations. I knew that the success of the clinic would depend largely on publicity, for which I got some good ideas from pamphlets issued about the vaccine. I loaded up with hundreds of these propaganda publications, and also had some coloured slides made for screening at outback picture shows. I then got some special notices printed and wrote dozens of letters to local newspapers, shires, stations and the Royal Flying Doctor Service, giving details of proposed clinics.

I knew from previous nursing trips that the average person is averse to the idea of a "needle" for any purpose whatever, so my advertisements emphasised the fact that Sabin vaccine, looking and tasting rather like raspberry cordial, was taken by mouth.

On a system of eight-week rounds, making three visits to each of these eighty-odd centres, I calculated that I had two years' work ahead. "Oh well," I consoled myself, "bit by bit." I then loaded the Cessna with equipment, including two heavy ice boxes containing 10,000 doses of vaccine for the first area, and reported back to Dr Davidson. I told him I was ready to go, and with a rather uncertain look he wished me luck.

9

SUGAR BIRD LADY

"I COULD TELL YOU SOME FUNNY STORIES ABOUT CARNARVON," the local undertaker said as he led me around the township. He was also the Public Health Inspector, and helped manfully to organise my clinics in this north-west port.

It was 23 May 1967, and I had left Perth the day before, flying into heavy showers and overcast weather but feeling as though I was vibrating with as many horsepower as the engine of the Cessna.

I spent the first day organising immunisation schedules at schools, infant health clinics, and the Native Welfare Centre; hiring the "town hall," and sticking up notices in every available position. The undertaker took me around the town, barely interrupting his flow of gruesome anecdotes to introduce me to one or another of the local personalities.

"There was this Pommie parson," he said. "Fresh out from England. Not long after he got here, there was a chap disappeared overboard on a fishing trip. Never thought we'd see *him* again, but about ten days later they found him floating outside the mouth of the Gascoyne River. Beats me why the sharks didn't get him.

49

"Well, the poor feller was a bit bloated, as you might say, and it was no use trying to fit him into a regular coffin. So someone got the idea of putting him into this old refrigerator crate.

"We dug a nice big hole and started on the funeral next day, six of his mates carrying the crate and the new parson following behind. As soon as the blokes got to the grave they saw that a big bungarra—a whopping great lizard about six foot long—had fallen into it during the night.

"When you scare a bungarra, the first thing he does is run up the nearest tree. And if there isn't a tree handy, he runs up *you*. Well, when the blokes saw the parson standing there all stiff and reverent, looking a bit like a dead tree, they reckoned that the moment they lowered the crate into the grave the bungarra would hop on to it, jump out, and run up the parson.

"So they give each other the wink, and drop the crate down hard to knock the old bungarra out. But they can still hear it scratching around underneath, so they heave on the ropes and bounce the crate up and down a few times, good and heavy. The parson is looking horrorstruck by this time, so one of the blokes says, 'Don't worry, Reverend. It's an old Aussie custom. You know—ashes to ashes, dust to dust. Just to let him know he's back in good old Mother Earth.'

"But the best of it was later on, when the word got round about what had been done. They're talking about it in the pub, and someone pipes up: 'Hey—that's *my* refrigerator crate you pinched. I was wondering where it'd gone. And I never even *liked* the bastard. You can darn well put him in something else.'

"Of course, they tell him he can go and dig it up again himself, but he wouldn't do that, so finally they fixed him up for it."

The rain that had followed my flight north must have been falling all over the area because the town began buzzing with rumours that the Gascoyne River—whose bed, except for a few stagnant waterholes, is usually bone dry—was "coming down." The timber and corrugated iron township stands on the Gascoyne banks and further up are the tomato and banana farms of settlers, mostly Yugoslavs and Italians. Everyone gathered to watch as the water began to trickle down from the Kennedy Ranges far inland, then a yell of delight heralded a wall of chocolate brown water about two feet high. The settlers, armed with spears, waded in and soon began landing a good catch of eels that had mysteriously manifested themselves from goodness knows where.

I had tried to work out my schedule so that my visits would coincide with cricket and football matches at the different centres. This was not because of a fanatical interest in sport—as some people interpreted my earnest enquiries—but because these attractions enabled me to "catch" a majority of the local population.

After an initial hesitation, the Carnarvon people were encouragingly enthusiastic about attending my first clinic, and so many of them appeared that I had to call on the generous help of the local Red Cross. I soon discovered an unexpected problem. In order to keep check on immunisation figures, the Health Department required proper records, to which end each applicant had to fill in two cards, giving his name, age, address and signature of consent.

This sounds simple enough, but I found that many people were unable to give their correct names and addresses, and had no idea of the meaning of the word "signature." When parents had to fill in permission for their children, they did not know the difference between "Christian name" and "surname" and very often could not give an exact date of birth.

It was difficult enough with the white settlers, but almost impossible with the Aborigines. Mostly they would just giggle, or mutter some name which I would vainly try to interpret. "Is it Jarry or Jerry?" I would ask, and the black face would split in a beaming smile. "Yeah, yeah—thass right, Harry."

"Sure it's Harry—not Jarry?"

"Yeah, yeah—thass right!"

"Which one—Harry or Jarry?"

"Yeah, you got 'im."

I thought I had the problem solved when I found a native girl who had been to school to interpret for me, but when I returned to give the second course of immunisation some of them flatly denied the names she had recorded, while others seemed to have changed their names for quite unfathomable reasons.

Part of the problem was the Aborigines' generally arbitrary use of all vowels and a good many initial consonants. I also discovered that many tribal names are virtually impossible to write down except in phonetics. An even greater stumbling block is that even semi-tribalised Aborigines have a number of different names which serve different purposes and signify different aspects of their tribal background.

Every man is given at least three names at birth—the one by which he is generally called, another signifying his food totem, and a third, known as his "skin name," which he shares with every member of his special kinship group. At initiation he acquires a secret or "private name," while some tribes go so far as to bestow a special "night name" as opposed to the "day name" by which a person is usually known. (This last appears to have something to do with misleading evil spirits that haunt the darkness.) To make things even more difficult almost all Aborigines now have a "whitefella name" to which has been added of recent years what is termed a "gubmint name," the latter serving the purpose of a surname for the benefit of official records.

I found that an Aboriginal was liable to give any one of his names more or less as the mood took him. No one was deliberately unco-operative unless he suspected that I was "getting at" him to reveal his "private name," in which case he was likely to give the first name that entered his head.

I began to sympathise with the pastoral pioneers who named Aborigines with such easily spelt and remembered appellations as Spider, Whalebone, Fishhook, Snowball, Sugarbag and Onegun-dun, all of which cropped up in my records, having become common family or "gubmint" names in the process of time.

I'll never forget the excitement and confusion of my first clinic in the Carnarvon hall. More and more people crammed in, peering over each other's shoulders, nursing wailing babies, slapping noisy children, gossiping, laughing and chattering as Mrs Betty Baker, a Red Cross assistant, and I wrestled with the problem of filling in the cards.

"What age are you, Nugget?" I asked an Aboriginal who had endeared himself to me by giving that single, simple name.

"Dunno missus," he grinned. "Might be t'ousand. You." (This meant that the problem had been thrown back to me—in other words that my guess was as good as his.)

"'Bout fifty?" I hazarded. "That all right?"

TOP: Captain & Mrs H. C. Miller with their four daughters. *From left:* Robin (the author), Patsy, Julie, and Marie Rose. BOTTOM: Growing up with aircraft. Julie, Robin, and H. C. Miller on Broome airfield

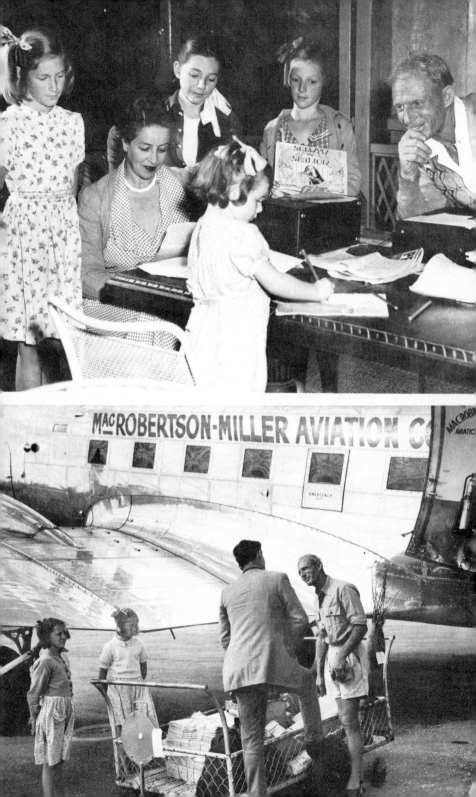

He nodded cheerfully, but one of his more sophisticated mates corrected me: "No, no missus. He got that name from Hall's Creek gold rush. Must be over eighty now."

I soon found that filing the cards in alphabetical order during the clinics was impossible, and deferred the job to after hours. The department also required numerous other statistics which, though important and useful, were mighty difficult to assess on the spot. "Number of people in each age-group" was a figure I was never able to work out while a restless throng of all ages from babes in arms to wizened great-grandmothers was waiting for treatment.. I was to work until many a midnight sorting out records and files.

The Aborigines around the township soon heard that it was "good medicine," and began to flock in for immunisation. As a general rule, because of their simple faith in us and love of free benefits of any kind, they are less resistant to the idea of taking medicine than are Europeans. They will even line up for inoculation by needle, whereas some whites are most reluctant to suffer this extremely minor operation. During an anti-tetanus clinic one native was heard exhorting a doubtful white mate to submit to the treatment on the grounds that it was bound to do him "the world of good."

These first days began to set the pattern, although I was surprised to find that some people in the white community were reluctant to take the spoonful of vaccine. The mystery was solved when people began to ask me, "Why do the doctors tell us not to take this stuff ?"

I could hardly believe this at first, but found that the word had gone around that the doctors were against the immunisation programme. Later, a hospital sister enlightened me on the mercenary considerations behind this attitude—a complicated story which for ethical reasons is better left untold.

I carefully explained the purpose of the vaccine to every enquirer, and diplomatically placed a number of pamphlets where the doctors might read them and perhaps regret their selfish sabotage. Slowly, the doubtful began to join the rest—though there was always a contrast between the eagerness of Aborigines to be treated and the somewhat suspicious approach of the white population.

The Wackett aircraft in which the author learnt to enjoy the thrills of flying. TOP: With her father, Captain H. C. Miller. BOTTOM: Just landed after a flight with the girls in rear cockpit

Word of the "sugar medicine" travelled fast, and sometimes, having retired for the night, I would be startled by the sudden appearance at my window of an Aboriginal anxiously claiming to have "missed out" on his dose.

Schoolteachers were always co-operative, and would line up the children to accept the spoonsful of vaccine or the pink-soaked sugar lumps. Some children didn't like sugar, and gave their lumps to others—who would thus receive a double dose. Others tossed them into garbage cans, from which the lumps were rescued by teachers who made the children eat them all the same. Sometimes I would see a black hand creep up over the edge of the table and whip away one of the untreated lumps of sugar, while wherever I walked I would be followed by a group of whispering children with wide, longing eyes. At first my heart melted and I doled out extra sugar lumps all round, but I soon found that my supply was running so low that I had to break all the lumps in half. This led to fights among the kids when one got a slightly smaller piece than another. I considered even bringing extra supplies but the boxes of sugar weighed about 300 pounds and my poor little aircraft was hard put to get off the ground as it was. So I had to harden my heart to those appealing eyes.

It is hardly to be wondered that, in the strange way people acquire labels outback, I came to be known to all the Aborigines as "the Tchooger Bird Lady."

10

LANDINGS HAPPY & OTHERWISE

"JUST DROP DOWN A BIT SO I CAN GET A LOOK AT THE BRAND ON those cattle, will you?" the station manager asked. I thought he was joking, but a glance at his face told me that he was serious. He was also very pale. I began to feel apprehensive, as when asking me to take him up for a quick look over his property he had warned me that he could stave off airsickness for no more than twenty-five minutes.

Maybe some pilots don't mind people being sick in their aircraft but I do, so I came down very gently to a level just above the big ghost gums. "We're off our place now," he informed me, after an anxious scrutiny of the land below, "but those cattle down there look like ours. Just get down a bit lower, so I can see the ear marks."

They were not his cattle, and I made the station airstrip just before having to surrender my only sick bag. My passenger climbed out, mopping his brow, and waved me a shaky farewell. I thought it would probably be the end of flying for him, but when I next heard of him he had conquered his airsickness, obtained a pilot's licence, and purchased a plane of his own.

Increasing numbers of private planes are being operated on

outback stations and, like the transceiver radios first installed in 1928 for communication with the Royal Flying Doctor Service, have done a great deal to change both the texture and tenor of life in these remote areas. On sheep stations the use of aircraft has reduced musters from four months or more on horseback to a couple of weeks, and as stock can be spotted so easily from up above, it has almost eliminated the need for a second round-up. The long hot drives to service station mills have been changed to short flips before "smoko," while quick maintenance assures the stock a constant supply of water in the thirsty summer months.

From a woman's point of view, travelling to town high above the hot, dusty track means that she can arrive looking smart and fresh and, having picked up the mail, shopped for stores and completed any other business, still has time to relax with friends.

One can safely assume that aircraft owners will report faithfully on the condition of their landing strips, in which after all they have a vested interest. Others, with no actual experience of aircraft, are often less trustworthy. Once, having been assured that a station strip was quite O.K. I did my usual short field landing, stopping just in front of a patch of grass midway. While pegging down the machine I discovered to my horror that the grass concealed a deep "crab hole," which, had I gone into it at any speed, as I might very well have done, would undoubtedly have flipped the aircraft over. I pointed this out to the station manager, who was waiting nearby to take me to the homestead. "Oh yes," he said, quite unconcerned, "we get a lot of these sink holes around here. Actually, we haven't done anything to this strip for over twelve months. You would have done better to come in on the side."

The strip at Dirk Hartog Island was one of the oddest I was required to use. Only about four feet wide and very short, it curved between the sand dunes like a bicycle track.

The island is a long, narrow strip, about forty-eight miles long by three to seven miles wide. The little port of Denham, twenty-five sea miles away, is its nearest point of contact on the mainland. On Dirk Hartog I found a self-contained community living in the mellow stone buildings of an old sheep station, built on early colonial lines, complete with a little church of which only the ruin remains. They grew their own meat and vegetables and had a plentiful supply of oysters and seafoods of all kinds. It seemed to me an almost idyllic place for anyone really wanting to "get away from it all."

A brass plaque affixed to the lighthouse on its outermost cape commemorates the Dutch skipper of the merchant vessel *Eendracht*, who gave his name to the island when he landed there in 1616. In fact Dirk Hartog is the first European known to have set foot on the west coast of Australia and to commemorate his landfall he had left an inscribed plate that was returned to the Netherlands in 1940.

At the time of my visit the station was carrying about 10,000 sheep, for which the sea formed a natural boundary fence. They were hardly prize looking specimens, since grass on the island is sparse and they seemed to subsist mainly on hardy scrub.

I discovered that from time to time the old sheep were herded together on the northern tip of the island and driven over a 200 foot cliff into the sea. When I asked why the islanders practised this ruthless form of euthanasia, I was told that it was a matter of economic necessity. "By the time we get the stock shipped to the nearest port and trucked away to Perth we finish up with a bill for cartage over and above the market price. If we didn't get rid of the old animals there'd be no feed left for the younger ones."

"But doing it like that!" I demurred. "Surely there's some other way?"

"Well," I was told, "if you can think of something cleaner, quicker and cheaper you might let us know."

Since my last trip to Dirk Hartog the island has been purchased as a holiday resort by Perth's remarkable and benevolent Lord Mayor—Sir Thomas Wardle—otherwise "Tom the Cheap" of an Australia-wide empire of supermarkets.

While conducting clinics at Exmouth and on surrounding stations I stayed at the hospital, where I met some friends of my Royal Perth Hospital training days. They volunteered to come along and help me on their days off. In fact it was a place of happy meetings, for one day, while administering vaccine to employees of the local prawn processing factory, I had a surprise visit from a friend of my schooldays in Broome. He was Dick Morgan, son of a Broome pearler. At that time he was pioneering a culture pearling enterprise in the shallows of Exmouth Gulf, and with his wife Dinali was living in a caravan on the beach at the Bay of Rest. He told me that there was a flat stretch of claypan near his camp, which he would mark out with old tyres if I could manage to visit them. So I took an afternoon off and flew down with Vivian Cay, one of my young nursing friends.

I never tired of looking down on the jagged outline of this coast, eaten into by bays, creeks and inlets; the sea itself streaked with the varying blues, greens and indigos of depths, reefs and shallows and in places blurred by the sandy tidal churn. By contrast the land is stark and forbidding, at least in the arid region south of the Kimberleys. The climate is a bitter antagonist, not only in its pitiless heat but in the cyclonic storms of the summer months. These strike the coast with sudden and terrible fury so that its waters are dotted with wrecks. Some people say that ships from ancient Egypt and Phoenicia lie amongst them.

But the day Vivian and I flew down to the Bay of Rest the sky was innocent of a single cloud, and the sea serene and calm with huge sharks and turtles to be clearly seen cruising around the edges of the submerged reefs. The area that Dick had marked out for us on the claypan was only just long enough to get down on and had a good number of bone-shaking tidal corrugations. However, as "natural airstrips" go it wasn't bad at all.

Dick was keen to go up again to spot new reefs where he might plant some of his seeded pearl shells. So together with a sea chart of the area we took off and criss-crossed the bay, enabling Dick to mark out likely places. As I didn't have the right eyes for reef spotting, I let Dick fly the plane. He managed very well, and I was surprised to hear that it was his first attempt. He was obviously a natural flier and what's more he caught the flying "bug." During the next cyclone season (at which time he always packs up his camp and heads south) Dick learned to fly in record time and gained his full private flying licence. He is now in the "frustrated flier" category; isolated at the Bay of Rest for most of the year with no aeroplane. But they are provided with at least the sight of one from time to time, as I never fail to buzz the camp in passing. I've often wondered if they know who it is that regularly disturbs their peace; anyway their frantic waving indicates that it gives them as much of a thrill as it does me.

It was so hot when we returned that Vivian and I got into our bikinis and plunged into a part of the bay guaranteed to be shark free. We swam out to the raft on which Dick performs the operation of inserting tiny beads into the oysters of the big pearl shells. These beads act as an irritant, causing the oyster to cover them with layer upon layer of nacre, in the same way that "natural" pearls are formed over foreign particles that get into the oysters by accident. Vivian and I were fascinated to find how similar the operation was to a gastrostomy, and that afterwards the oyster shells, like human patients, were removed to "recovery beds."

Though it was late afternoon when we set off on our return flight to Exmouth the temperature was still 105 degrees—in fact rather more for us because of the sunburn we had acquired during the day. So we didn't bother changing out of our bikinis. We were just about to land on the Exmouth strip when another aircraft came nosing up to within a few feet of our wing and a passenger began filming us from the window. This machine landed just ahead of us and as I braked the aircraft to a stop the cameraman sprang out and ran towards us filming rapidly. As we emerged, however, he stopped dead, almost dropped his camera and stood gaping open-mouthed at we two bikini-clad maidens. We discovered later that he was a minister of religion who was making a film of mission activities in the north!

The airstrip at Exmouth was one of the worst on the run. This was hard to understand because it was often used by light aircraft in connection with the United States communications base then being built at Northwest Cape. Right on the edge of the gulf, the strip was covered with huge, ugly stones which could easily have burst a tyre, cracked a propeller, or done something equally disastrous. I complained several times to the Base Colonel, but as nothing practical was done about it I had to borrow a broom and literally sweep myself a clear path before each take off. This meant that I was pouring with sweat, caked with dust, and in a thoroughly bad temper by the time I was ready to get away.

There was a somewhat strained atmosphere about this base. The Americans were living in air-conditioned houses while most of the Australians were in caravans or stark mobile huts. The Aussies marvelled endlessly, with a curious mixture of envy and contempt, at the luxuries which the Yanks considered necessary to existence. It seemed to them some sort of affront to fair play that these blow-ins from overseas should be supplied with duty-free liquor and cigarettes, extravagant food, vegetables at city prices, and petrol at twenty cents a gallon. Among the incredible goods that were being sent direct from the States was a consignment of pianos that I saw piled up beside the jetty, and—even more astonishing—200 lawn mowers! As I watched the latter being unloaded I wondered what purpose they could possibly serve in that sun-baked country where it was hard enough to discover a single blade of grass. When I returned some time later, however, I was amazed to find green lawns flourishing under rotating sprinklers. I had to hand it to those "new chums" for enterprise, and wondered whether our Aussie attitude were not a rather absurd hangover from frontier times when the ability to rough it under crude, makeshift conditions was seen as a proof of stamina; a virtue to be cherished long after its purpose had disappeared.

There were two airstrips at Gascoyne Junction; one close to the township and another, much more suitable, about five miles away. The former strip was very short and had nothing to recommend it except its proximity to the centre of the town, which meant that aircraft could be taxied up and tethered to the gate-post of the Shire Hall! In wet weather a creek ran across the far end of the strip, and once, if my wheels had not sunk in deep mud, I would have skidded nose first into it. Another hazard was the horses that were always grazing in the area. At first, I managed to scare them off by buzzing the strip two or three times. But they soon got used to these tactics, and came the day when buzz them as I would they simply tossed their heads and went on feeding. I resigned myself to having to come down on the other strip and was flying towards it when I saw a willy-willy racing towards me across the plain. The whirling column of red dust seemed possessed of some evil spirit of Aboriginal legend. It hurled itself straight at the aircraft, enveloped it, whipped it around 180 degrees, and tossed it upwards in savage contempt. This was most unusual and certainly unexpected but I regained control and managed to land without mishap. I was shaking at the knees when I opened the door, to be met by the Shire Clerk who had kindly come out to fetch me back to town. As the only person in sight he collected the reaction to my shock: "Why the hell can't you keep your stupid horses off the airstrip?" I yelled, with a vehemence that I reserve mainly for the family.

He told me they belonged to the adjoining station and that it was the owner's job to control his stock.

One of my favourite places on the route was the port of Onslow, about 900 miles north of Perth. It is one of the few north-west towns that has somehow managed to retain a pioneering atmosphere—a feeling of every man, woman and child being part of a community that by sheer refusal to give in has come to terms with that inhospitable land. In the eighty-five years of the town's history it has been destroyed by cyclones more than ten times. On the last occasion Nan Corker, the hospital matron, was delivering a baby when the building collapsed about her. Somehow she completed the delivery and mother and child came through all right. I loved listening to Nan's stories of courage and resource told with a wealth of humour and homely philosophy. Her theory was that a good stiff brandy and a yarn to an understanding listener was the best medicine for most ailments. For me her prescription was "breakfast in bed"; a dose of spoiling that set me up for the next round of my relentless schedule.

But the best place of all for me was Broome. Mum was sometimes there and Dad never failed to be around the aerodrome when he heard I was due. He always had the kerosene refrigerators ready for my vaccine, which saved me having to find space in hospital or hotel freezers. I enjoyed the chance of quiet talks with him on topics ranging from flying to the state of the sad old world. Although he had not encouraged my flying in the first place he was now more than reconciled. In fact our mutual enthusiasm for aircraft brought us into an even closer relationship than we had known before.

11

CHOCOLATE KOATED PILL

"OH—YOU'RE THE GIRL GIVING OUT THE PILL," A NORTH-WEST school-teacher said when I introduced myself. By this time I was quite used to explaining that my job was concerned with the prevention of polio—not pregnancy.

The "Pill" story had preceded me around the north, no doubt propagated, to embarrass me, by my flying associates. The registration number of my aircraft—VH-CKP—encouraged further witticisms at my expense. Whenever giving my call sign—Charlie Kilo Papa—by telephonic alphabet, some voice would break in on the same wave length asking: "How's the Chocolate Koated Pill today?"

More people in the north-west were aware of the danger of tetanus than of polio and seemed disappointed that my scheme did not cover this hazard. I therefore began carrying a supply of tetanus vaccine and gave out triple antigen inoculation to children, many of whom had not been immunised against anything.

In fact as my job progressed I received an ever increasing number of enquiries about health problems of all kinds. Despite the splendid work of the R.F.D.S. many of the small communities never saw a nurse or doctor unless a sufferer was flown to the nearest centre for emergency treatment. During or after every clinic there was the inevitable hesitant question: "Sister, I wonder if you'd mind . . . ?" This would precede a description of a symptom or series of symptoms suffered by the speaker or some friend or relative.

I was always quite happy to help but had to be careful sometimes of overstepping the "nurse's prerogative" with which most doctors are so concerned. One can easily be trapped into a situation of the kind that caused me on one occasion to be asked to report to the Matron-in-Chief at the Medical Department in Perth. She had, she informed me, received a complaint from an irate doctor in one of the north-west ports to the effect that I had behaved in an unethical manner.

The incident referred to had occurred in the early hours of the morning at an hotel in one of the ports. I was awakened by the anxious wife of the proprietor—who happened also to be the mayor. She told me that her husband, while trying single-handed to eject some drunken customers from the premises, had received two black eyes, a number of minor abrasions, and a gaping wound in the forehead. I considered that the latter required immediate stitching. My advice to call a doctor was dismissed because of a dispute between the mayor and a local medico, reputedly over the latter's refusal to extend the facilities of the hospital X-ray unit to an injured race horse. So I produced my first aid kit without further ado. It was short of a few items, but with the help of a pair of pinking shears and some eyebrow tweezers, I made a pretty neat job of the stitching up.

"What can we do about his poor eyes?" the wife enquired, looking pityingly at her husband's grossly swollen countenance. "He's got an important lunch engagement, too—some businessmen arriving on the plane in a few hours' time."

Nothing in my nursing curriculum had covered treatment for this condition but my grandmother, who claims often to be in telepathic communication with me, at this moment transmitted a very useful piece of old world advice: "Make a strong cold tea compress!"

After several hours of this treatment the improvement was so remarkable that the mayor was able to keep his luncheon appointment with befitting dignity. In the ensuing court case it was stated that the proprietor had received numerous injuries one of which required stitching. The local doctors questioned each other concerning this repair which was finally traced to myself. Hence the complaint.

The Matron accepted my explanation of the circumstances and I later had the matter out with the doctor in question. I had the better of that argument.

Of all the health problems I encountered in the north none was as distressing as the incidence of trachoma. This is an infectious eye disease of mysterious origin which, although probably non-existent in Australia before the advent of white settlement, is now almost endemic in the north-west and Kimberleys. Sometimes misnamed "sandy blight" (a local name for any kind of conjunctivitis), trachoma is caused by a micro-organism and often results in blindness. It spreads rapidly in conditions of poor hygiene and is passed on by such agents as flies, personal contact, or towels shared with an infected person.

Aborigines and teachers in bush schools of from twelve to sixty pupils often asked me to have a look at the children's "sore eyes." Always, it was trachoma, on which I had received careful instruction from Professor Ida Mann, a W.H.O. expert on the detection and treatment of this disease.

The infection is discernible long before the patient complains of soreness and irritation. When the upper eyelid is rolled back, tiny white spots can be seen on its inner surface. These become gelatinous lumps which scar and contract the eyelids, so that the lashes turn in and cause irritation and ulceration of the eyeballs. Sometimes, if there is an improvement in general hygiene, the disease will clear up by itself. If not, the end result may be blindness—and, of course, the sufferer can in the process of time have infected many others.

Luckily the disease responds to treatment with eye drops and sulpha tablets and although these are no protection against re-infection, it is easy to prevent by the observation of ordinary hygiene. Even the ironing of clothes and towels will control the organism.

"Ordinary hygiene," however, is not always easy for people living in outback conditions, especially Aborigines, and it was pathetic to see so many children with badly damaged eyes, a condition which could have been avoided by standards that any city dweller demands as a right.

It became an increasing worry to me and a considerable addition to my load of work. I reported the situation to the Health Department, and was told, "Do what you can."

So, with the aid of the dedicated teachers of bush schools, mostly quite young men and women, I began my own programme. This included health talks, with slide shows demonstrating the progress of the disease. The children responded enthusiastically. Many were better and more intelligent about treating themselves than were their parents. In fact they often treated their parents too.

Then there were other problems: "Sister, the Aboriginal children are scratching their scalps all the time," a girl from the Native Welfare Department told me, and the reason wasn't hard to find. As the children lined up for their Sabin vaccine we examined their heads, and any discovered to be harbouring nits were sent home for treatment with D.D.T. powder.

Not so simple was the case of the child whose ear was a running mass of suppuration. Something was obviously lodged just inside, but I was not carrying a complete medical outfit and saw no way of getting it out—until I remembered the long-nosed pliers in the aircraft tool kit. The obstruction proved to be a pocket of dead flies lodged just behind the ear drum into which their activities had perforated. After this first experience I found the condition to be quite common and was ready to meet it with a pair of surgical forceps. It seems that the flies actually deposit their larvae in the children's ears, and eat through the ear drums in the same way that they "blow" sheep or cattle. No good station manager allows flyblown stock to go very long without attention; nor have I met any so callous as to knowingly permit the condition to go untreated in a station Aboriginal. In the cases I encountered the children and their parents seemed to have accepted the affliction—unlike such things as 'flu and bad colds, in which they readily seek advice—as something about which nothing could be done. It was "just one of those things" that the victim had to learn to live with and shut up about.

I began to understand why so many of the children I encountered were hard of hearing. Luckily the school teachers are now on the look-out for such defects, instead of blaming their slow learners for being stubborn, stupid, or inattentive. In fact the efforts of many teachers to improve conditions and open new vistas of enlightenment to outback children show a degree of dedication of which far too little is known.

It is gratifying to see the neglect of the past being tackled in other ways as well. Modern services, such as the appointment of Public Health Sisters in key towns, are doing much to improve the general welfare of our backward people.

But many years of neglect cannot be made good overnight. Nor should such deficiencies as a high infant mortality necessarily be attributed to the white man's disregard. There is a great deal we do not yet understand about the Aborigines' physical and psychological make-up; characteristics acquired over countless centuries of adaptation to highly specialised conditions, and within a social system in which survival of the fittest was a primary law of life.

IN A TOUGH
COUNTRY

OF THE FLIGHTS BETWEEN CENTRES I NEVER TIRED, AND HOW familiar I was to become with the defiant face of that ancient, parched and ravaged land. Travelling north from Perth I was soon past the areas of intensive agriculture, divided by the geometrical hand of man into farms and stations from five to ten miles apart. Then would come the scattered plots of the bolder experimentalists that ran out into an arid never-never of marsh and scrub.

From here on could be seen the tracks of that spirit hero of Aboriginal myth who had emerged from Shark Bay, once upon a dream, leaving the evidence of his journey in a trail of white saltpans that shine like giant coins.

From this point I always longed, when flying north, for two free hands—*and* the talent of course—to sketch the elaborate meanderings of tidal channels and creeks that seldom run; their intricate courses finely etched in shapes resembling the forest trees that flourished here in the geological past. For vast areas the hand of man is still nowhere in evidence, but the sprawling landscape looks from the air like the palette of a frenzied artist; splashed, blobbed, and smudged in ochre shades of yellow, red and white. Here and there the flat plains give place to low, rugged hills; sometimes convoluted and fissured like cerebral cortex, sometimes ranged in the long, dark structures of ironstone outcrops—ancient symbols of the country's future wealth.

Then come the new mining centres, twinkling from afar like clusters of bright, glass beads, to shape up on approach into neat rows of rectangular buildings with roofs glinting in the sun.

Iron ore has completely changed the way of life in much of the north-west, and to a great extent the outlook and tenor of the entire State. By this time everyone must be familiar with the story of how the discovery of the world's largest reserves of this and other minerals triggered off what is probably the greatest prospecting boom in history. At first few Western Australians realised what had hit them—and some still haven't. I had only a vague impression myself until I actually encountered the reality of these crude, noisy towns and centres. The many new names on the map —Port Hedland, Dampier, Mount Tom Price, Mount Newman, Mount Goldsworthy, Cape Lambert, Karratha, Pack Saddle, Paraburdoo and the rest of them—are all growing in the dust of urgent industry, shaking with the thunder of explosives and the rattle of half-mile-long trains of mineral cargo, ringing with the sound of prospecting machinery and the roar of giant earth-moving equipment. The harbours are busy as never before with ships being loaded up for Japan, Great Britain, and Europe.

When carrying out my vaccine programme in the more exclusively male of these communities I was usually escorted to the first aid post by the camp boss and left to carry on. During my first encounter with the situation I recalled an interview with the Mother Superior of Loreto Convent at the end of my schooldays, in which we were given what seemed at the time quite an outspoken talk on general behaviour and were each presented with a little book called "How to Say No". As far as I can remember the summation of the advice was that the best way to stay out of trouble was to keep men "at arm's length." Well, here I was, surrounded by men at very close quarters indeed, though my problem was not of having to say "no" but of persuading them to say "yes."

Most of the mine workers were big, robust young men, to whom the suggestion of being saved from a crippling disability

The author loading her Mooney aircraft VH-REM before taking off for a bush clinic from Port Hedland airfield

by a drop of vaccine seemed so much "bull-dust." They treated it as some wacky new notion on the part of the "heads," that they were inclined to buck on principle. I delivered my spiel and looked around, feeling as embarrassed as on my first day as a trainee in a Perth hospital ward. No one moved until a burly bloke began to elbow his way through from the back.

"My oath, I'm on!" he said. "My best mate got polio and hasn't walked since."

After that the show proceeded without a hitch. It taught me that the best way to persuade a doubtful group of the value of the service was to find someone who had had personal experience of the disease. After that it was plain sailing.

The end of the day's official programme was often as described elsewhere; only the beginning of another day's activity for me. If it was not advising on an assortment of ills and ailments, it was involvement in some local happening. One day while I was distributing vaccine in the Port Hedland Town Hall, Bill Neech, the Native Welfare Officer, asked if I could help search for a missing Aboriginal woman. She had been last seen wandering off into the bush in the general direction of Marble Bar, and her relatives were getting anxious for her safety. The police knew there was precious little chance of spotting her in the scrub, but reckoned that to take the plane up would at least give the impression that something was being done. Bill, an ex-R.A.F. pilot and a keen flier, was all on for it too. Any excuse for some low flying was O.K. by me, so I set off with him beside me and two policemen in the back.

We had worked out a square search pattern covering the areas that the woman was reported to have been seen in, and rose through a blast of heat under boiling summer cumulus that were a sure sign of turbulence.

The aircraft bounced and juddered as we flew out over the thick scrub. We circled bores and windmills, and looked for signs of camp fires, rubbish dumps, big shady trees, dry creek beds, or the flocks of crows and hawks that inevitably gather around carrion. We saw plenty of animal carcasses and tracks, but no sign of human footprints or remains.

After about an hour we spotted the fire of a native camp by a creek bed and swooped over it hopefully, catching the occupants

TOP: The author at work with "McLeod's Mob," in Wodjina Hills, Pilbarra district, Western Australia. BOTTOM: With Aboriginal children at Balgo, Western Australia

at an awkward moment when most of them were squatting comfortably behind rocks. We were low enough to see the whites of startled eyes as they leapt to their feet and ran for hiding, trailing their trousers as they went. Bill and I glanced back to see whether our companions were enjoying the joke, but found them seated miserably with their heads in their hands, all sense of humour or interest in the search lost in agonies of airsickness. They were only too grateful when we called it a day and restored them to their equilibrium.

But the police in those parts are normally a hardy bunch and need to be. They have some tough characters to deal with and some mighty unpleasant jobs to grapple with.

One of the worst of these is looking for—and sometimes finding—bodies in the bush. During this time I heard the story of an Aboriginal who had been seized by religious mania, and had disappeared after telling his mates that he was going to shoot himself for Christ. The police set out in blistering heat and eventually came upon the body with a gun close at hand. The man had been dead for about a week, but they could not bury him before finding the fatal bullet and matching it to the weapon in the remote possibility of establishing foul play.

Somehow they got the corpse back to town and handed it over to the doctor, who found that the bullet was lodged in the head. As a proper post mortem was beyond him at that stage of decomposition, he asked for a prospector's hammer. With this he cracked the skull open like a nut, found the bullet, and took off as quickly as possible.

At the door of the hospital he was met by a Native Welfare Officer. "One of the old men of the tribe has been on to me for a hank of the dead man's hair," he said. "It's some tribal business he has to carry out and he won't take 'no' for an answer. He says he has to get it himself."

"No fear," the doctor groaned. "Not after what I had to do to get that bullet."

They managed between them to persuade the old man that there was an evil spirit in the mortuary that only the doctor could handle. The doctor then slipped quietly into the women's ward, snipped a lock of hair from the head of an unconscious Aboriginal woman, and delivered it to the tribal elder with solemn ceremony.

70

They make a speciality of crude humour in the outback, maybe as a defence mechanism against the harsh realities of life. And of course no one caught in a predicament likely to make a good yarn need expect it to be kept dark. On one of my visits to Dampier, the two nurses with whom I was billeted told me that a few nights before they had been awakened by two men carrying in an injured mate. "What happened to him?" they asked the men, who answered, "No idea. We found him lying outside his house. He's quite conscious, but he seems too shocked to talk."

Having got the patient to bed the girls found that he had a curious assortment of injuries; a lacerated scalp, a broken leg and third degree burns to his buttocks. He refused to explain to them what had happened, nor would he tell the doctor whom the nurses called.

"Well, I just can't treat you until I know," the doctor said. "It might be a police matter."

The patient rolled agonised eyes towards the nurses: "All right," he moaned, "I'll tell you, but get *them* out of here first."

The nurses retreated to their living quarters, whence they heard a mumble of voices followed by a bellow of laughter from the doctor. When he called the girls back to assist with the treatment, he had regained his professional composure, but when the job was done and he was about to leave he could contain himself no longer. "I promised not to tell," he said, "but I just can't resist it."

It seems that the patient had been engaged in the routine procedure of killing mosquito larvae by pouring kerosene on to his water tanks. This done, he decided he might as well clean the bowl of his w.c. with the kerosene left in the can.

He then disposed himself comfortably on the toilet with a magazine and a cigarette. After a few minutes he eased up, dropped the butt into the bowl and returned to his reading. Twenty seconds later there was a shattering explosion and he was blasted from the seat. This accounted for the burns on his bottom. He had been sitting with his ankles crossed and came down with one leg under him—hence the broken leg. The scalp laceration was caused by striking his head on the lavatory pan as he came down.

The patient had concluded his tale of woe with a plea that was

71

as piteous as it was vain: "Don't tell anyone, Doc, or I'll never live it down."

The poor fellow had my sympathy, because as often as not the joke was against myself. An incident I found hard to live down happened on a flight to Mount Goldsworthy. It was one of those days of turbulent flying when the hot air, rising from the ironstone hills and sun-baked ground, seemed to lift the machine like a gigantic hand and drop it just as suddenly. At a particularly alarming stage of this process something shot from under the seat and nipped me sharply on the ankle. I was wearing only sandals, so was able to observe that my attacker had left two distinct punctures. My first thought was that it was probably a death adder, of which variety I had heard some hair-raising stories of recent weeks, so without further reflection I lifted my mike and announced that I thought I had been bitten by a snake.

I was the only woman flying around those parts so Port Hedland came back immediately with an anxious enquiry: "Charlie Kilo Papa. Are you all right?"

My condition seemed normal—except for a somewhat accelerated heartbeat. I could not feel any of the paralysis or shortness of breath associated with an injection of snake venom.

"Yes—all right so far," I replied shakily, feeling rather like the man who had jumped from the top of the Empire State Building. I put my legs up on the seat and scanned the red earth and scrub below for a place to land if I felt any more definite symptoms.

The aircraft droned on. Port Hedland called every two or three minutes with another anxious enquiry, to which I replied that I was anyway still alive.

Suddenly the aircraft gave another almighty leap, and as it dropped a mouse was flung skittering from its hiding place under the seat. In a moment of blind relief I grabbed the mike and blurted, "It's all right—it was only a mouse!"

I could hear loud male guffaws coming from all directions, and one M.M.A. pilot enquiring: "Are you standing on a chair?"

I came down as soon as possible to investigate whether the mouse had nibbled the control cables. I found it had behaved itself in this regard but had been living off my emergency rations. I meant to buy a trap but somehow didn't get around to it and by the time I returned to Perth, six weeks later, had become so used to its company that the idea of trapping it seemed like treachery. I searched the plane, with the idea of catching it by hand and releasing it to raise a family at Jandakot, but it had forestalled me by disembarking apparently by instinct on the southbound flight.

The weather, always a major concern to a pilot, was actually more of a worry to me when I was on the ground than in the air. A pilot's options in bad weather are pretty well defined; he must either battle through it, return to base if he has enough fuel, or, if there is a convenient landing-field, set the machine down.

The real problems began when I *was* on the ground. I spent many sleepless nights worrying about the safety of the aircraft, pegged down on some remote airstrip and with howling winds trying to whip her away like a kite. On one occasion, when flying home to Perth, the turbulence was so severe and the wind so strong that I was making little headway and was obliged to turn back and land at Mount Magnet.

This wasn't easy, as every time I lifted the wing in an attempt to turn, the wind would catch it and try to keep the aircraft rolling. But we made it back, and landed in rain that was being swept ahead of an oncoming cyclone. By the time I had hammered in the pegs I was drenched and freezing, but dared not leave the plane. So I sat out the night in the cabin; cramped, cold and shivering, feeling the constant jerking vibration, and crawling out to hammer the pegs down again whenever it seemed that the aircraft was about to drag them out. The fact of having to spend a good many nights in similar conditions was another good reason for my preferring to continue the job alone. I could never have expected anyone else to feel the same way about my aircraft and to share such discomfort on its behalf.

Nor was wind the only hazard. As every pilot knows, horses and cattle find the wings and tailplanes of aircraft convenient back-scratchers. I once found a donkey stretching itself with its forefeet up on the wing and another time, at Fitzroy Crossing, discovered that my fibreglass wheel spats had been chewed up by goats. Birds, of course, make a point of honouring the polished surface of an aircraft with their "mark," and find air vents and undercarriage fairings the most desirable of housing sites.

13

McLEOD'S MOB

"YOU'VE HEARD OF DON MCLEOD?" BILL NEECH ASKED IN THE
Native Welfare Office in Port Hedland. "I've arranged for us to
give out vaccine to his mob. They're a nomadic tribe now, you
know—out beyond Abydos Station at present."

Before 1946 few people in Western Australia had heard of
Don McLeod, but after that time most of the nation was aware
of him. Interpretations of his activities and his motives differed
considerably, but at least it was agreed that, for one reason or
another, he was passionately involved with the Aborigines. In
1946 he had organised a strike for wages and better conditions
that brought out 600 Aborigines from stations throughout the
Pilbara. Actually the dispute was to go on for years, during
which time some of the natives drifted back to the stations, others
broke into a separate co-operative group, and some stuck with
"McLeod's mob," and formed themselves into the Pindan
Mining Company. It is a long and complex story, much of which
has been related in the novel *Yandy*, by Donald Stuart, and which
has been otherwise dealt with in two comprehensive theses by
anthropologists John and Katrin Wilson. Don McLeod himself
doesn't, as I later gathered, appear to go far along with any of

these versions of his struggle to raise the Aborigines' level of independence. The full truth, as with all other controversial aspects of history, will never really be known. But I was interested in the opportunity to form a personal impression of McLeod and such of his people as remained with him.

"I'll meet you at the Abydos strip," Bill told me before I left his office. "It should be an interesting experience."

From Port Hedland I took along with me two nurses named Meg Cheesman and Penny Webb who were hitch-hiking around the North West. En route to Abydos, a sheep property about eighty miles south-east of Hedland, I had to take in the township of Marble Bar, about 114 miles from the port. This is reputedly one of the hottest spots in the world, with a summer temperature often running over 100 degrees Fahrenheit for weeks on end.

The town, which sprang up after the discovery of gold in the Pilbara district in the late 1880s, once boasted a boom population of 1500, but this was short-lived. It is now the centre of comparatively small scale mining, but the surrounding district is known to be rich in minerals and some residents prophesy another boom in the near future. The marble from which the town derives its name is actually a bar of jasper that runs across the nearby Coongan River.

While there on this trip, my two young friends and I were pressed to attend a party at an outlying property named Coongan Station. We were assured that it would be great fun and that the landing strip was "perfectly O.K." In fact it proved to be so overgrown that we could not even locate it, so we had to come down in a gymkhana paddock fairly ploughed up by horses' hooves and we narrowly missed a couple of nicely camouflaged goal posts.

The occasion was a big celebration dance, held in traditional style in the shearing shed. Actually it *was* fun, especially as I was able to combine business with pleasure by doling out doses of vaccine to be washed down with beer. I knew from past experience that the vaccine would be blamed for every hangover, but felt I had somehow to justify the frolic and the risk incurred on landing.

Bill was awaiting us next day on our arrival at Abydos. Meg, Penny and I secured the plane and boarded his vehicle, and were driven along an almost imperceptible track between scrub and hills, deep into the Tinstone and Wodgina Ranges. At intervals an Aboriginal would appear from nowhere, and without a word leap onto the Landrover and solemnly point the way ahead. These living roadsigns brought us at last to Don McLeod's camp of which my first impression was the absence of animals. Most "black camps" I had visited had been plagued by dozens of half-starved, half-wild dogs and cats, that made life a misery for themselves and everyone else but from which the natives refused to be separated. Somehow Don McLeod had managed to persuade his people that they were better off without them—a thing no station manager I have yet encountered has been able to do.

It was a remarkable camp in many ways. We found about two hundred people living in the rocky gullies among the sunparched hills and looking, despite having to trek a long way for water, surprisingly clean and healthy. The women's clothes were un-ironed but fresh and their hair brushed. There were no sick babies and none of the belligerent alcoholics who were all too common in some Aboriginal communities. "All the people here know that a blackfella can't take alcohol," Don told us. "If they can't do without it, they can go somewhere else."

Don is nuggety, sunburnt, and as spare as the native vegetation. Probably in his sixties, he is direct and fluent of speech, and extremely widely read. He shook his bearded head when we asked him to share the lunch we had brought along with us. "I eat the same as the rest of them," he said. "I led them out here and I won't have them think I'm taking favours from anyone. One of the women will bring me over something soon."

He explained that they all lived by collecting tin from the creek beds. The pieces of metal were separated from extraneous matter by a process known as "yandying," which entailed placing the material in a curved sheet iron container and shaking it expertly until the metal was at one end and the discard at the other. Each member of the group had his own specially labelled jam tins, which with infinite labour and patience were filled with tiny pellets of tin. A 44-gallon drum full of these tins would eventually be taken to Port Hedland and sold for about $2,000. From this each man would receive his rightful share.

"Everything they make goes back to them," Don told us.

"We have a store here and I've taught them the value of money so they don't splurge it on rubbish. I choose clothes for the girls and the kids when we go to town." He smiled. "They think I've got good taste."

He then told us something of the co-operative system they had developed over the past twenty years. This was administered by a committee elected by an interesting adaptation of the old tribal system, but in which women, though still excluded from traditional ritual spheres, occupied positions of complete equality.

After lunch Don called them all over and, speaking slowly and carefully, explained the purpose of the vaccine. We distributed the impregnated sugar lumps which were by that time saturated with as much red dust as vaccine; then he asked: "Would you mind having a look at my head man's eyes? His name's Crow. He's a good man and I hope he'll take over here when I'm finished. He's been complaining of sore eyes for a good while now."

This had an all too familiar sound. I examined the man's eyes and then, with the help of Penny and Meg, looked at those of all the other people. "I'm afraid the whole camp's got trachoma," I told Don when we'd finished. "We'll get some eye medicine out to you, but you'll have to use it properly if it's going to do any good at all."

I then explained to Don and four of the most responsible members of his group about the necessary sulpha tablets and eye-drops. One of the main problems about leaving Aborigines to treat themselves is that they tend to take all the medicine at once, forget about it altogether, or to give it to the children— perhaps with the idea that it will save them from similar symptoms. These practices have been known to have fatal results.

As an isolated community in the process of "guided social change," I thought it might have more chance than the average of eliminating trachoma altogether. They were so touchingly eager to understand and to help themselves that when I returned to Perth I mentioned the matter to Dr Ida Mann, who had taught me a lot of what I know about the detection and treatment of eye diseases. She had met Don on a previous tour of inspection for the Department of Health, and as she was going north around' that time decided to pay him a friendly call. She was able to confirm that the whole camp did in fact have trachoma.

About two months after my first visit, Don granted Dr Mann and myself permission to return to his camp. We were delighted to find that the treatment was being carried out meticulously and was working well. We both felt privileged by Don's trust in us and respectful of the tenacity with which, through thick and thin, he has stuck to the controversial course on which he embarked so many years ago. There was no doubt whatever that he had succeeded in instilling a new pride and confidence into the members of his group. He had shown that Aborigines, under consistent guidance and separated as far as possible from the temptations offered by degraded whites, are perfectly capable of responsible planning and action on their own behalf.

I visited them four times in all, both to continue the trachoma treatment and to give the booster doses of vaccine. On each occasion the camp had been shifted to a different part of the hills, but I welcomed the chance of seeing more of that intriguing wilderness that was still, for its original people, rich in the traditions of their dream-time. During this period Meg and Penny had arrived in the Kimberleys, Meg to become Matron of the Wyndham Hospital and later to marry in that town; Penny, after some time working in the same hospital, to marry Jan Ende, the R.F.D.S. pilot stationed in Derby.

I ran into them both again from time to time while I was in that part of the north, and we were able to exchange notes on medical cases and social problems. These we discovered to be more and more complicated as we delved into them. It might appear from what we had observed of Don McLeod's group that the key to the Aboriginal problem lay in getting the people off the stations or away from the towns, and into community enterprises. But it was by no means as simple as that. What was right for "McLeod's mob" could be quite wrong for people in other areas and different circumstances. McLeod's plan for guiding his people towards self-determination within a segregated situation had shown impressive results in the face of incredible setbacks and a deal of opposition. It was his opinion that the formal education being received by young Aborigines in towns, on missions and settlements served only to confuse and corrupt them. He told us that a few young people of his group who had gone off to missions had come back destroyed and had been voted out of the community.

78

ments served only to confuse, unsettle and corrupt them. In fact he told us that the few young people of his group who had gone off to missions had come back destroyed and had been voted out of the community.

One would need to be very brash indeed to argue the point with a man who had cut himself off from his own people in order to understand and to live the life of his followers. It seemed, however, that the education he rejected as wrong for his group could well be the best, if not the only course, for Aborigines born and bred within mixed and competitive communities, and in areas where there was no such simple economic outlet as alluvial mining.

Co-operatives, to help Aborigines take their first steps into our complex economy, need the guidance of men like Don McLeod; dogged, one-eyed individualists. But where are these to be found? Even the most dedicated missionaries have to toe the line in obeying their superiors, not to mention departments and governments on which they are, to some extent at least, dependent for support. They must also consider the goodwill of the outside communities—a thing from which McLeod's people alienated themselves when they began their stand against the system.

Then there are the problems of where and in what industries such co-operatives can be set up in regions other than those of alluvial mining. Cattle stations? Fishing enterprises? Cottage industries? Such things have been and are being considered and may come to something eventually, but in the meantime history is moving quickly, tribal groups are becoming scattered, and the Aborigines are increasingly attracted to the towns.

Don McLeod's fight for wages and improved conditions in the North-West had reactions in the Kimberleys, where a complete walk-out of Aboriginal workers would have been more serious than on the sheep properties further south. Limited payment was introduced after the war, and in 1968 a Bill was passed by which all Aboriginal employees were to receive award rates.

Viewed from the outside, this might look like an all-out victory for the forces of enlightenment, but there were other sides to the situation that I was soon to experience at uncomfortably close quarters.

14

"DURACK TIME"

I ARRIVED AT A WEST KIMBERLEY STATION ONE DAY TO FIND THE manager faced with the heartbreaking task of selecting nine Aboriginals from the hundred or more who had been attached to the station for well over half a century.

"The ones I choose can keep their immediate families here," he said, "but the rest will simply have to go. The new law stipulates that all native workers must receive award rates from now on, and we can't afford more than nine of them. How the others will get on, heaven only knows. The station has been their life."

The "blacks' camp," usually situated on the river bank near every main homestead, was a carry-over from "the early days" when the white settlers came in with their flocks and herds. They had encouraged able-bodied Aborigines to work for them, which meant that the families had to come too—not just wives and children but parents, uncles, aunts, cousins, and a complicated variety of tribal relatives. The younger men worked mainly as stockmen, and many soon developed a skill to rival that of the Wild West cowboys. The women were trained in household tasks, and the older folk would potter around at various jobs such as gardening, milking, and carting wood; sometimes working for only an hour or two a day or as the mood seized them. They took it for granted, in accordance with their true community outlook, that all received the same benefits by way of payment. These were regular distributions of clothing and blankets, tobacco, medicines, tucker, and a little pocket money. The station owners claimed that it was not cheap labour and this was probably true, but as time passed it began to appear from the outside very much like the former slave labour conditions in America. Just as on many of the plantations in that country, however, the dark-skinned workers were if anything more reluctant to alter the status quo that they had come to understand and to accept as a way of life, than were their white employers.

I was inclined to agree with the station manager that only needless hardship all round could result from the new legislation. On reflection, however, I guessed that my reaction would probably have been the same to Don McLeod's organisation of the Pindan strike in 1946—had I been around at that time. This stand had also resulted in cases of individual hardship. Many of the North-West station people were devoted to their Aboriginal workers and the workers to them. Numbers had not wanted to strike but dared not stand out. Some went back to the stations, only to discover that improved mechanisation had superseded them, so they drifted into the settlements and town reserves. Nonetheless, McLeod had forced the wheel of change that was in many respects overdue to turn.

The same might well have been said of the introduction of award rates. The change had to come, for it was difficult in a democratic country to uphold a law that maintained differences of race, status and education. The trouble was that, as with many similar reforms in other parts of the world, it had come without the gradual upgrading of education and living standards by which many of the unfavourable aspects of the new régime might have been avoided.

Writing of the situation in her book *The Rock and the Sand*, my mother put it this way:

"Post war Australian policy, in a precipitate effort to prove its social conscience to the world, had so far done little more for the natives of the north than to deprive them of the few important things they had clung to in their subjection. They had acquired a sense of importance without incentive or self-respect, freedom with nowhere to go, a living without a way of life."

The immediate result of the new law, as I saw it, was a pathetic maladjustment. Being thus cast adrift from their homes and cherished communities and deprived of their jobs, however menial or insignificant they may have been, the Aborigines had lost their identity and all sense of meaning in life.

A few found jobs elsewhere but the majority began drifting into the town reserves, mostly to subsist on government handouts and to spend their time in gambling, drinking and prostitution. Others "went bush" and lived for the most part by spearing stock on the stations that had once supported them.

I was holding an immunisation clinic at Kalumburu Mission when a police party staggered in after a sixty mile walk. It appeared that their vehicle had broken down while they were looking for a group who had been "bushranging" on Gibb River Station. They were generally in a pretty bad way; painfully sun-burned, and with shockingly blistered feet. I imagine that the Aborigines in question had probably observed their predicament with some amusement, as perhaps too had the shades of the old Mounted Police who carried out their job on horseback and were renowned for their bushcraft.

Flying over the Kimberleys my feelings were an inexpressible mixture of sadness and exhilaration. So different from the red spinifex stretches of the North-West was that 283,000 square mile area. Its immense plains are interlaced with an elaborate complex of river systems; its skyline broken by the dramatic contours of mountain ranges, sometimes rounded like batches of bread prepared for giants, sometimes flat-topped like the tables on which they might be served, the sides sloping sharply like draped coverings embossed with a textured patterning of vegetation. I was thrilled by the wild colours and formations of this lonely landscape, with its expanses of park-like savannah dotted with white gums, bauhenias, paper barks, grotesquely spreading boabs and improbable ant-hill empires, the water courses darkly etched with a tropical profusion of trees, creepers and pandanus palms, and speckled with ubiquitous flocks of black crows, white cockatoos and eagle hawks.

It was incredible to me, moving 5,000 feet above at 130 miles an hour, the shadow of my aircraft a small swiftly moving cross far below, that the pioneers had ever found their way or lived to tell the tale of the land they had discovered and believed to be the answer to the Australian pastoralist's prayer. I thought about Alexander Forrest and his little survey party, trailing with their horses and packs along the big rivers from the west coast across to the overland telegraph line in the Territory in 1879. And I thought of my great-grandfather Patsy's brother Michael, two years later, leading a party from Cambridge Gulf, the first white men to follow the course of the Ord and to strike out west to the coast at Beagle Bay. I thought of the stocking of the country in the following years, the sheep men shipping their flocks from the south-west and driving them inland along the course of the Fitzroy while the cattle men struck out overland from Queensland to settle on the fertile pastures of the Ord and the Margaret.

It was especially moving to me to visit at last the stations pioneered by and, until 1950, controlled by members of my mother's family. Different branches, with their partners, had originally settled millions of adjoining acres of leased grazing land in East Kimberley and the Northern Territory, their original properties having been Argyle, Ivanhoe, Lissadell, Rosewood and Dunham River. Grandfather Patsy Durack and his sons held Argyle and Ivanhoe, and later joined the owners of Newry and Auvergne, in the Northern Territory, to form the company of Connor, Doherty and Durack.

It didn't really prove to be the gilt-edged asset of their dreams. They still faced hazards of uncertain seasons, stock diseases, marketing, poor prices, isolation and the rest, so I suppose it is little wonder that Grandfather, having seen the company through the trough of the depression and the war years, decided to sell out while the going was good. Only his eldest son, Reg, and his family retained a material interest in the north. Their property, Kildurk, on the Northern Territory side of the border, had been a part of the million acre Auvergne station run.

I had been particularly anxious to visit Argyle and Ivanhoe

stations, where my mother, aunt, and uncles, and of course my grandparents, great-aunts and great-uncles before them, had spent so much of their lives. The Ivanhoe Station homestead of those times was destroyed by fire, coincidentally on the day of Grandfather's death in September 1950, and a new place had since been built on the river bank. Argyle, however, I recognised at once from photographs; a simple stone building, with wide verandahs paved with flat slabs from the river bed. As it was the first real home to have been built in the East Kimberleys, and held so much of the history of the district, it was sad to think that it would soon disappear under the waters of the new Ord River dam. It has since been decided, however, that it will be removed and set up again on another site to become a pioneer museum.

Many stations in the north were, and some still are, owned by outside companies employing managers, not all of whom had the same attitude to the Aborigines as owners who maintained an immediate association with their properties. It is fashionable these days to assume that all station owners were unvarying exploiters of Aboriginal labour, and to scoff at the possibility of a family relationship existing between natives and white employers. I might even have had doubts about this myself had I not experienced such an affectionate welcome from the old station people who referred nostalgically to "Durack time."

As so many of these people had become scattered of recent years I made a point, everywhere I went, of asking "Are there any Durack time people here?" There usually were, and when I introduced myself there would be great excitement. I would find myself fondly embraced as "belong Mary little girl," and bombarded with questions about different members of the family and with memories of other days. Eyes would overflow with tears at mention of those who had passed on or met with misfortune of any kind, while there would be exclamations of joy at news of births and marriages.

On one station I was invited by the Aboriginal community to afternoon tea, which was served with the care and ceremony no doubt taught them by Durack women of long ago. They found it hard to believe that I actually flew an aircraft, but vividly recalled my father having stunted over Argyle and Ivanhoe before dropping down to call on Mum and Auntie Bet.

Top: Captain Miller helps the author to load the Mooney; Broome. Bottom: Trying to solve a problem on the Mooney

"One time," an old retainer named Duncan recalled wistfully, "we reckon 'im bin bugger up properly." He then described with expressive gestures how the aircraft had appeared to drop from the sky in a dizzy whirl towards inevitable doom, only to regain equilibrium just above the level of the trees and to slip down safely in the horse paddock.

They had all decided at the time that such deeds of derring-do must surely be to impress "the girls," though which one especially they could not agree upon.

Old Duncan was eager to take me to some family grave on a river bank, which he told me had become obscured by silt in the last flood. I could not make out whose grave he was referring to, though I gathered that the occupant's untimely end had been due to the machinations of an evil spirit known as "Red-legs." I did not have time to embark on the expedition they suggested, but I was really enjoying my talk with these dear old people when a rather cross voice interrupted us: "Clear off now, you all about! Missus can't waste time talking to you."

I was embarrassed and distressed, but the people themselves took it all in good part. "Yes, well, you got a big job to do," Duncan agreed, and diving into his little house brought me out a boomerang. "This might come in handy," he said, "s'pose you got to come down in the bush sometime."

I guess he thought that if I could fly an aeroplane I could surely manage such a simple device as a boomerang!

I once came upon an old "Durack time" woman in the Kununurra hospital, where I was staying during that stage of my programme.

"That's old Lizzie from Ivanhoe Station," I was told in explanation of the terrible wailing that had arisen from a room down the corridor. "She's about eighty and there doesn't seem to be much we can do with her. If we don't lock the door she gets out and makes bush. She spits out her tablets, throws her food over the floor, and wails like a dingo day and night."

I asked to see her, and found the poor dishevelled old soul crouched rocking to and fro in the corner of a room she had turned into a shambles. When I spoke to her she glowered suspiciously through her tangled hair.

"I know you, Lizzie," I said. "You belong Ivanhoe."

Typical outback country over which the author flew on her vaccination rounds. Top: Mount House Station, Phillip Range, Kimberley. Bottom: Kennedy Range, east of Carnarvon

"What name you?" she asked sullenly.

When I explained who I was her face became transformed and she flung her arms around my knees in delight. Then followed the ramifications of family trees in her world and my own and a flood of reminiscences.

"Look missus," she confided at last, opening a tobacco tin into which she had spat out a number of tablets. "They been giving me this bad medicine. I reckon might be poison."

I pretended to examine them carefully and critically. "No," I said, "that good medicine. That same like I give my Mummy and Daddy when they have bad cold."

This so completely satisfied her that I had to prevent her from taking all the tablets at a gulp. For the rest of my time there I brought my "book work" to do in her room and slipped her an occasional sugar lump which she devoured with relish. She would fall asleep as I worked, still rambling on about the past. By the time I left she was obviously on the mend and has since returned to her family on the Kununurra reserve, a few miles from the Ivanhoe Station homestead.

I don't tell this story to reflect credit on myself as someone with a special understanding of the Aborigines. In fact I must confess to having very little real understanding of these interesting and complex people. But I have learned one thing about them which no doubt applies to all other human beings: that they need to retain a link with their past, a sense of identity that can be restored in some measure by such a simple thing as recognition by an old acquaintance, or even a meeting with someone who knows their country and can spare the time to let them talk of it.

15

HAPPY HOUR

ONE OF THE BEST PARTS OF LIVING AWAY FROM HOME WAS THE joy of returning for short intervals between clinics. My first stop, after landing back at Jandakot, was always the Medical Department. There, having extracted my precious collection of stones and other souvenirs, I would leave a heap of surgical towels covered with grease and red dust to be laundered, and the heavy insulated boxes to be refilled with vials of vaccine. Sometimes I would be properly dressed, but would mostly be wearing the stained operating gown I put on when cleaning out the plane and making running repairs.

The first time I reported back to Dr Davidson, he had asked whether I needed an assistant. "No thanks," I told him. "I'm getting on all right, and by going it alone I'm risking no one's life but my own." I didn't say that the risk I most feared was being saddled with an assistant who was either incompatible or prone to airsickness—possibly even both. There was also an element of pride in my independent attitude. The southern territory was being covered by teams of three, so I was proving something to myself by working singlehanded.

I didn't realise how hungry I was until I got home. When on

the job I mostly stayed in outback pubs where, since I came in at odd hours when the staff was either asleep or busy in the bar, I as often as not cooked my own meals. My first concern after arriving at a town was always to find a big refrigerator in which to store my vaccines, so during those two years I became familiar with the inside of almost every refrigerator in the North-West and Kimberleys. In the hotels, these were usually situated in the "slum and slop" areas behind bars and kitchens. I had the doubtful privilege of seeing what went on behind the scenes, and would sometimes recognise food being served up in the dining rooms that I had last seen covered with ants and dead flies.

I used to think that some of Mum's culinary tricks were a bit dubious, but I just didn't know how the other half lived. I was very glad to get back to some wholesome home cooking.

Mum is a quick, practised but rather unpredictable cook. Mostly her concoctions turn out surprisingly well, but occasional accidents occur in the general confusion, like too much chilli sauce, too much salt, or no salt at all. Once, when she was actually following a recipe, the strangest thing of all occurred. My youngest sister, Marie Rose, had just returned from school holidays on a station in the Murchison, and this was a sort of welcome home. The meal was proceeding happily until everyone began removing foreign particles from the mince.

"It's full of grit!" someone complained.

"Nonsense," said Mum, always ready to defend herself. "Those little bits are only pepper-corn. It was in the recipe."

"Not out of a pepper tin on the kitchen shelf?" Marie Rose asked in shocked tones.

"Where else do you expect?" Mum said.

Marie Rose dived into the kitchen emitting a terrible wail. "Oh NO! You *couldn't* have! That was my Yalgoo gold dust! It's worth a fortune!"

With more eagerness than she had ever before displayed for the job she removed the plates and made vain efforts to salvage what specks of gold remained. I draw a veil over the suggestions put forward for the recovery of the specimens that had already gone down!

In our house dinner is cooked—usually without much fore-thought—in what is known to us as "happy hour." Julie first gave it that name and it has somehow stuck, even though it's not as happy and hilarious as it used to be. It's a kitchen-based evening ritual during which friends and family drift in and out, talking loudly and, if so inclined, drinking anything they can find in fridge or cupboards. Although mostly interested in talking about themselves they are usually prepared to lend an ear to the traveller returned—the sailor from the sea, the hunter from the hill, the flier from wherever it might be. When both Patsy and Julie were working with M.M.A., it was mostly fliers. My sisters had inherited much the same feeling towards the north as myself, and during their school holidays had sometimes taken governessing and child-minding jobs on outback stations. Patsy later went off to England and joined a group of young Australians intent on "finding themselves" abroad, which in almost every case amounted to finding someone else. During this period she met the young Australian Fleet Air Arm pilot whom she was later to marry in Canada, but in the meantime she had returned home and donned the uniform of the M.M.A. flight hostesses.

Julie had completed her Commercial Art course at the Perth Technical College and spent some time teaching at various schools. She was a gifted artist, full of energetic originality, but her exuberant, gregarious and restless spirit sought outlet in a faster moving and more extrovert role. She had therefore thrown herself wholeheartedly into the flying job, and was at that time the chief checking hostess for the company.

Julie, more than any of us, enjoyed her inherited identity with both the land and the air. Although interested in such things as wealth, possessions and titles as part of other people's backgrounds, she envied no one anything. I remember her indignation when someone once asked Mum whether she shared the problem of children wanting "to keep up with the Joneses." "Phooey," said Julie, "blow the Jaguars and the luxury launches—as far as I'm concerned we *are* the Joneses." She had a way of transmitting something of her own cheerful confidence to less assured friends and relatives, a thing that made life seem, for many, almost insupportable when she was no longer around.

She treated all passengers, business tycoons, government officials, workers of all colours and nationalities like VIPs. Always vitally interested in anyone travelling into "her" country on "her" airline, she would launch into a conversation with anyone at any level and would reward the feeblest attempts at humour with her specially encouraging brand of laughter.

She would dole out advice to her workmates on anything from how to get or keep husbands or wives, how to pack in five minutes flat, remove stains from fabric, or pull themselves round from heartbreaks and hangovers. She would turn from initiating a bush Aboriginal in the use of a knife and fork to advising a travelling politician on the problems of the country and how to remedy them, or a perilously expectant mother on how to delay the progress of labour while in the air. She would harangue company chiefs on working conditions in the tropics, and tell mechanics what needed to be done to the aircraft.

Needless to say this habit of expressing herself fully and forthrightly did not endear her to all members of the staff. The efficiency she expected, in a country where high standards were hardly traditional, caused some people to duck for cover at the sight of her.

In addition to her normal duties she had taken a special interest in the improvement of flight safety precautions and the evacuation of aircraft in the event of emergencies. It had not been enough for her enquiring mind to accept the advice issued in the operations manual. She had to assure herself that escape hatches and chutes would indeed open in times of crisis. It did not make her especially popular with the management when she discovered that in several instances this was not the case, and also that the evacuation procedures could never have been carried out in the given time. She therefore set herself the task of redrafting the manual on more realistic and up-to-date lines and she personally trained the girls until they had attained a standard of competence unequalled by that of any other air hostess staff in Australia. As President of the Air Hostess Association (W.A. Branch) she fought tirelessly for the improvement of flying conditions and was instrumental in effecting a general upgrading of wages and accommodation and in setting a more reasonable limit to flying hours. She and Patsy worked together to bring about the proper organisation of their Association and to update the award to meet modern conditions.

Julie was born as extrovert as Patsy and I were introvert. She loved big parties as much as we shrunk from them. She could cope and cater on any scale and go "kicking on" as long as there was anyone left to keep up with her. I came to appreciate her social aplomb as a special and sometimes valuable gift, but as a child I found it both alarming and embarrassing. She started making an impression on aircraft travellers on the first flight we made together to Broome when she fell madly in love with the hostess, Kitty O'Neill. She insisted on "helping" her with the passengers and having been put tactfully back in her seat beside me made an announcement that caused me to fairly shrink with apprehension. "I've promised Kitty something special," she said. "I'm going to make her a pair of glubs." Julie's "glubs" consisted of a pair of men's socks slit open, cut in duplicate from an imprint of her own fat little hand, and cobbled together again. I was worried that Kitty might expect a proper pair of gloves, not two for the same hand which wouldn't fit anyway, but I comforted myself with the thought that Julie would probably forget about the deal after she got to Broome. No such luck! She was determined to get on with the job immediately and with this aim in view approached one startled male passenger after another asking if he would mind giving her his socks. "Dad says you don't need socks up north," she said. "It's too hot." Her blandishments proved unsuccessful, but once in Broome Dad was only too glad to supply her with all the socks she wanted to keep her quiet. So Kitty, making suitable noises of surprise and delight, eventually received her "glubs."

In later years I often had occasion to bless Julie's loving heart and impulsive generosity. It was always a thrill to meet up with her along the track when she would give me not only moral but physical support in the form of fruit and chocolate which were hard to come by in the outback. Sometimes I would return tired and hungry to my parked machine on some out-of-the-way airstrip to find a bag of goodies and a note to say that she had spotted my plane when the aircraft she was hostessing dropped by. Once she actually loomed up in front of me as I was about to take off from Carnarvon across Shark Bay in very bad weather. "You'll have to run over me first if you try to take off in this," she said. "They don't call that 'Shark Bay' for nothing. You'd be just mad to fly anywhere today."

91

I promised to take her advice, but once she was on her way could not resist trying to make up for lost time. I soon regretted my foolhardiness. Half across the bay, something shot past me at a rate of knots, and for a moment I thought I'd seen a flying saucer. I soon realised that it was the windsock torn loose from my immediate destination, the Denham airstrip. This meant that it must be blowing really hard down there; also that I would have to land without knowing the exact wind direction, and risk running off the strip into the bush if I came in on the wrong one. The airstrips—two narrow clearings on a salt pan— are bad enough at the best of times and very slippery when wet. I solved the problem by flying over anchored fishing boats which always face into the wind, but as I came down and gave my call sign and time of arrival to Carnarvon air radio I heard Julie's scolding voice through the aircraft speaker, "Mike Mike Romeo to Charlie Kilo Papa. No more bickies for naughty girls. And what's more I'm going to tell Gran."

When I got back I always knew immediately when Patsy and Julie were home because I would hear their voices from the kitchen intent on outdoing each other with accounts of their latest adventures. It's a pity we didn't tape record their more hilarious experiences, which lost nothing in the telling. Patsy specialised in revolting stories about flights with dead bodies, people getting trapped in the aircraft toilet, or losing their false teeth in sick bags and demanding that they be retrieved. Julie always seemed to be on board when criminals were being escorted south for trial, Aborigines armed to the teeth with ceremonial weapons taken to the city to perform corroborees, premiers being flown to open things or lunatics to be shut up.

Once she had to deal with a schizophrenic who had been at different times a dog, a horse and a bull, but was then being an elephant, in which role he had wrought havoc in a general store. The young policeman escorting him knew him to be a decent enough fellow in his right mind, and enlisted Julie's help in trying to talk him out of his illusion. Game for anything, she put forward a number of what she thought would be key questions.

"Going to Perth are you?"

"Trapped me, the bastards! Taking me to the South Perth Zoo."

"How many wives have you got?"

"Elephants mate for life, don't they?" he said, and went on swinging his trunk.

"What religion are you?"

He looked her suspiciously in the eye: "Whatever religion elephants are, I s'pose."

"What do you want for lunch?"

"Have you got any bananas?"

I would have thought she was drawing the long bow but for an experience I had not long before in Shark Bay, when asked to prescribe for someone with "touch fever."

"You mean he's got a touch of fever?" I asked.

"No, *touch fever*," I was told earnestly.

Alert to the outback habit of leg-pulling—and having done some of it myself—I made a quick mental check on all the diseases of the area. "Touch fever" was not amongst them and I was about to dismiss the subject when an old part-Aboriginal laid a hand on my arm. "Fair dinkum, missus, you wanna be properly careful with that feller. Touch him and tell him to do something and he'll keep on doing it 'til you tell him to stop."

"Or other way round," another volunteered. "Jus' lay your finger on him and say: 'You can't walk!' He'll sit there like he was paralysed."

"Someone told him he was a dog once," another chimed in, "an' he down on his hands and knees and run after a car barking till he collapsed."

"Everyone's scared some nut might tell him to kill someone," the story went on. "You know—for a joke like? Or even serious. He'd do it all right."

"What's the cause of it?" I asked. They shook their heads, and threw the problem back to me with the typical Aboriginal rejoinder: "We dunno. You!"

It was later suggested to me that "touch fever" is a possible manifestation of the Malay blood strain in a number of Shark Bay people. Stories of the early pearling fleets indicate that members of the Malay crews were subject to this kind of hysteric suggestibility. A man would sometimes brood over real or fancied wrongs until he worked himself up into a killing mood and would "run amok" with any weapon he could lay hands on. An old

Shark Bay resident told me that she had witnessed an "amok," and their policeman had felt obliged to shoot the afflicted man.

In our younger days we suspected that some of Mum's "happy hour" visitors were also suffering from one or another form of madness, but we later came to appreciate that their symptoms were merely manifestations of the creative spark. We got pretty used to hearing wild-haired poets declaiming their immortal works, novelists unfolding endless intricacies of plot and character, actors putting on real-life turns of temperament and painters calling curses on the heads of Philistines. They had the effect on Dad of an electrical discharge, and, on sight or sound of all but a few deemed for some reason acceptable, he would dart into hiding like a crab into its hole. His reactions did not always go unnoticed, with the result that Mum received a certain amount of sympathy both ways—from Dad for having to suffer lunatics, and from her artistic friends for having married one.

Then in and out the strata of older Millers and friends would weave the younger fry. Andrew, who came fourth in the line of family, never made very close contact with his sisters. He was an odd boy who lived a sort of outside tribal life with a group of undistinguishable friends known collectively as "the Cnaws"—a name derived from the frequent telephonic enquiry: "C'naw please speak t'Andy?"

Mum held that the Cnaws were "the revenge of the Bibbulmum," the vanished tribespeople of the South-West whose spirits seemed, all out of time and context, to have taken possession of them. They were a foot-loose lot, eschewing anything in the nature of study, organised sport, wholesome activity or hobby groups. Not for them the Boy Scouts, the Sea Scouts, the Wild Life or Junior Rock Hunters clubs, though they followed, in their feckless fashion, certain aspects of all these worthy bodies. They could make fairly water-proof cubbies and light camp fires with anyone; they could swim, and paddle dinghies; they knew a good deal about birds and their nesting habits and could track snakes and lizards as well as any Aboriginal. They could also net crabs and spear cobblers, and were possessed of a few special gifts such as the ability to move soundlessly, to merge with the landscape, vanish into thin air at the prospect of a job and to communicate with each other telepathically regarding this danger.

Apart from bone laziness there was little actual vice in the Cnaws. They weren't the positive kind of no-hopers who got into trouble with the police or did anything actively anti-social. In fact the few people who managed to communicate with them found them likeable enough, and they were not lacking in the occasional kindly impulse—such as buying birthday presents with borrowed money.

John, the youngest, though showing a number of Cnaw-like tendencies, somehow missed out on the capacity to vanish and has always been too eager to enter into and dominate "happy hour" ever to qualify as a true member of this exclusive and elusive tribe. Moreover, whereas Andy's pets—things like lizards, beetles, birds' eggs, tadpoles, and grasshoppers—were seldom in evidence, John's menagerie of tropical fish, guinea pigs and Priscilla Botulinis, the incontinent duck, are a communal responsibility and the constant subject of controversy.

Now and again a Cnaw, by inherent impulse or parental influence, would show ominous signs of industry, at which he was either prevailed upon to revert to type or excluded from the tribe and condemned to the awful fate of having to "make the grade." Andy, as unopposed King of the Cnaws, escaped every assault on his freedom and soon after leaving school set forth on a rambling odyssey to make contact with other members of his tribe scattered throughout the Continent.

This leaves only Marie Rose, who came between Andrew and John and was spoilt by us all as a sort of glorious live doll, her every whim indulged, her every utterance hailed as the expression of budding genius. So sure were we elder sisters that she was destined for fame that we would sit patiently taking down her confused, nightmarish ramblings, one of which, founded on the fact of a tribal vendetta that occurred in Broome when she was about five, I have kept to this day. Herewith a brief extract:

"In this country there's very dark things—trees and things. They can't help it. They grow in the creek. The black man was finded in the creek, stabbed and sticked. They pulled him out and got poisonous and died too. (It's coming beaut, isn't it?)

"In this country every peoples have spears, arrows, guns. T'wang! T'wang! You've got to say 't'wang' because they're

Indians. They shoot everyone—bears, woofs, horses, mans. . . .
The story of all these things was done by Marie Rose. It was
very good."

Marie Rose's early literary promise was swamped by pre-
occupations arising from the natural increase of two white mice,
some of which escaped to beget champagne coloured progeny
from the common cupboard variety. At one stage she had over
200—every one named and cherished and the frustrated cat
trained to allow them to crawl all over her. The loss of a single
mouse was a calamity and if it was a nursing mother the young
were fed to maturity with an eye-dropper. Wherever Marie went
the mice went too, and she had reached her latter school days
before she could be prevailed upon to accept an invitation to visit
relatives in Queensland, leaving all but two mice behind. During
her absence the rest were "donated to science."

Very much a part of "happy hour" associations are inevitably
my artist aunt, Elizabeth Durack Clancy, her children Michael
and Perpetua with whom we had grown up, and the four uncles
who dropped in from time to time from various parts of Australia.
A specially strong influence in our lives was my Uncle Kim
Durack, the pioneer of agricultural development on the Ord River
and later at Camballin in West Kimberley. His story will no doubt
one day be told in full as his inspiration was far-reaching and his
dream only now beginning to be understood.

Even as children we were fascinated by Uncle Kim's conversa-
tional range and the flattering way in which he would assume we
could follow his philosophical and scientific discourses. Topics
embarked upon in the kitchen at home would be continued
during holidays when we sometimes went from Broome to visit
him. While his Camballin rice project was in the first experimental stage he lived in a caravan under a big boab tree, which also
gave shelter to his precious kerosene refrigerator. During this
time, with the help of a Spanish builder, he was gradually erecting
his dream house—a spacious rectangular stone place with pillars
inspired by the Parthenon, and which he foresaw as the centre of
an agricultural experimental village.

But when his crops began to flourish beyond expectations,
others took over and his dream was shattered. It was discovered

too late that his prophecies were correct—that the time had not come to reap a rich reward from his experiments.

When I returned to Camballin in May 1968 to conduct a clinic for the little community that was soon afterwards to disperse, I seemed to be moving in a melancholy dream. I remembered Kim's careful scientific instructions as we helped him shift the heavy sacks of earth that controlled his irrigation system—and Julie's delight when he said she had a better sense of hydraulic principles than I, which really meant that she had a stronger pair of arms. I remembered the Christmas party he had thrown for neighbouring station friends when he had taken for granted that Julie and I would act as caterers and hostesses. It was wonderful training in the art of improvisation and one of the most memorable Christmases of my life. I remembered his passionate insistence on what seemed to us totally meaningless formalities—including the "bread-and-butter" letters after reciprocal parties which he made us write and re-write until they met with his approval. Part of his grand plan had been to build a little temple—"a place of rest and contemplation"—on top of the nearby hill where we had one day stumbled on a cave containing some Aboriginal sacred weapons and boards. Knowing nothing of their significance we had bagged them gleefully and were astonished to be told by our uncle that we had committed sacrilege, and we were made to put them back. I can still hear his indignant voice thundering after us: "And *exactly* where you found them, what's more!"

I returned to Derby in an unusual state of depression—only to hear over the radio that Uncle Kim had died suddenly that day in Canberra, at the age of 49.

I learned that Mum and Julie had flown off to attend his requiem and pack up his modest worldly goods. Julie, who had loved him so devotedly, was heartbroken, but as always a tower of strength.

She was to follow him little more than a year later, a bride of five months, in a swift and inexplicable knife thrust of destiny.

16

MANTLE OF
SAFETY

I WAS DISTRIBUTING VACCINE TO THE CHILDREN IN THE LITTLE
school at Onslow when the telephone rang. I heard the teacher
pick it up and speak a few words, and then she exclaimed, "It's
San Francisco—calling Sister Miller!"

Communication with Onslow is carried out by a radiotele-
phone system which allows only one person to talk at a time, and
the reception is usually poor at that. I picked up the phone, heard
"Hallo? Hallo?" and then the line went dead. All the kids were
chattering, the switchboard operator was flustered by the first-
ever call from America to Onslow, and finally I gave up and went
back to doling out my doses of vaccine.

The call came through at last but the line was very bad. I could
just hear Doctor Dicks saying: "Could you get away for two
weeks between clinics and help fly a Beechcraft back to Australia?
If so I could arrange your airline booking. Please confirm."

"O.K. I'll manage somehow," I replied, and turned back
breathlessly excited to the children. "I'm going to America!"

I knew that the Beechcraft referred to had been secured for the
Royal Flying Doctor Service to cope with demands of the rapidly
increasing mining and industrial activity in the North-West. The

story of the R.F.D.S., one of the most romantic in medical history, is well known, but a few important facts are worth repeating.

Inspired by the Reverend John Flynn, the service began operating in outback Queensland in 1928. Its aim was to overcome one of the greatest drawbacks to development in Australia's isolated areas; the almost complete dearth of medical facilities. If people fell ill in the far outback they either recovered with the help of what patent medicines lay to hand, or died—often without anyone knowing the cause. "Fever" was the most favoured description of illness, which was usually treated with liberal doses of quinine and Epsom salts. Naturally enough this did not always effect a cure. In an even more hopeless situation were the victims of accidents, who were entirely dependent on the rough first-aid of their mates.

If it was bad for men, it was worse for women and children. The sick often had to be taken for hundreds of miles over rough bush tracks in a desperate attempt to get them to a doctor. Often, as in the tragic story of Pastor Strehlow of Hermannsburg Mission, told by his son in his moving book, *Journey to Horseshoe Bend*, they died and were buried on the way.

Pastor Strehlow's trouble was almost certainly that of congestive heart failure, which, with the advent of the Flying Doctor, could have been diagnosed in the early stages and the patient soon restored to more or less normal health by a course of digitalis, diuretics and suitable diet. Instead, he set out on a long buggy ride over rough bush tracks, in the last stages of an agonising disease, to a destination he did not live to see.

John Flynn saw that the age of aircraft and radio might conquer such problems, but there were plenty of difficulties and disappointments before his dream became reality. To this end, every isolated community required a radio which could send and receive messages, but the equipment of that period was too clumsy and complicated for use by complete amateurs. Alfred Traeger, an Adelaide engineer, developed a transceiver worked by a tiny dynamo which was operated by a stationary bicycle, but it took hard pedalling to keep up the power to send a message for 300 miles or more. Modern equipment is much simpler and more efficient.

The first base was established in Cloncurry in 1928, and was so successful that more bases were opened to entirely cover the outback areas of Australia. The organisation was known first as the Australian Aerial Medical Services, and was changed to the Flying Doctor Service in 1942. The prefix "Royal" was granted by Queen Elizabeth in 1955.

Today the Service is divided into seven sections, with a total of thirteen bases. Each section is independent of the others, and is registered as a non-profit organisation in its home State. The sections are administered by councils made up of honorary members, who are usually leading business and professional men.

The R.F.D.S. costs more than a million dollars a year to run. This money comes from the Commonwealth and State Governments, from donations and bequests, and from a share in the Post Office revenue gained from more than 300,000 telegrams sent over the R.F.D.S. radio network every year to outback communities.

The Flying Doctors and nurses in R.F.D.S. aircraft now cover something like one and a half million miles a year, and as many as 3,500 patients are flown in to hospitals each year. Thousands more are treated on the scene of illness or accident, and a great many by means of advice given over the radio and implemented by people on the spot. Special medical chests, the contents of which are free, are provided for such places as sheep and cattle stations, mines, police stations, prospecting and survey parties, oil rigs, lighthouses, and so on.

When one of these outposts reports a medical problem, a doctor who may be anything up to 300 miles away will ask a series of careful and patient questions, and will use the bush-dweller at the other end of the radio link as his eyes and hands. It is remarkable how often this combination of the doctor's trained mind and his interlocutor's commonsense will arrive at an accurate diagnosis. The doctor will say something like: "It sounds to me like a renal colic. Give the patient two of the number forty-four Pethedine tablets from the medicine chest, and keep him in bed. Measure and strain all his urine and report back to me in four hours' time. If he's no better we will send the aeroplane out to bring him in to hospital."

The motto of the R.F.D.S. is: "When in doubt, go." Unless the doctor is absolutely certain that it is only a simple injury or illness, which can be treated by radio advice and prescription allied to one or more of the numbered items from the medicine chest, he will go as quickly as possible or send an aircraft with a nurse and ambulance facilities to bring the patient to him.

Sometimes it is only an hour or so from the time of receiving the call before the patient is resting comfortably on a stretcher aboard the aircraft.

The Flying Doctor contacts his far-flung "practice" during regular daily radio schedules, but if an emergency crops up at any other time the outpost presses the emergency button or blows a special two-toned whistle into the microphone. This rings an alarm bell at the R.F.D.S. base, which alerts the radio operator. He answers the call, and "patches" the radio link into the land telephone line so that the outpost can speak directly to the doctor at his home or surgery.

The R.F.D.S. has developed enormously in scope from those first mercy flights. Nowadays, the aim of the Service is to provide the full range of medical requirements over the millions of square miles which it covers by air and radio. Routine flights are made to isolated communities and townships, some of which have small hospitals with qualified nursing staff. Regular clinics are held at these and other centres, and people travel up to 100 miles by car for advice and examination. This is particularly useful for those who suffer from chronic complaints, and are thus able to obtain regular treatment. Other services include examinations for the early detection of cancer, antenatal supervision, various immunisation programmes, and aerodental clinics.

The people of the outback even have specialist services brought to them—which was one of Dr Flynn's ambitions. Among the first organised visits of a specialist to the outback was that made by Professor Ida Mann in 1953, to investigate and treat eye problems throughout the North-West and Kimberleys.

A flying consultant surgeon is now stationed in Queensland, and other specialists make periodical visits to some of the R.F.D.S. bases and outposts. Altogether, the effect of the Service has been to rid the outback of one of its most haunting problems: the fear of illness or injury without hope of skilled treatment.

"Send for the Flying Doctor," is the first impulse of many when faced with any unusual emergency, even when it is not really

101

medical at all. One such case was when a doctor was called to an outpost station to rescue a cook weighing seventeen stone, who had fallen into the cesspit. It appeared that white ants had weakened the wooden seat to the degree that needed only an overweight sitter to cause its collapse. Station hands had heard the poor woman yelling for help and having failed in all attempts to heave her out, had put over an emergency call to the Flying Doctor. All that was required was a bit of common sense, to contrive the use of planks and ropes with which to lever the victim out. Fortunately only her dignity was hurt. She resigned the minute she had been extracted, and returned to base in the aircraft with her rescuer.

A Flying Doctor team soon develops versatility. Pilots become accustomed to landing anywhere within reason, and often at night, with car headlights or fires providing the only illumination. The doctor and nurse must be prepared for anything—including pointless calls from people with the same mentality as those who report a fire for the fun of seeing the fire brigade turn out.

Then there are the "acute appendix" cases who are miraculously cured by the sound of the Flying Doctor engine, and who stroll out to meet the doctor looking perfectly fit. The attitude of the Service, however, is that it is better to make a dozen wasted flights than to ignore a call that might prove to be a genuine emergency.

There have been some beneficial side-effects, too—or, as Dr Flynn called them, "pups." One of the most important of these has been the overcoming of that terrible sense of loneliness and isolation—in itself amounting almost to a sickness—which afflicts people living far from other human beings. Dr Dicks once received an emergency call in which a man gasped out that he felt like death, and doubted whether the doctor could reach him in time. The doctor took off immediately, and as soon as he landed at the lonely station a utility came speeding out to meet him. A healthy-looking man jumped out and ran over with outstretched hand, saying, "Thanks for coming, Doc. I've felt better ever since I knew you were on your way." He had been alone for several months.

In lighter vein, Dr Dicks also recalls being one day summoned by the manager of Balfour Downs Station, out on the edge of the

102

Great Sandy Desert. He found on arrival that the patients were four undernourished Aborigines who had wandered in seeking treatment for the sores with which they were all afflicted. The Doctor, while getting the natives into the aircraft, explained to the enquiring manager that they had a bad case of yaws.

Not long afterwards there was another urgent call from Balfour Downs, and Dr Dicks flew out to find the manager in a highly nervous condition, awaiting him on the airstrip.

"What's your problem?" he asked.

"If I've got the same as those natives," the manager said, "I need treatment too."

"But you look all right," the doctor said, "no sores or rash that I can see."

The manager was not to be put off. "*You said* they had the same as I've got and I want to be cured."

It was only then the doctor realised that the poor chap had mistaken the word "yaws" for "yours," and that having no one with whom to discuss his problem he had worked himself into a state of neurosis.

The direct radio contact between outposts and bases, as well as between the outposts themselves, has helped to make such loneliness a thing of the past. During the gossip or "galah" sessions, people can hear the cheerful voices of their "next door neighbours"—who may be more than 100 miles away. They can listen to normal broadcast programmes, too. If a homestead does not report each day on the roll call the base operator will soon become concerned and send someone out to investigate.

Dentists now make regular visits with R.F.D.S. aircraft to isolated towns and stations, with their coming heralded over the radio network. In the early days of the aerodental service, dental troubles had been so long neglected in the outback that dentists extracted three times as many teeth as they filled. Now, they fill three times as many as they extract.

The "School of the Air," which enables bush children separated from each other by hundreds of miles of desert, hills, and scrub, to participate in classes run by specially trained teachers, is conducted through the R.F.D.S. radio network. It has brought new horizons to young people whose interests might never have had a chance to blossom beyond the narrow confines of stockyard, station homestead, and the "blacks' camp."

The co-ordination of search and rescue work for people lost in the bush, the dropping of food to homesteads cut off by floods or bushfires, the spotting and reporting of such fires, passing on warnings of bad weather or emergency reports of various kinds —all these have become part of the R.F.D.S. service to the outback community. On the lonely obelisk erected to the memory of Dr Flynn, part of the inscription says: "He brought to lonely places a spiritual ministry, and spread a mantle of safety over them by medicine, aviation, and radio."

He, and the Royal Flying Doctor Service, have in fact done far more than that. That "mantle of safety" has helped to attract men and their families to the outback, and has consequently played a large part in the development of Australian resources such as oil, livestock, and minerals—the raw materials upon which so much of our prosperity depends.

For some time before getting that call from San Francisco, I had known that since the R.F.D.S. could not afford a new aircraft the council was considering the purchase of a slightly used one from the United States. A reliable dealer in the U.S.A. had been asked to look out for a suitable machine which had done about 500 hours. If this was found it would be fitted with extra tanks for the Pacific flight and flown back by a member of the R.F.D.S., thus saving about $30,000 on the new price. I had guessed that this member would probably be Dr Dicks, and that he would no doubt find a co-pilot to return with him from America. That the chance to make the flight should be given to me seemed too good to be true.

17
FAREWELL
SAN FRANCISCO

LUCKILY I WAS DUE FOR LEAVE, BUT I COULDN'T MAKE ANY arrangements until my airline booking was confirmed. I was fishing off Shark Bay jetty when another fisherman put a hook through his finger and went up to Denham Hospital to have it cut out. He returned with a bandaged finger and a telegram. This had arrived from Doctor Dicks via Perth, then via Carnarvon Hospital. The Carnarvon airfield radio operator, who knew that I was at Shark Bay, had forwarded it to that Post Office, whence it was sent to Denham Hospital and finally delivered by the injured fisherman.

The message confirmed the booking, but left little time, after the scheduled completion of my current immunisation clinic, for me to catch the flight out of Perth. It was nearing the cyclone season, and I flew north from Shark Bay into rain which had waterlogged many of the airstrips I had to visit. As I landed at Mundawindi the aircraft skidded on the wet ground, and one wing hit a tree on the side of the strip. I leapt out, took one glance at the five-inch hole in the wing of my poor little aircraft, and burst into tears.

But after examining the airframe manual I managed to convince myself that the damage should not have affected the main-spar, and that the wing was therefore not likely to fall off. I could not bash or bend the holed aluminium back into shape, so decided that a professional job of bandaging was in order. I stuffed a lot of white surgical napkins into the hole, strapped them over with scotch tape, and then covered the "wound" with paper and white plastic to camouflage the problem as far as possible. It looked as frail as a politician's promise, but I thought that it would get me to Perth.

I had five more stops to make en route, and had an embarrassed certainty that the eyes of every other pilot were focused upon my wing. At Wittenoom Gorge, I asked a young engineer to inspect the damage, and he said, "I think it's all right. You'd better tell the Department of Civil Aviation, though. There's a big fine for not reporting accidents."

I rang up the Chief Accident Inspector in Perth, and said, "I have a small dent in my wing, but I'm more or less on my way to Perth and I'm sure that it's okay."

"What size is the dent?"

"Oh . . . not very big. A couple of inches . . . maybe."

"You can fly it direct to Perth," he said at last, but I managed to convince him that I'd *have* to make a few stops for "fuel."

. My luck seemed to be running out though. I flew on to the iron ore town, Mount Tom Price, for the night, and knew that I would have to leave at first light—i.e. shortly before sunrise the following day—if I was to have any hope of catching the 1 p.m. flight from Perth for overseas.

So I arranged with the senior transport officer in the town to pick me up for the airfield at 5 a.m. I waited outside the hospital from 4.30 a.m. until the sun was glaring brazenly over the horizon. But the dusty road remained empty. I would have walked the five miles had I not been laden with cases of heavy equipment and valuable vaccine. There were no telephones and I didn't know where my driver was staying anyway. When he turned up eventually two hours late I was too furious to speak. I could hardly see for tears of rage and disappointment as I climbed into my aircraft and took off at full throttle. Perth was five and a half flying hours away, with one refuelling stop at Meekatharra, thus missing the overseas flight by about twenty minutes.

Still, there seemed to be no point in giving up, so I kept the aircraft flat out all the way. I got a clearance for landing at Perth Airport, and as I cut the engine after taxi-ing in heard a loud-speaker announcement that my flight was delayed for, "Another thirty minutes."

But I was not out of the wood yet. The D.C.A. Accident Inspector was waiting for me, grim-faced as he saw my bandaged wing, and proceeded to uncover the shameful wound. As he helped me push my aircraft into a hangar he administered a severe ticking-off. I heard him out meekly, then rushed for the jet wearing summer clothes and bound for a northern hemisphere winter.

The relief of having actually *made it* and of finding myself headed for America, even though I carried nothing but a dusty overnight bag and a life vest from my aircraft, made me feel quite light-headed. The stare of obvious disapproval from the smartly dressed Adelaide-bound woman next to me decided me not to let on that my destination was any farther than her own. I rang home from the Adelaide airport and asked Julie to unload my aircraft, refrigerate the vaccines immediately, and line up some-one to repair the damaged wing.

"Where the hell are you, and where are you going?" she asked.

"I'm on my way to America. See you in about ten days—with any luck."

"Good Lord!" she yelled. "Have you told the Health Department?"

"No," I said. "There's a couple of weeks' break before the next clinic. I'll send them a post card from Hawaii."

I arrived in San Francisco sunburnt and pretty spare after a year of outback flying, and shivering from the damp cold of a Califor-nian winter. After the enormous emptiness and timeless silence of the bush, my first sight of San Fancisco traffic made me feel that I was entering some kind of nightmare. But we were soon so busy that there was little time to think about the atmosphere of panic and chaos which seemed, at first glimpse, to be typical of America.

Dr Dicks had been in the U.S.A. for about three weeks, looking for a suitable aircraft, and had found a Beechcraft Baron down in Albuquerque, New Mexico. She was at Oakland

International Airport, on the other side of San Francisco Bay, and although lovely to look at, the space in her cockpit was severely restricted by the two 103-gallon ferry tanks installed behind the pilots' seats. They were essential for the long ocean flights, but did not even leave room for seat backs, so two half-inch thick pieces of foam rubber were stuck to the tanks instead. These were to cause uncomfortable flying, with cold aviation spirit sloshing against the thin metal behind our aching backs.

Two twenty-gallon tanks had been installed in the nose, and emergency equipment such as a two-man inflatable dingy, radio sets, flares, water, sextant, maps, charts and emergency rations had to be stowed around the floor and the ferry tanks. All this took up even more space, but had to be placed carefully for quick accessibility yet so as not to interfere with the dozens of valves, cocks, and delicate fuel lines needed to switch over from one tank to another.

The aircraft was approximately 1,200 pounds above her normal gross load, so we decided to take off from Oakland, which had a runway 12,000 feet long, with the advantage of another airstrip across the Bay to land on if the Baron couldn't gain sufficient altitude, or if anything happened on take-off.

When all was in readiness except for the filling of our long-distance fuel tanks we took off on a dummy run to get some practice over our expected departure route via Port Reeves and "The Faralons," a group of rocky pinnacles about twenty miles out to sea. These have the last radio navigation beacon before the mid-Pacific weather ship *November*.

It was a bright morning, and we had a fantastic view over the hills, bridges, and San Francisco Bay. The sights below us were breathtaking—but those around us were terrifying. The air was thick with everything that could fly; jet aircraft, military aircraft, single and twin-engined private aircraft, gliders, and great flocks of large and small birds, flapping and gliding nonchalantly amongst all their man-made counterparts. To pilots used to the clear skies and comparatively empty airlines of Australia, it was almost paralysing. On another of the trips which I was to make to pick up aircraft for the R.F.D.S. I went up in a glider in the same locality, and the noise of engines all around was deafening.

But we reached the Faralons without a collision—even though there was one period when a Fokker Friendship was flying on the same course and at precisely the same level about 100 feet to starboard, and we could see that the pilot never even sighted us.

On returning, we were told to orbit over Dumbarton Bridge to lose altitude and wait our turn for landing. This we did amongst a swarm of aircraft which seemed to be going upwards, downwards, backwards, forwards, and sideways. We planned to make a quick landing at Palo Alto to pick up some essential radio spares which were waiting for us, and at 1,000 feet were told to join the airfield circuit. We were going round and round with eleven other aircraft, visibility restricted by turning, smog, and the great flocks of birds, every circuit becoming wider and wider so that eventually we became mixed up with aircraft waiting to land at an Air Force base nearby.

We gave it up, and returned to Oakland with our problems compounded by trying to understand the men in the control tower. They spoke very fast, their American accents often difficult for us to follow as they passed from one set of instructions to another without a second's pause. We felt that we could hardly keep on asking, "Please say again," and eventually decided to risk it. On the whole, however, I think that the Americans are more patient and understanding than Australian aircraft controllers, even though they deal with about a hundred times more traffic.

When we let down above Oakland we found that we were landing in a train of aircraft, which touched down one after another and almost nose to tail. The jet which followed us down might have given us a little more leeway had the pilot known that we were scared-stiff foreigners, but we made it at last and skidded off the runway to let him and the other jets come roaring and whining in behind us.

We had become quite *blasé* about such conditions by the time we did our third and fourth ferry flights, but we had a lot to learn during that first one. For me it was not simply a matter of learning about flying under international conditions and over the huge lonely stretches of ocean, but also of learning about myself. I find it difficult to define just what or how I learned, but

109

in my own mind I liken it to the case of the unfortunate foreign professor whom I once flew on a tour of the outback.

I was asked to take him north so that he could see the Royal Flying Doctor Service in action and examine the medical situation in the base hospitals. He was arrogant, rude, and self-opinionated, and scoffed at the somewhat crude facilities which were often the best arrangements possible in difficult circumstances — and which were infinitely better than none at all. In fact his whole attitude was one of: "If only *we* were doing this, how much better it would be."

On the way back to Perth at night we encountered a line of severe electrical storms. It was like being in the middle of a battle. Thunder bellowed all around us, from tumbling black clouds lit by savage flares of lightning; hail and rain slashed on the thin skin of the machine. I had my hands fully occupied, trying to work out from the constant lightning flashes where the worst storm cells were and which was the safest route through, while struggling to keep the aircraft right way up. Once, I glanced at the professor, whose grey perspiring face betrayed his fear.

After we landed he climbed out shakily and gave me a ghostly smile. He was now very silent, and I felt somehow that he was a changed man. Perhaps it was the best thing that ever happened to him; something which taught him that, compared with the monstrous forces of the elements, he was a very unimportant human being indeed. The machine, which at first might seem to isolate man from the great problems of nature, can actually plunge him more deeply into them. For some, as indeed it was to me when tackling those perilous ocean flights, this can be an enlightening experience. Man's transient strivings, all his ambitions, satisfactions, and frustrations fade into insignificance as one hovers in that vast eternity between sky and sea.

When setting out on such a flight, fraught with many unknowns, and with little hope of survival in the event of misfortune, the pilot is not really risking his life for the aeroplane. As Saint Exupery puts it ". . . a pilot's business is with the wind, with the stars, with night, with sand and with the sea. He strives to outwit the forces of nature. He stares in expectancy for the coming of dawn, and truth for him is what lives in the stars."

Ever since my first experience flying the Pacific I felt that I had come to grips with nature, with life and with myself, and have not been able to attach the same significance to many things which I once thought to be of importance.

In some ways, the three first flights have blended into one in my memory, since they all followed much the same pattern and the adventures and accidents of one could have happened on any of the others—except insofar as we learnt from them.

They all began in much the same way; a period of waiting for that all-important weather pattern. Morning after morning we would creep from our beds at 3 a.m. to ring the weather bureau and receive some such report as: "Strong headwind components," or "Complicated frontal systems with rain, low icing, and turbulence." As we had to cover one of the world's greatest stretches of ocean, and one which can develop savage weather conditions, we had to be reasonably certain of the overall pattern, since even quite a brief period of strong head winds could mean a fatal cut in our range.

Of great value in this respect are the satellite pictures, obtainable in San Francisco and Hawaii, which show the entire Pacific and its areas of weather disturbance.

At last we would receive a report that gave us reasonable winds and weather, so that we were able to take off for Hawaii.

The first task on the morning of take-off was to stow everything aboard, check that the inflatable dinghy, knives, spares, and other emergency equipment were handy, and stash away some goodies to eat *en route*. I don't believe in starvation flights. Fifteen or sixteen hours is a long time to sit in a cramped cockpit, and bringing out something nice every now and again provides a welcome break.

Flight plans, almanacs, maps and charts, sextant and other navigational gear we placed to hand, and stowed last minute odds and ends in the nose or on top of the reserve fuel tanks— hoping all the time that the extra ounces would not be the last straw to break the Baron's back.

Then we topped up the fuel tanks, squeezing in another ten gallons where the air bubbles had settled since filling them the previous night. The total load was 380 U.S. gallons, which are slightly less than Imperial gallons.

111

Next we hosed the ice from wings and fuselage, as this can add much unwanted weight, and rang through to the tower for clearance—which we discovered was easier than trying to understand American spoken at machine-gun speed over the radio. Then a last cup of coffee, and into our flying suits. I wore a bright orange model, purchased for four dollars at a hippie junk shop in downtown San Francisco, which I prize greatly for its multitude of handy zips and the many pockets which I crammed with further odds and ends.

We almost needed shoe horns to ease us into the cockpit, where we sat bolt upright, backs against the fuel tanks, an H.F. aerial reel and the numerous fragile fuel cocks and lines, maps and star tables between our feet.

We taxied out onto the runway, with clearance to Hawaii and a requirement to maintain a minimum rate of climb of 250 feet per minute to clear mountains between the airfield and the coast. And then—off, the engines propelling us down 5,200 feet of runway until the airspeed indicator read 100 knots. Despite her heavy overload, the Baron took off with the ease and grace of a bird.

18

WELCOME
TO HAWAII

Rising smoothly to about 1,000 feet on our first pacific flight, the Baron took a bite of the cold morning air, settled into her stride, and soared to a safe height towards the mountains.

The first three hours of a ferry flight are hard, concentrated work. A heavy load makes an aircraft less stable, and the pilot has to keep both hands on the stick. Meanwhile the second pilot watches apprehensively to see that all fuel systems and engine dials are working as they should, sorts out the instrument flight charts, handles progressive clearance and radio frequency changes, tunes in the navigational aids and keeps an eye out for other traffic.

"Crossing the coast over Half Moon Bay," I was able to say at 7 a.m. It was then just first light, and we were already well launched over the blue-black Pacific.

California, with its smog and fog, dense air traffic and suicidal flocks of birds, was dropping behind us, but it was not yet time to relax. Even though the weather pattern had looked favourable, a line of heavy cloud loomed ahead when we were only about one hour out from the coast. Rain battered against the windscreen as soon as we plunged into it; herald of hour after hour of solid downpour and instrument flying. There was not much turbulence, but the rain soon found its way into the cabin through the nose locker, soaked feet and legs already numb from the cold, and crept aft to turn my stock of cakes, biscuits and sandwiches into one big soggy inedible trifle. We were as cold as Antarctic explorers and could not use the cabin heat, as it was a fuel burner system located right under the nose tanks. So to the drumming of the rain and the growling of the engines was added the rhythmic chattering of teeth.

Luckily there was plenty to do. I had to make a regular check on the fuel tanks, which was an acrobatic stunt in itself and involved squirming round to remove each tank-cap, inserting a steel tape to measure the depth, and inhaling quantities of petrol fumes. A regular change over from tank to tank was required to maintain an equal load, and we encountered problems in this until it was discovered that our main right and left tanks had been wrongly labelled. We then had to work out a cross-feed process to get back to normal.

There was also navigation, which involved the use of radio beams which send out dots and dashes. A special map and formula is employed to work out a position by counting these signals. This system can be used, even when the signal is too weak to be heard, by placing a hand over the loudspeaker and feeling the vibrations.

We were well-equipped with radio gear, both high and very high frequency. The trouble with the former was that it relied upon an aerial which had to be wound out during flight. When unreeling it not far off the coast of U.S.A. I felt a *twang* which meant that the drogue steadying the aerial had departed, so communication by this means became a problem. But we had a few friends on Pan Am or Qantas flying the same route, so could talk to them on V.H.F. as they cruised along a few miles above us in warmth, style and comfort.

Having heard that airlines were rather fed up with having to relay position reports for ferry aircraft with unserviceable or bad radio equipment, we felt diffident about asking them. However, the sound of a female voice must have been something of a novelty in that situation, as we always got instant attention from anyone within range.

On one occasion, the drogue jammed in the hawse-pipe as I was winding it out, and after shoving half our stock of pencils down after it in an attempt to push it clear, I cast about for some other method. Dr Dicks found a piece of hacksaw blade in his pocket, and with great difficulty I managed to saw off a metal curtain rod and hammer it down the hawse-pipe with the aid of a can of drink. These were the unpredictable happenings for which one simply could not be prepared, and had to solve by improvisation or quick thinking.

On another flight we were sailing peacefully along in moderate turbulence when we heard a sudden "bang" behind us, and a moment later our faces were pressed against the dashboard. We soon realised that the "pull to inflate" cord of our rubber dinghy had caught around a fuel line, so that the dinghy had inflated. We had to force ourselves back against the bright yellow bulk of rubberised canvas and stab it to death with our knives.

The Pan Am pilots cheered us up with a few well chosen words every now and again, and passed on rather discouraging information about the weather. After roughly seven hours' flying it was with great relief that we heard the ocean ship *November*, stationed half-way to Hawaii for navigation and air-sea rescue operations. Because of weather interference our auto direction finder did not home in on *November* until we were about thirty miles away and we then discovered that we had been blown somewhat north of our course. It is an unwritten law that if a pilot fails to pick up the ocean station on his navigation aids he must return to the mainland and try again.

We took turns at flying and navigating as the Baron rumbled onwards through rain, cloud and occasional sunny patches, any chance of relaxation being ruled out by the constant crashing of fuel in the thin-walled tanks against which we sat.

Evening came on after thirteen and a half hours aloft and we could see fair-sized tropical thunderclouds scattered across the route, with dazzling displays of lightning against the darkening sky. Earlier, we had taken a sextant sun shot which showed us as being 150 miles behind schedule, but we disregarded it in the belief that the windscreen refraction must have given us an error. When we had been flying for fourteen hours, and there was still no indication of land, we began to believe that the sextant shot had been right and that we must have struck a very strong headwind.

"Ferry tanks are dry now," I announced as the engines started to splutter, and Dr Dicks hurriedly turned cocks to change to the aircraft system. "Just over half the main wing tanks left."

We were well past our estimated time of arrival, but there was nothing to be seen except a starry sky reflected in the sea below, so that it was impossible to tell where sky and sea met. Every time I lifted my head from trying to tune in to one of the Hawaiian stations I became strangely disorientated, and was sure we must be flying upside-down or at least sideways. The stars seemed to be hanging beneath us, as if we were rolling, lost in space, and at other times we appeared to be diving into the sea.

We hoped that we were heading straight for Hawaii, but since the island towers 13,000 feet out of the sea, and we were flying at 6,000 feet, we were afraid that unless we could see lights or pick up radio guidance we might find it all too abruptly. Dr Dicks flew with his eyes glued to the instruments, while I strained mine into the darkness and longed to see the yellow gleam of man-made lights instead of the mocking silver twinkle of the stars.

"We should have been there an hour ago," he said. Neither of us liked to suggest that we might have passed well south of the islands and be heading on into the Pacific until our wing tanks ran dry, for to change direction offered no greater chance of salvation than to carry on.

The minutes passed with leaden deliberation. I glanced at the instrument panel, hypnotically attracted by the pointer on the fuel gauge, which was leaning further and further to the left. Then we both saw the tiniest movement on the Visual Omni Range needle; a radio navigation aid. It was like the smile of a friend as it began to move in definite response to impulses from the station. The automatic direction finder also came to life, and all of a sudden we were no longer flying blindly into the darkness, but following the radio beams which seemed to promise life and landfall ahead.

"There's a light!" I said at last, and at the same moment heard Hilo airfield calling us. The light was an aerodrome beacon that, together with the radio voice, seemed to beckon us in through

TOP: The Mooney on Mount House airstrip, with vaccines in shade under tail. BOTTOM: Scene from a great height, this river of North-West Australia resembles a brancheole of a human lung

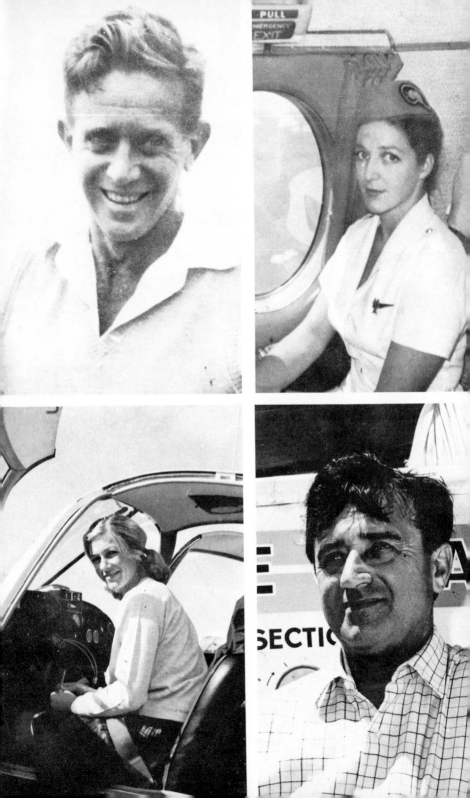

the misty tropical night. We started our descent towards increasing numbers of lights that shone dimly ahead, and were just receiving landing instructions when our V.H.F. set cut out.

Luckily we had an answer to this small problem. I groped around amongst the soggy junk on the floor and fished out our portable Bayside transceiver, which has saved the day so often that we carry it on every flight. I dumped it in my lap, pushed up the telescopic aerial, and we were back in business.

Hilo airstrip runs straight out to sea, and we lined up nicely on a long final approach which brought us down to 300 feet, at which point the aircraft began to heave alarmingly about. We had hit what is known as a Katabatic wind, whirling down the 13,000 foot mountain beyond the airfield. There was a bad moment in which everything loose in the cabin, including the Bayside, took off for the roof. The Bayside's aerial was bent at right angles, but when we regained control I found that it still worked. We came very close to landing the wrong way up, but at last felt the blessed shudder of wheels hitting tarmac.

With groaning muscles we clambered out of a cockpit that was as untidy as my young sister's bedroom, and jumped off the wing. The air was moist and warm and heavy with the scent of frangipani. A cheery voice was saying, "Aloha, aloha! Welcome to Hawaii!" and the first stage of our Pacific haul was over. We discovered that an unexpected head wind for most of the way accounted for our having averaged only 122 knots ground speed instead of our expected 170 knots, and that our fuel situation had been on the point of becoming critical.

The Pacific had many more surprises in store for us. We took off from Honolulu at 2 a.m. one morning, with the help of radar vectors to get us clear of the islands and other traffic and to put us on course for our next refuelling point on Tarawa Atoll. In an attempt to save time, we had unwisely obtained our weather information several hours before departure, and were somewhat worried because of lightning seen through the misty rain on the windscreen. But we droned along on an even keel until a sudden flash glared eerily, lighting up the face of a huge black mass head. It looked pretty solid and within a few seconds we had flown out of the calm, moist air into the heart of a tropical thunderstorm.

TOP LEFT: The author's uncle, Kim Durack. TOP RIGHT: Her sister, Julie Miller, when she was a MMA hostess. BOTTOM LEFT: The author in the cockpit of F-OCLA. BOTTOM RIGHT: Doctor Harold Dicks, President of the W.A. Section of the Royal Flying Doctor Service

Hailstones bombarded the fuselage, the aircraft was forced upwards at 2,000 feet a minute, and then dropped again like a stone. "Well, this is it," I thought, almost certain that at any second the load factors on the heavy machine would cause it to break up or go into a fatal spin.

I observed that the face of my watch had been smashed but didn't suppose that time would be of much more concern to me. I don't know what I looked like and didn't care, but I noticed that Dr Dicks' face wore its usual hopeful expression and that his hands on the controls were as steady as ever. I soon discovered, while radioing Honolulu for a safe course through or out of the storm, that he had somehow eased the aircraft onto a reciprocal course.

We were out of the immediate "panic" area when a voice from Honolulu came through genially: "Our radar blots out weather to concentrate on air traffic. I'm afraid we can't be much help to you but stand by and I'll get a report from a U.S. Navy C-37 with weather radar."

The information came back that there was a line of heavy tropical thunderstorms, 200 miles long and fifty miles wide, across our track.

I have little doubt that Amelia Earhart encountered such a disturbance, and after experiencing the forces of these storms can understand how a comparatively low-powered aircraft, such as she was flying, could have been dumped down into the sea as the forces of nature outwitted those of humanity.

We both agreed that we couldn't possibly circumnavigate the storm and still make Tarawa with the available fuel; also our main ferry tanks had shifted in the turbulence and the securing cables needed checking. So it was back to Honolulu.

This wasn't exactly a straightforward procedure. We were grossly overloaded with aviation spirit, so there was a risk of undercarriage failure on landing. We had no dump valves fitted into the ferry tanks but had, by a stroke of luck, been talking to another ferry pilot in a Honolulu bar the night before. He had been flying an aircraft out, mismanaged his fuel system, and nearly finished up "splashing down" in mid-Pacific. We were now able to put his experience to good account. His engine, like ours, was a fuel injection type, which automatically feeds back any excess fuel into the auxiliary wing tanks. Unless one keeps an eye on the amount of fuel in these tanks and burns it off as necessary, they overflow through special tubes under the wings. Our friend's near disaster was caused by losing his gas this way.

It now occurred to us as the ideal method of getting rid of our surplus to enable us to effect a safe landing. We were instructed to fly back to the islands and to hold at 6,000 feet over Koko Head radio beacon until we had reduced our supply to the required level. Koko Head is actually a live volcano, to whose fire we contributed fuel at the rate of 102 gallons an hour instead of the normal 22.

After a couple of hours of this carry-on we were given permission to land. We were still flying in heavy cloud and had just turned onto a course for the airfield when the controller of the radar frequency to which we were tuned shouted, "November Five One Kilo. Bear right — bear right! Traffic at twelve o'clock!"

Dr Dicks turned the stick hard right, and almost immediately the aircraft was shaken violently by the slip-stream of another machine. "That's one of the closest shaves I've ever seen," the controller said. "It was unidentified traffic coming towards you at 300 knots."

Our lives had been saved by the quick reactions of the controller watching the radar screen, but I felt pretty shaken as we went in to land. For some time after that I had to force myself to fly into clouds, fearing a sudden encounter with "unidentified traffic" or with malicious monsters pelting hail and hurling lightning.

On our next two Pacific flights we had special dump-valves installed on the fuel system so that we could get rid of surplus fuel in emergency. Dr Dicks got the bright idea that these would also come in handy for disposing of personal surplus on a long flight, but we were warned about this in the nick of time by a pilot who had tried it out, to find that the valve exerted powerful suction that had dramatic and painful results.

19

PACIFIC PARADISE

DRONING SOUTHWARDS FROM HAWAII IN THE DAWN, ANXIOUS eyes and ears strained for tiny Johnson Island en route to our next landfall at Tarawa, I only wished we had been furnished with a safety device once recommended to me in a letter which ran as follows:

"Dear Miss Miller,

I have invented a set of parshoot *harness* to save the lives of parashoot jumpers. 12 months or more ago a young french man jumped to his death beacuse his parashoot failed to open, 12 months later his young lady did likewise. Now girls like you are too valuable to lose like that so when you get a chance you could put it to the Cheifs, I have never seen a parashoot, I have aerophobia so I cannot go up in lifts or planes or escalators, this is a part of this affair a seat like a Bycycle with stirup straps made of *nylon* stirup irons made of Alluminum. This harness is to releave the person of the weight of their legs and body as the harness go up to the parashoot, and the parashoot take all the weight and the top part of this affair opens the parashoot after a few feet and the person lands safely. After they land they pull a yellow cord and a window in the parashoot opens and that lets the parashoot go flat instead of dragging the person along the ground for 100 yards perhaps a mile according to wind force, this could be tried on dummies. I will watch the papers to see how you are getting on, I am in touch with L.B.J."

Our first sounds of Johnson Island were the faint, tinkling strains of "Waltzing Matilda"—whether Radio Australia's signature tune breaking through, or played in our honour by the island airbase, we never knew. This island, a coral mass more like a giant aircraft carrier than the classic picture of a south sea tropic paradise, is equipped only with an airstrip and a few concrete buildings—not, I should imagine, a popular military posting. However, the sight of any land at all in that lonely expanse of ocean was welcome indeed, and we were greatly heartened by the friendly chatter of the radio operator as we approached.

Civil aircraft are permitted to land at Johnson only in emergency, but we considered the slight diversion from our direct route advisable in case of trouble. Valuable information regarding winds and drift could also be obtained by using its naviagtion beacon.

I enquired about the fishing and hinted to the radio operator that it would be great to come down and stretch our legs. He replied regretfully that he had no authority to permit our landing, much as he wished we could join them in the ham, eggs, and hot coffee they were about to enjoy. I told him sadly that we couldn't, for obvious reasons, allow ourselves the luxury of drinking coffee up aloft, but were just breaking out some tired-looking cheese rolls bought four days ago in San Francisco and now tasting strongly of petrol fumes.

"Ah! San Francisco," he replied wistfully. "What wouldn't I give to be spending Christmas back State-side."

He gave us the latest weather report, stayed with us for a hundred miles or so, then advised us to call Honolulu or Nandi with our next position. His voice faded out on the friendly note with which it had come in: "Nice meeting you guys. Goodbye now, and good luck!"

We then settled down to some serious navigation and fuel calculation. When flying in the tropics, petrol fumes rapidly develop in the ferry tanks in spite of air vents. So the caps must be released frequently to prevent pressure building up, and expanding the tanks with a startling "bang." This process results in a fume-filled cockpit and splitting headaches for the occupants.

We made a practice of running all our ferry tanks dry before using the integral wing tanks. This enabled us to know exactly how we were going and also improved our centre of gravity situation. However, the ominous cough and splutter of fuel-starved engines, the signal for a quick switch onto another tank, somehow always took us by surprise and had a knack of happening at awkward moments. Once, when I was making a steep turn to pass through the only gap in a line of heavy clouds, both engines cut out together. It happened at one of those rare moments when my companion was having a nap. He woke with a start and our hands met on the fuel cocks.

Only once, on all three Pacific flights, did the engines cut out for any other reason. On this occasion we were flying through bad turbulence when both engines ran rough and we began, for no apparent cause, rapidly to lose power and altitude. It is in such an emergency that one appreciates the insistence on detail and engine failure checks that underline a pilot's training. Our first thought, as the Baron vibrated and the altimeter started to unwind, was that there might be water in the fuel, but a quick cockpit check revealed that the ignition switches turned to only one magneto a piece. They had been knocked off by the pilot's knee bumping the dashboard during the turbulence, and the engines roared healthily once more as soon as they were flicked on again.

South of Johnson Island we ran into the "intertropical front"—an area which stretches for more than 500 miles north and south of the equator and develops, with little warning, into cyclones and typhoons. We could see build-ups ahead of us in the form of huge, solid-looking masses of cumulus cloud from sea level to 35,000 feet—beautiful but perilous. We tried at first to fly around the more isolated storms but it soon became obvious that this caper could take us well off course. Ahead lay an unbroken black wall of rain but there was no alternative than to slow to turbulence penetration speed, tighten seat belts, and head into it.

It was as though night had come upon us instantaneously, so we turned up the cockpit lights. Entombed as we were in cloud and pelting rain, the occasional dazzling flashes of forked lightning came as a relief. The hideous crackle of radio static that made communication between us almost impossible reminded me that trailing aerials can act as lightning conductors. There was also a danger of our 60 feet of aerial becoming wrapped around the aircraft. I started to wind it in, but Dr Dicks shouted that we'd better give some sort of position report to Nandi before doing so. Suspecting we had drifted somewhat to port, I worked out a rough "guesstimate" and radioed the information. There was no reply but this was hardly unexpected since we usually had to repeat our 150-mile position reports at least six times before getting through. There was always a chance that some other traveller would hear our signal, though, and we knew that we would be mighty fortunate, in the event of a splash-down, to be found in this loneliest of all ocean stretches.

After a perilous hour and a half we broke through the other side of the front as abruptly as we had entered it. We emerged into a soft, blue day, with a few innocent fleecy clouds drifting between sky and sea. Light-heartedly I dug out my camera and took some shots of clear sky against the darkness of the receding front.

Within about 400 miles of Tarawa, in the Gilbert and Ellice Island group, we established communication with the New Zealand run radio station situated on the island of Beito. Shortly afterwards the radio compass needle ceased its aimless wandering around the dial, flickered uncertainly and finally locked on zero, indicating Tarawa straight ahead.

About an hour before our expected time of arrival we spotted the unique cloud formation that reflects the soft green shades of a shallow island lagoon. Before long we were within V.H.F. radio range and enthusiastic voices began coming through clearly, welcoming us to Tarawa and giving us the terminal forecast. We had already given our E.T.A. on first contact with High Frequency radio, so that customs and quarantine officers would have plenty of time to don their whites and travel several miles by boat and jeep to meet us at the aerodrome. A fire truck had also to be brought out and warmed up and fuel drums rolled into position. The New Zealanders in charge of this radio station really sweat out a ferry flight, and for fourteen or fifteen hours beforehand start relaying weather conditions through Nandi or Honolulu and monitoring their radio beacon which is especially turned on to guide the aircraft in. It is most reassuring for ferry pilots to know that these conscientious men provide such a splendid service.

Ours being one of the first ferry aircraft to come through direct from Honolulu, our first visit caused great interest in Tarawa. Apart from a monthly mail service from Fiji, visiting aircraft were relatively few, and we were asked to make a low pass over the radio hut so that the operators could have a look at our new machine. This seemed the least we could do for their services so, after locating the right hut on the long chain of islands around the lagoon, we came in for a traditional salute. In the sheer excitement of having battled through to this exquisite atoll, however, I forgot to wind in the trailing aerial. As we soared in over the palm trees there was a sudden "twang!" and about forty feet of wire scrambled back into a loose knot between my feet. Luckily our interested watchers managed to rescue the drogue, but—shame upon me—I did precisely the same thing on our second visit to Tarawa!

The main village and administration area of this island group is situated on Beito, the coral airstrip being on another island about ten miles away. The narrow strips of land around the large lagoon range from about 100 yards to a quarter of a mile wide, and some of the islands lie so close together that they are connected by coral causeways. The colouring is the predominant Pacific harmony of blue, green and white, in a multitude of varying shades; the dark green of palms and taro plantations, the translucent green of the lagoon, the deep, almost purple blue of the surrounding ocean and the white of the surf breaking on the narrow coral beaches.

As we stepped out of the Baron into the humid tropical air we were watched by crowds of islanders; officials dressed in their starched white shorts and shirts, others in cloth sarongs. To our great relief—and to onlookers' amusement—we

124

struggled out of our heavy flying gear and gratefully accepted some fresh, cool coconut milk, while a customs officer sprayed the aircraft to destroy any bugs we might have transported into their remote paradise.

One of those to receive us was an Englishman who had come all the way from a neighbouring island to question us on behalf of its inhabitants. "What do you want to know?" we asked.

"As a matter of fact," he said, "ever since hearing you were coming, three days ago, we've been laying bets on how you *managed* during the long fourteen-hour flight."

"*Managed?*" I asked, as though I had no idea what he meant. That was, of course, a secret reserved for the family "happy hour."

On our third Pacific ferry flight we were so tired on reaching Tarawa that we decided to rest there for a couple of days in the Otintai Hotel, an idyllic tropical bungalow between the ocean and the lagoon. Every move we made was watched with absorbed interest by groups of islanders either wandering around the hotel or paddling past in canoes. That worried us not at all, as they were delightfully happy, friendly people and refreshingly unspoiled. It was not long, however, before we realised that for people associated with the medical profession there could be no such thing as rest—even on a remote island.

The notice: "Birth Control Clinic," attached to a grass hut attracted our professional interest and in passing we got into conversation with the English doctor in charge. He took us along to the island hospital and showed us through airy wards with coral floors and bamboo ceilings. The surgeon of this establishment was a New Zealand-trained islander named Timone Flood who told Dr Dicks that he had a patient urgently requiring a cholecystectomy (removal of gall bladder). "I've only done one myself," he said, "I was hoping he'd hold out till we could get him to Suva, but I'm afraid he won't. Would you happen to have any experience in this line?"

Dr Dicks, a practised surgeon, readily agreed to assist, and arrangements were made to excise the gall bladder later that day. The patient, a Gilbertese weighing eighteen stone, was brought to hospital by canoe from a neighbouring island. He looked a poor prospect for anaesthetic, let alone for major

125

surgery, but it was obviously his only chance. The gall bladder, revealed at last under inches of subcutaneous fat, proved to be not only diseased and full of stones but adhering to a hob-nailed, friable liver. Dr Flood told us that this type of cirrhosis was very common in the islands and that many died of it. Its cause is no doubt a lack of protein in childhood, combined with later indulgence in the all too popular coconut palm toddy that has a high alcohol and chemical content. During the operation the liver began bleeding so badly that a transfusion was necessary. Luckily there was a donor at hand so Dr Flood attended to this aspect while Dr Dicks finished sewing up.

We had been invited to dine with the acting Resident Commissioner, and when everything possible had been done for the patient we were already overdue. By the time we had showered and changed, the native driver who had been sent to fetch us, no doubt fearing that he would be blamed for the delay, was sweating with nervous agitation. He took off at a terrifying pace which was maintained through scattered villages beside the narrow road that wound along the spine of the islands. The dark boles of palm trees whizzed past in the dim light and we missed groups of children seemingly by inches. There was a sudden "thump" and a howl that made my blood freeze. "Only a dog," the driver said, and accelerated, almost instantly hitting another one, followed by an unfortunate chicken. I felt in greater peril than ever in the air, but our complaints were ignored until, on entering yet another tiny village, we were forced to a skidding stop by a group of frantically waving inhabitants. A flickering orange glow at one side of the road turned out to be a burning motor-bike with a man pinned underneath. Three more bodies and another motor-bike were scattered around. Our driver seemed quite exasperated when we insisted on jumping out and pulling the burning man clear of his machine. While I was inspecting one of the other casualties an onlooker pushed me aside and made a sign of the cross in the air. The poor fellow certainly looked dead, but I had felt a pulse fluttering under my fingers and caught the smell of alcohol on a wavering breath.

The other three victims were unconscious too and all four had a catalogue of injuries rivalling a Saturday night in the Perth casualty ward: fractures, burns, lacerations. We were still

126

discussing what to do, with the Commissioner's driver plucking anxiously at our sleeves, when we heard the clang of an ambulance bell. Since we knew that there were no modern methods of communication near by, this seemed at first like a fortunate coincidence. We later found, however, that the islanders have a "telephone system" of their own by which they shout a message from village to village, so that it travels the seven miles to the hospital in as many minutes.

None of the onlookers spoke English and, ignoring our pleas, they began dragging the bodies about like rag dolls, then tossed them into the ambulance where they hit the floor with resounding thumps.

As soon as the ambulance drove off our driver forced us back into the car and covered the rest of the distance at nightmare speed. We explained the circumstances of our delay, but I'm afraid the Commissioner and his wife must have found us rather ungracious guests, as we were both preoccupied with the fate of the accident victims. We excused ourselves early and returned to the hospital, where we found that the four men, owing to lack of other accommodation, had been placed in the Labour Ward. Their heads were resting precariously on the footrails of the beds, and they appeared to be in the same condition in which they had arrived. It appeared that the staff had decided there was no point in doing anything about them until they either recovered consciousness or died, and in the circumstances there seemed nothing we could do either.

We found our cholecystectomy patient, however, to be pulling round fairly satisfactorily. His wife was camped under his bed, and the five other patients in the ward were watching him with keen interest. Reluctant to leave him at such a critical stage, we decided to stay another couple of days. The story had a happy ending as after our return to Australia we heard from Dr Flood that the patient had been discharged from hospital within ten days and had subsequently made a good recovery. Dr Dicks was very relieved to receive this news, as it meant that he could confidently show his face again to the charming people of this island group.

During our two extra days in Tarawa we met an Australian named Barrie MacDonald who was writing a thesis on the area and who told us a great deal about it. Most people will remember Tarawa as the scene of a bloody battle in World War II, in which U.S. marines conquered the atoll after wading for nearly a mile across a lagoon in the face of Japanese fire.

Dr Dicks was especially interested in the island story, because his brother Alan had spent many years in the British Colonial Service on Tulagi in the Solomons and on Ocean Island in the Gilbert and Ellice group. Barrie MacDonald urged us to visit Tabiteuea, saying that it was one of the few remaining unspoiled Pacific islands. It lay 200 miles south-west *en route* to Port Vila, in the New Hebrides; our next refuelling stop.

"They have one radio on the island," Barrie said, "and they love getting telegrams. Let them know you're coming and they're sure to give you an interesting time."

The post office clerk's eyes fairly popped as he read the wire we had made out. He called to a group of islanders sitting in the shade of the verandah and translated the message into their own language. It was greeted with awed gasps and grunts, after which the clerk returned to us with a worried look: "Excuse me," he said, "but does this mean you're going to *Tabiteuea?*"

When he was assured that that was our intention, his big eyes rolled again. "But the people are very cruel there," he told us. "It is not a nice place to visit."

He thought for a moment, then added: "But you are strangers. You are white. Perhaps you *could* visit Tabiteuea with safety. But maybe we could write the telegram in a different way."

He called his friends, who crowded around eager to assist. Teak-coloured fingers traced imaginary words on the counter as each one had his say. After some fifteen minutes of earnest and animated consultation, they had worked out a message that was greeted with general approval. "It is agreed that you shall send this telegram," the clerk informed us:

GREATLY IMPRESSED BY G. & E. ISLANDERS STOP REQUEST PERMISSION VISIT YOUR ISLAND MEET PEOPLE HAVE A FEAST SEE DANCING STOP ESTIMATE ARRIVAL ELEVEN O'CLOCK TOMORROW.

We nodded, everyone else nodded, and the clerk gave a sigh of smiling satisfaction.

128

The telegram was despatched, and the form was then pinned on a public board in the post office. Apparently this was standard procedure in Tarawa as it joined a number of telegrams which had been sent out of or into the area. We scanned them with interest, including one from ourselves which read:

TO RESIDENT COMMISSIONER: NOVEMBER 4827 JULIETTE ARRIV-
ING TARAWA THURSDAY PLEASE TURN ON DIRECTIONAL BEACON.

Beside it was another:

SHIP ARRIVING TOMORROW TEN PIGS FIVE LUNATICS GENERAL
CARGO.

20
A CRAB IN
THE TOILET

A STORM OF APPLAUSE FROM AN AWED ASSEMBLY OF OVER 200 islanders greeted us as we closed down the engines and stepped out onto the new airstrip at Tabiteuea.

Confronted in my hilarious flying suit and Mae West by an impressive line-up of six chiefs, I felt like a member of the royal family caught out wearing the wrong clothes. Mindful of the ominous comments of the post office clerk at Tarawa, we tried to recall all the hints Barrie MacDonald had given us about local customs.

We were trying to guess which of the six chiefs was the oldest or most important when a strong young islander sprang forward, and with a flourish drew a sharp knife from his belt. I was afraid that for some reason they hadn't liked the look of us or that we had made some unforgivable mistake, but he flashed a wide smile, picked up two coconuts, slashed them open and handed them to us to drink.

To our relief we found that the island "President" or main chief, Peter Kanere, could speak English and was able to interpret what the young man was trying to tell us. "He says he is very strong man. He will guard your aeroplane today and tonight. There are some bad people on this island. I advise you to accept his offer, and I think perhaps one dollar for payment."

In addition to the dollar, we gave our guard, to his boundless delight, a packet of rather petrol-flavoured currant buns and two tins of soft drink. We then boarded the island's only truck, a wobbly-wheeled veteran in the back of which had been placed the seatless frames of three ancient armchairs. The islanders themselves never use chairs, but were very proud of having been able to produce these specimens of "white man's sitting." Three of Peter Kanere's sons, crouching on the truck tray, held the chairs steady as we trundled slowly on our way, pursued by hordes of children shrieking with delight at the amazing spectacle. Nodding, bowing and smiling in regal style and ducking under palm fronds which rasped overhead, we were driven to the "Transit House." a small hut of thatched bamboo with a coral floor. We were told that it was reserved for specially honoured guests.

Here we were helped off the truck and the President showed us inside, indicating two cubicles divided by a palm partition and each containing a bed made of coconut posts with a fibre base, a table, two stools of woven coconut fibre, and a shower recess. The latter contained a suspended paint tin with a string attached. The string was pulled, the tin up-ended, and a trickle of water fell upon the expectant bather.

Big openings in the bamboo walls provided generous peep-holes for interested spectators, mostly children, who clambered suffocatingly around until shooed away by our interpreter.

No sooner were we inside than we were served a thick mass of pandanus fruit, rolled and marinated in coconut oil (practically pure carbohydrate and very sickly), accompanied by a platter of saltless, fly-covered fish, a hunk of taro root, some rice, and coconut milk. We ate as much of the food as we could and tried to look as if we were enjoying it.

The curious children had by this time congregated around another hut about ten feet away. Attracted by their wild shouts of laughter, we found that the object of their excitement was now a man, handcuffed and stark naked, who kept jumping up and down, emitting animal-like noises and finally chasing the teasing, shrieking kids around the yard.

"Take no notice. He is mad," Kanere told us casually, and then on a note of—could it have been modest pride?—"We have a lot of lunatics. There are nine now under restraint in the jail over there." He pointed to a small stone building only a few yards away.

"Are they dangerous?" I asked.

He thought for a moment before answering: "No, not dangerous, only cruel. But they are handcuffed, as you see."

The distinction seemed rather too academic for comfort and I saw Doctor eyeing his bag, obviously wondering whether it contained anything with which to meet an emergency. But the time had now come to resume our triumphal progress and we drove on over the rough coral track through closely situated villages, almost hidden in high, green vegetation, and each containing all the members of one family.

Before long our progress was arrested by an old man standing in the middle of the road waving his arms. For a moment we feared it might be another island accident, but Kanere smiled reassuringly. "An invitation," he said, and helping us from the truck escorted us to the big, open "Maniaba," or village meeting house. We hoped we were about to see a dance, but Kanere said that unfortunately the islanders did not perform on Sunday. They would, however, entertain us in other ways.

We removed our shoes before entering the crowded hut, where we sat cross-legged on grass mats. Every dark eye was fixed on us with piercing curiosity. Kanere was soon translating a barrage of eager questions. Who were we? Where from and where to? Why had we come to Tabiteuea? Formal speeches of welcome were made by various chiefs, and we reciprocated.

We had brought with us coloured pictures of the first men on the moon, which proved a wonderful talking point. They were handed around for inspection and examined with intense interest. Kanere said they had heard over the radio about these men landing on the moon but had not known whether to believe it. Even now some of the villagers seemed to suspect they were being fooled. "There are two men in the pictures," someone observed shrewdly. "If there were only two men on the moon, who took these photographs?"

We explained this to their apparent satisfaction. They then

TOP: Arriving at Honolulu on the first ferry flight. BOTTOM: Tarawa Atoll from the air, showing the lagoon

turned their fascinated attention to the photograph of man's first footprint in the grey moon dust and asked if there was wind, water or vegetation up there. By the time Doctor had answered all these and other questions to the best of his considerable ability, our audience got the impression that he was Neil Armstrong himself and regarded him with greater awe than ever.

During this interlude my every attempt to ease the cross-legged posture, to which I was unaccustomed, was rewarded with peals of laughter. Various elders made more speeches, everyone sang for us, and I was handed baby after baby to examine and admire.

We then asked whether they would accept the gift of some tobacco and popcorn that we had brought with us. This was seriously discussed, and an affirmative decision was followed by speeches of thanks.

Now ready to move on, we found ourselves trapped by the arrival of another feast. The food was the same as before, quite palatable, and, we realised, specially prepared in our honour, but for us, far too sickly and much too much. Shooing away the thousands of flies we ate with uneasy forebodings. Stomach upsets are bad enough in any circumstances, but when in the air are quite unspeakable. I thanked myself for having some sulphadiazine in my handbag.

We emerged at last into the fresh air with well-concealed relief, but our day had hardly begun. News of the invitation had spread back along the track so that on our return to the "Transit House" we were stopped at every one of fourteen villages and were obliged to spend at least half an hour in each of them. In every "Maniaba" we listened to the same sort of speeches, answered the same sort of questions, and were served the same specially prepared food and fresh coconut milk.

At some of our stopping places, village jesters provided comic relief by mimicking our movements and throwing in a few inventions of their own. The star turn was an imitation of myself at the aircraft controls, meanwhile attempting to roll pandanus cakes, feed a baby, and nag my co-pilot, wiggling my bottom seductively the while.

We had been advised, as part of our briefing in Tabiteuea manners, that it was extremely impolite to ask to go to the

TOP: The welcoming party at Tarawa. BOTTOM: Typical Tarawa scene

toilet during one of these village feasts. In any case we had seen no sign of anything in the nature of a loo and by the time we had been eating and drinking steadily for over seven hours the situation had become serious.

Back at last in the guest house, some urgent questions elicited the information that the local sanitary facilities consisted of a communal hut perched above the sea on the edge of a short, coral jetty. As I hurried in this direction a number of islanders, wielding their fishing rods on the beach, rushed for strategic positions and, gazing eagerly upwards, cast their lines. I was past caring and wished them good fishing as I contributed the bait. A small supply of toilet paper was then cheerfully handed in to me by a little boy. I wondered what sanitary arrangements were made for the lunatics and what sort of conversation to strike up if I were to encounter one of them there on my next visit. "Have fun," I told the Doctor as I met him on my way back along the jetty.

Surprised that we had not brought our sleeping mats, Kanere sent one of his sons to borrow some from the jail and these were spread over the bare springs of the beds. The hut was now filled with the high whine of mosquitoes, so I put on slacks and a long-sleeved shirt and despite the comfortless arrangements, slept soundly until dawn. I was awakened by a chorus of giggles, to see about thirty pairs of eyes peeping through the bamboo walls at my incredibly amusing night attire.

There was nothing for it but to repeat the public ritual on the jetty. The only occupant of the hut was a large crab, which quickly scuttled under the seat and obliged me to perch myself at a precarious angle to the intense glee of the onlookers below.

"Watch out—there's a crab in the toilet," I warned the Doctor on my way back. He did not seem to understand, but enlightenment was in store for him. Seconds later I heard a wild yell and saw him erupt in some confusion from the hut. As far as the onlookers were concerned this was the highlight of our visit.

21

ISLAND HOP
TO SYDNEY

"COME BACK AGAIN, AND STAY. YOU ARE ACCEPTED HERE," Chief Kanere said, shaking hands warmly as we returned to the plane. We only just managed to clear the strip with our heavy fuel load and in spite of the interesting experience we were thankful to be heading towards Port Vila and "white man's bathing."

Before long we had entered the convergent zone between the Gilbert and Ellice Islands and the New Hebrides—another bad weather area of great cumulus build-ups. As before, there was no choice but to strap down, plunge in, and sit it out. In such conditions it is best to fly at about 1,000 feet in order to keep below the worst of the lightning, hail and convection currents inside the storm clouds, leaving sufficient height to manoeuvre in case of being driven seawards by turbulence. The technique in rough weather is to maintain a level attitude and the correct turbulence penetration speed, in order to minimise the danger of structural failure or loss of control.

We made it through with no more than a few anxious moments, and soon observed a thick haze ahead. This was Nature's own smog, rising from the many active volcanoes of the New Hebrides area and becoming almost as thick as cloud. It was exciting to look down on the volcanoes; some quite new-born, one smoking away in vigorous maturity, another extinct, with its crater now a lake. On our first flight in this area we began to sniff anxiously around for the source of a smell of burning, but finally decided that it was only the volcanoes which were on fire, not the Beechcraft.

The volcanic islands rise to considerable heights, so that we were obliged to fly over 7,000 feet in order to maintain a safe clearance. The peaks rise out of masses of lush tropical foliage, surrounded by the blue-green sea which rushes between the islands in channel currents as strong as those in the air above.

A precise, French-accented voice cleared us to land at Port Vila, and directed us around the circuit as efficiently as if we were coming in to land at an international airport. When we had come to a stop on the well-kept airport lawn, we were met by French and British officials who seemed to be trying to outdo each other in carrying out the letter of the law. New Hebrides is a condominium (or "pandemonium," as some unkind critics say), governed by both the French and British. We gained the impression that this sense of competition extends even to the shine on a belt buckle and the razor-edged crease on a pair of shorts.

But this immaculate crispness does not extend to everything in the vicinity. On our first visit we met Dr Ted Freeman, of Sydney, who took us to see the hospital to which patients must be taken by boat, since it is on an island in the bay. An old, somewhat decrepit building, with narrow corridors, it had a small and poorly-equipped operating theatre and a matchbox labour ward and nursery. Most of the patients were lying on mats around the verandahs, with post-surgery and post-natal cases chatting to those recovering from such diseases as hepatitis, malaria, and dysentery. Tubercular patients were theoretically isolated on one side of the hospital, but wandered around to talk to their friends.

Dr Freeman was coping remarkably with problems of over-crowding and the treatment of tropical diseases, including malaria, elephantiasis and meningitis, but it was obvious that he was desperately tired. He was helped by four Australian

136

sisters, and by native girls who, in addition to their medical duties, acted as interpreters. They talked to the patients in their own language, and to the doctor and sisters in pidgin English-French.

We heard that a new hospital was to be built by the Government, but Dr Freeman thought that the islands were badly in need of something like the Australian Flying Doctor Service and was very glad to talk over his problems and dreams with us. The people are widely scattered through the New Hebrides, and it is impossible for the few doctors to make regular visits to the many small communities. Most babies are born without medical care and there is consequently a very high infant mortality rate. Many maternal deaths are due to lack of quick medical aid, and tropical diseases are rife.

Dr Freeman thought that a Flying Doctor Service would be the first step towards essential health control, and had actually submitted a proposal for such a service to the Australian Board of Missions. Most members were sympathetic, but the island institution had to be deferred owing to a diversity of aims and scarcity of funds.

The experience made me realise how very healthy, by comparison, we are in Australia, and how easily solved are our medical problems compared with those in such tropical communities. In fact, as we were later to learn, all Dr Freeman's dedicated work for this island community was doomed to disappointment. Some time after this visit he left with his wife and six children for Scotland to study for his F.R.C.S., having first laid the foundation stone for a new hospital. On returning in 1970, he discovered that the stone had been stored away and no progress whatever made on the new building. A few weeks later he was himself seriously smitten with meningitis and was forced to leave the Hebrides. One wonders whether the islanders will ever again find such a selfless and devoted friend.

A pleasant aspect of our stay at Port Vila was the delicious home-cooked French food at the Rossi Hotel, something we looked forward to and spoke about for thousands of miles. Less appealing, however, were the great rumbling jerks as earthquake shocks passed through the island's stony bowels. The inhabitants appear to ignore the phenomena, having

137

become quite accustomed to earthquakes which would cause chaos in an Australian city.

Our next scheduled stop was Sydney, via New Caledonia; another such rugged island but an entirely French possession. En route we detected a smell of burning for which we could not blame the volcanoes. Our radio had fizzled out, so instead of passing straight over Caledonia we had to land at Tontouta for repairs.

The delay at Tontouta meant a night arrival at Sydney and on this last lap we met some of the worst weather we had experienced during the entire flight. Cloud was down to 600 feet over the Sydney airport so we came in under radar control and were guided to the instrument landing system for Runway 07. Flying down the glide path in thick cloud and rain we expected we would have to overshoot and try again, but just as we were about to do so we saw the lights of the runway gleaming dimly below and came straight down. We stepped out with a sigh of relief, at which moment a great jet screamed past in the cloud above, overshot the runway, and had to go round again as we had expected to do. Elated at being back on home soil again, and there being no one else around to do so, we congratulated ourselves.

After the journey from San Francisco to Sydney, our flight from Sydney to Perth seemed as straightforward as a bus ride and the friendly, familiar face of Australia was all the map we required. As we approached Perth, the airport came through with repeated requests for our estimated time of arrival, so it was not hard to guess that some kind of welcoming ceremony had been planned. Dr Dicks decided to smarten himself up, and insisted on recovering a bottle of water jammed under the seat in order to slick down his hair. He got hold of it and sat back, so intent on his titivations that he ignored the bumping of the aircraft over the updrafts of hot air from the earth below. Just as he unscrewed the top, the plane jolted and dropped sharply, causing the water to leap up and saturate his pants. A mental picture of the undignified figure he would cut on arrival concerned him as much as it amused me and he began to scrabble frantically among the gear in the cockpit. As I circled the airport, not failing to remark on the big reception committee assembled near the Flying Doctor hangar, he managed to wrench off the wet trousers and struggle into a dry, but extremely crumpled pair, breathlessly completing the operation just as we touched down.

On seeing the line-up of familiar faces it seemed almost as though we had never been away. Next day, with hardly time to outline our adventures to the family, I was busy preparing for my return to the north.

22

OLD LAW
IN A NEW AGE

I WAS STILL FLYING THE CESSNA IN WHICH I HAD CARRIED OUT the first vaccination project, but she was becoming a little worse for wear. I knew that she had a fairly rough history, and could sense that the control cables were slack. On one occasion, her reluctance to come out of a turn caused me some anxious moments and I realized that she needed a good overhaul.

Dad was also worried about this, and urged me to change to another aircraft before starting the Kimberley vaccinations. About this time, a party of tourists in a Mooney aircraft landed in Broome. Dad was much taken by the machine, and, when he found it was for sale, we arranged to buy it.

Though smaller than the Cessna, she was a honey to fly, and felt solid and reliable. I knew that I would have a problem fitting in all my gear as well as a passenger if I ever had to carry one, but I was so confident about my new bird that I didn't worry too much about that. It seemed to augur well that I was able to obtain a registration to match my initials: R.E.M. In the radio telephone code, these became Romeo-Echo-Mike.

The Mooney was due for a major inspection and this was done in Perth before beginning the Kimberley run, but as we had to wait for parts from the U.S.A. the job wan't finished until the very morning on which I was to fly north. There was little time for a proper test flight, but I decided to risk it.

On application of full power for take-off, the engine began popping and banging like a badly-tuned T-model Ford. I aborted the take-off, taxied off the runway, ran the engine full bore, tested the magnetos, and leaned off the mixture. She was still coughing and banging, but the problem seemed to me to have improved somewhat. I thought that the plugs had probably oiled up during a prolonged ground run whilst we were swinging the compass and waved off the mechanics who came running with frantic gestures. I cleared for departure again and managed to get her into the air, aware that the engineers were gazing after me in horror as I went stuttering off to the north. It was an awful thing to do to them, but my schedule was fixed and I couldn't afford another lengthy delay. I was sure, as proved to be the case, that the oiled plugs would soon clear.

But as soon as I tried to level out into cruising flight I sensed that the trim was wrongly adjusted, and in spite of putting on full forward trim it was hard to keep the nose from forcing itself up. Having to push the stick forward all the time made flying extremely tiring, but I consoled myself with the thought that Dad would fix it as soon as we got to Broome.

After landing there, we tried to remove the belly panel, but found that the screws were frozen solid. The easy way out seemed to be extra weight in the aircraft to keep her nose down, so while flying around the Broome area Dad always came with me as ballast. When I began to go further afield, we loaded about 200 pounds of rocks onto the floor in front of the co-pilot's seat and, being a "rockhound," I eventually made a rockery out of lovely Kimberley stones.

It was good to be based in Broome, because I could live with Dad. Amongst my first jobs was a vaccination visit to a native reserve near the port, and I was asked to hurry as they were all going to the funeral of a well-known Aboriginal. The day before, he and his friends had been staging a corroboree for tourists off the liner *Centaur*. A highspot of the performance had been a bone-pointing death dance, and much to everyone's horror, this man had dropped dead in the middle of the act.

141

While I was talking to the Aborigines about it, one of them said, "I dunno . . . might be something in this blackfella magic!"

Stone-ballasted like an old sailing ship, and with the engine running sweetly after some friendly paternal persuasion, I set off to two Kimberley missions—Lombadina and Beagle Bay. I had to come down at Cape Leveque, the only airstrip in the area, and a short one at that. It runs across the Cape, with 100 foot cliffs at either end and much of the surface loose and boggy. Fortunately I had been warned of its peculiarities by Bishop Jobst, who is in charge of the Catholic diocese of the Kimberleys and also a keen flier. Because of his good advice I managed to come down, cunningly, on the "good side."

There is a lighthouse on the Cape, serviced by two families to whom I gave out vaccine before proceeding by road to the missions. I found them most pleasant people, but one member explained to me in some embarrassment that the families weren't on speaking terms. While greeting each group on opposite sides of the aircraft I could not but reflect sadly on the problems of isolation.

I was driven to the missions from the Cape by Father Peile, a Pallottine priest who was then the superintendent of Lombadina. In the tradition of his Society, he is a keen student of anthropology.

The nuns I met at the two isolated Dampierland missions belonged to the Order of St John of God, that entered the missionary field in Kimberley in 1907. My mother has written the wonderful story of their pioneering efforts to raise the standards of the Aboriginal and part Aboriginal people of this area and there is little I can add, except to express my own humble admiration of the selfless task they set themselves. They have flinched from no aspect of the Aboriginal problem, from the education to the care of the sick—including lepers.

I found them delightful to deal with, full of happy humour and humanity and most realistic about the problems and contradictions of the task they have undertaken. They are assisted by Pallottine priests and brothers who instruct the people in various trades such as carpentry, mechanics, vehicle maintenance, stock work, and gardening. At Beagle Bay they have set up a cool drink factory that supplies the local market.

142

I also visited Pallottine missions at Balgo Hills, in the lonely desert area south of Halls Creek, and at La Grange Bay, South of Broome. The latter mission is now staffed mainly by lay apostolate helpers—wonderful young people who have given up a period of their lives to the cause of the Aborigines.

I found that missions of various denominations share, for the most part, the same enlightened outlook. Their aim is to provide a bridge between the Aboriginal world and that of the white man. If they are to survive, our indigenous people have no option than to integrate in to the latter. Many missions now aim to become co-operative industrial centres, and the Aborigines are being encouraged, in every way possible, to take the initiative and leadership towards that end.

More importance is now being attached to maintaining a basic pride of race and a sense of racial identity, with less interference in tribal law than was considered necessary for "salvation" in days gone by. Upholding this enlightened approach, however, is not always as simple and practical as it might sound. There are aspects of the old law which are definitely retrogressive to integration and have, in fact, lost any sense or reason that they might once have had. Among these aspects are the claiming of young girls by the tribal elders, and certain painful and often disastrous operations performed on adolescents of both sexes.

I would soon be out of my depth in anthropological waters if I attempted to hold forth on Aboriginal tribal law. But I have tried, as a nurse, to understand something of the background to cases that frequently come my way. I have seen many tragic results from the practice of this "old law" that some people imagine to be a simple and wholly admirable structure that puts our so-called "civilised society" to shame. Many of its aspects are indeed admirable, but it is far from being simple and is subject to as many fads, cults and innovations as our own, some of them, as I see it, being downright mischievous. New "culture heroes," with attendant rites and practices of their own, are constantly being introduced to supersede those whose practices held sway in the past.

Although, in many parts of Australia, all aspects of the old law have been forgotten, there are areas in which it is still quite

143

vigorously upheld. In parts of the North-West and the eastern goldfields a sort of militant fundamentalism is expressing itself today, as though in defiance of the new culture in which the Aborigines see little virtue and can find no place. From time to time the elders get together and decide to revive practices that have died out, though they appear to have either hazy or non-existent memories of the reasons for them. It is obvious, anyway, that when it comes to carrying out operations connected with these rites they have lost any skill that their forbears may have possessed.

While stationed at Meekatharra, on the edge of the "rain maker" country, I came upon some distressing instances. In the hospital were three Aboriginal boys of about eighteen, who had undergone tribal initiation during a corroboree held near Wiluna. Members of station families, they had not been as smart in avoiding this ordeal as are young Aborigines closer to the towns. The result was that, some ten days later, all three were in such a shocking condition that they had approached the Meeka hospital for help.

They explained to the doctor that, according to tradition, they had been "run" to the point of exhaustion, and then held down while the tribal "witch doctor" performed the usual circumcision. This was followed by an embellishment, supposedly to increase the powers of manhood, that someone remembered having been carried out in the past. Using a blunt stone instrument the "doctor" had hacked out a section behind the glans penis and had cut the fraenum—a fold of tissue which normally limits the movement of the organ. In so doing he had succeeded in cutting right through to the urethra, with the result that the organs soon became so grossly swollen and infected that the boys could hardly walk and could urinate only with the greatest agony.

The doctor, having examined the appalling mess, and not wanting to cause trouble for the youths on their return to the tribe, asked what they wanted him to do; cure the infection and then attempt to make them as they had been before, or merely deal with the infection.

The poor boys, completely bewildered about the whole deal, were content to leave the decision to him. The doctor did his

144

best but feared that, as in many other cases he had seen, they would end up with chronic orchitis—a painful swelling of the testicles which would render them subject to frequent bladder infections and probably sterile.

Many of the missions, while appreciating the important aspects of tribal initiation, have persuaded the elders to leave the actual circumcision to a qualified doctor. Several elders admitted to me that the white doctor did a "better job," and that, provided the boys had been ceremonially "sung" according to tribal tradition, the new arrangement was a good idea.

The practice of "bone pointing" or "singing dead" is another aspect of the old law that dies hard and can result in much misery and endless vendettas. I was once required to fly an Aboriginal woman with four broken ribs and a fractured clavicle to hospital in Perth. It appeared that she had been "sung dead" for defying some tribal taboo, but had obstinately refused to die. The elders, therefore, having contrived to stupefy her with alcohol, had proceeded to kick her in the chest. She could not remember how it happened, but was told that the magic was taking effect. Evidently not convinced of this, she had presented herself at the hospital, been treated for severe bruising and sent home—only to return soon afterwards with more serious injuries. When the story eventually leaked out it was decided to send her to Perth, in the hope that by the time her broken bones were mended the affair would have blown over.

Another incident concerned an Aboriginal woman of about forty-five. With her elderly husband, she had come into a North-West station from the desert some fourteen years before. She had been trained by the manager's wife and had no desire whatever to return to her tribe, but after her husband's death bush relatives turned up and demanded that she return to her own country to carry out the traditional widow's ceremonies. When she refused they attacked her with a boomerang, and she had to be taken to the Meekatharra hospital where a large piece of wood was removed from her thigh. Having recovered from her wound, and knowing that the alternative was death, she returned to carry out the wishes of the desert tribe. When I last visited the station she had been away for several months, and her young son was being cared for by the Manager's wife as one of her own.

145

The Australian Inland Mission, a vigorous Presbyterian organisation, is one that extends its services to all members of the community—not specifically the Aboriginal. A.I.M. centres have hospitals run by minimum staffs of nurses who dedicate two or more years of their lives to work in the outback. They nurse, cook, wash and clean, with no mention of "overtime," and often have to face tricky medical situations without the advice of a doctor. Taking X-rays, plastering limbs, delivering babies, and sewing up lacerations are all part of the day's work, to be done without complaint and on their own initiative.

It was not at all unusual to find sick babies occupying the nurses' rooms so that they could attend to them in the night, or for the nurses to give their beds to visitors and sleep in a ward or on the verandah.

There was always work for another pair of hands, and I was only too happy to hop in and help with the eternal round of tasks on my visits to these places; anything from cooking or washing up to feeding babies or the aged. Sometimes the nurses would invite some of the young men in the area to dinner, but when the meal was served it was just as likely that they would be summoned to attend a casualty, or that a patient in the wards would have taken a turn for the worse. They would finish up being so busy that the dinner would go cold and the guests quietly disappear.

Even though there were so many men around, and some glad enough to help out if possible, the nurses were usually so busy that they had little chance to get to know them well. When they had any time off, they were usually so tired that they would sooner go to sleep than accept the eager invitations offering. Sister Elizabeth Burchill's book *Innamincka* tells the very interesting story of the early days of the Australian Inland Missions. I doubt whether things have improved very much since her days in Central Australia during the 1920s. Possibly the Government is happy enough to leave the work of medical care in isolated areas to such dedicated women as the St John of God nuns, the Catholic lay apostolate, and the A.I.M. nurses. Certainly they receive little in the way of comfort—as I can testify from numerous nights spent on the mission verandahs, surrounded by hospital screens which would crash over in a breeze, the barking of innumerable dogs, and the inevitable whining of mosquitoes.

One of the missions visited on my immunisation round was Kalumburu, on the extreme north western coast. Founded by Spanish Benedictine monks in 1908, this establishment has had a brave but chequered history and was the scene of a tragic incident in World War II.

As Japanese aircraft were known to be reconnoitring in the area, Allied bombers were stationed on the mission landing strip. In September 1943 these were machine-gunned by Japanese fighter pilots who, as well as destroying a number of aircraft, also wrecked the mission buildings and killed the Super-intendent, Father Thomas, an Aboriginal woman, and four children.

I took time off to explore the wrecks of the bombers that now lie rusting in the scrub beside the strip. What, I wondered, became of the crew of the "Mississippi Dream," whose names were stencilled on her nose?

The mission staff included two Spanish nuns who cooked delicious meals and made good use of the splendid vegetable garden maintained by the staff and Aboriginal people. The children, as at all such institutions, I found attractive and out-going, especially two whom the nuns had adopted as babies when their parents were taken to the Derby Leprosarium.

On one of my visits to this mission, Superintendent Father Basil arranged a fishing trip on which we set out to the beach with nuns, brothers, and children. As the day went on Father Basil and I got caught up with a party of anthropologists who were digging around the site of a camp thought to have been used by trepang gatherers from Timor and Macassar, when this wild coast was still a "terra incognita" to the European world. The scientists showed us a coin dated 1810, and pieces of pottery that had lain there perhaps for centuries.

Later we set off in an outboard dinghy into Napier Broome Bay to deliver mail and a bunch of bananas to a party surveying the prospects for a fishery industry in the area. After passing a number of Aborigines fishing from their dugout canoes with long, barbed spears, we were welcomed onto the survey boat to share a delicious meal of succulent prawns and scallops.

147

We found the crew so interesting that we talked on until Father Basil, with a startled glance at the sinking sun, remembered that he was to officiate at a funeral before nightfall. To save time we were towed close inshore, to be greeted on the beach by the anxious nuns, who had begun to fear that not only one, but three funerals were in store for them.

TOP: The author with Doctor Harold Dicks on their arrival in Perth after the ferry flight from San Francisco. BOTTOM: The Beechcraft Baron on the coral airfield at Tarawa

23

GREMLINS

Always conscious of my utter dependence on my aircraft, I took every opportunity of servicing her. However, ground facilities were virtually nil between main centres, so if anything went wrong I had to fix it myself or fly on and hope for the best. Quite early on one of my eight-week rounds a hydraulic cylinder began leaking, but all I could do was keep topping it up until my supply of fluid ran dry, then fly the rest of the round without flaps or brakes.

All the same, I was luckier than some. Once when flying fairly low over Exmouth Gulf I spotted a hut on one of the small islands in the area. I then noticed, under water on an offshore reef, the unmistakable shape of an aircraft. On landing at Onslow I was greeted by Ian Tonkin, officer for the local Department of Civil Aviation, to whom I excitedly conveyed this interesting information. It was no news to him. "I know," he said calmly. "It's my Fairchild."

He told me that the hut I had seen had been occupied by a hermit who normally kept in regular radio touch with Port Hedland. When he missed several calls, Ian and a friend flew across and circled the island in search of him, during which

Top: The cockpit of F-OCLA with all equipment tightly packed for the flight. The HF radio is strapped to the right hand seat. Bottom: F-OCLI and F-OCLA ready for the flight from Paris to Australia

manoeuvre the engine failed. Ian brought the machine down on a small, steeply-sloping beach, where she promptly rolled over on her back. The two men managed to scramble out just before she slid gracefully down into the water. They dived in an attempt to salvage some items from the cockpit, but got no more than the sodden log book before the plane sank still deeper into the sea.

They made for the hut, where they met the island hermit who told them casually: "I'm O.K. My radio's packed up—that's all."

I forgot to ask how Ian and his companion got back to the mainland.

Sometimes a flight seemed to be gremlin-haunted from the start. One morning, before take-off from Lissadell station in East Kimberley, I found that there was a drop of 280 revs on the left magneto. I hoped it was no more than an oiled plug and, worried about keeping the Ord River station people waiting, decided to push on and check the situation there.

No sooner had I taken off than I discovered that the under-carriage would not retract, and soon found that a big bag of sticky lollies, kept for raising my blood sugar in time of crisis, was jammed under the retraction lever. By holding the controls with my chin, thus freeing my hands, I was able to remedy the problem and carry on. I circled Ord River homestead to alert the folk of my arrival and came down on the station airstrip about ten miles up river.

I had been looking forward to seeing this station, of which I had heard a good deal from both Mum and Dad. They remembered it during the management of one Joe Egan, a redoubtable old-timer of tough bush philosophy and ribald wit. In the early days of the M.M.A. service, Dad had spent some time at the Ord with Joe while repairing a damaged aircraft. Up to that time he had never met such a character and some of the stories he recalls of him and his seraglio of native women would be material for a modern best seller.

I taxied to a clearing, unloaded my vaccines and equipment in the shade of the wing, and waited for the sound of an approaching vehicle. Time passed and I heard nothing but the "carking" of a few crows and the drone of a million flies; nor was there any sign of approaching dust. Glad enough of the opportunity to check the engine, I took out my tool kit and started unscrewing the aircraft cowls. Three hours later, hot, thirsty and covered in grease, I had discovered that the plugs were all O.K. I supposed it must be the ignition, and there was nothing I could do about that. So I put the cowls back, explored around for a while for interesting stones, then, concluding that everyone at Ord River must be away, gave the machine an affectionate pat and asked her to get me to the next place. Just at this moment I heard the sound of an approaching truck, ran over to the road and flagged it down.

The driver was a New Australian whose English was limited, so our conversation was brief and to the point.

"Could you drop me off at the station?"

He looked at me curiously, and enquired, "You okay?"

"Yes, thanks."

He looked at me again, shrugged, and said: "Okay. Hop in."

I grabbed my gear from the aircraft and jumped aboard, whereupon the driver rushed me to the homestead, let me out and roared away without uttering a word.

"Anyone home?" I called. There was no reply. It was only then I noticed that the garden was overgrown and as I approached the house the doors swung on their hinges and creaked eerily in the hot wind. Cautiously I stepped onto the verandah and went inside. There was a sudden agitated flapping of wings which I found to belong to a colony of bats that were nesting in the house.

It had a nightmare quality, like discovering an inland equivalent of the *Marie Celeste*. Dirty dishes and cutlery cluttered the table as though the occupants had left in the process of a meal. Dust lay thickly on the floor, and furniture and the contents of the medicine chest were scattered about.

I wandered around like a sleep-walker, not knowing quite what to do or what to think. The station, as Kimberley homesteads go, had obviously been quite well equipped. There was a reasonable kitchen and bathroom and several toilets, which, by way of amusement, I flushed to surprise the big, green bullfrogs that were camped peacefully in the bowls. I was preparing to face a ten-mile walk back to the airstrip with my gear when the truck driver returned, this time with a number of Aborigines. I asked him why the homestead was deserted, but his reply was unintelligible. He did, however, appear to understand what I told him concerning the purpose of my visit. So in an attempt to salvage something from the mix-up I asked him to call the natives together for vaccination.

"You blackfellows—come up here for needle," he shouted.

They promptly vanished, so I had laboriously to explain that the treatment was given by mouth—on sugar. When this message finally got through the men returned, and while I was handing out their doses they managed between them to explain something of the situation.

I gathered that the property had become eroded through overstocking and had been resumed by the Government, after which the manager had packed up his personal belongings and cleared out. My Aboriginal informants were among those employed to round up straggler cattle. There was now, I gathered, an Agricultural Department settlement nearby to which the truck driver consented to take me.

Here I met two families employed in reseeding the eroded river flats. They were most upset to hear of my long wait and produced a welcome cup of tea, after which I vaccinated everyone in sight.

"Where's your next stop?" they asked.

"Turner River," I replied.

"Well, you won't even find a dog there," they told me. "That station's been resumed too."

I only wondered what had become of the letters I had sent to Turner River and also to Ord River and which had never been returned.

Now ahead of schedule, I set out over rugged country for the next station, hoping that the aircraft, in spite of high temperature, high blood pressure and fibrillating pulse, wouldn't let me down. My eyes alert along the way for clearings in case of emergency, I buzzed the next homestead shortly before sunset.

I planned to stay at this station overnight but the only person to show up was an Aboriginal on horseback who, in answer to my question, informed me that his boss was at home. I asked whether anyone intended coming out to fetch me. He seemed to think not, so I climbed into the saddle behind him and he spurred his horse into a canter that soon got us to the homestead. I mounted the steps and cheerfully announced my arrival, but there was no sign of life. I began to think that the Aboriginal had misunderstood me and that this place was deserted too. A dubious peep inside revealed a scene of utter chaos. Papers, dirty clothes, empty bottles and glasses were strewn everywhere and it was not long before I discovered that although the manager and his wife were at home, they were in no fit state to interview anyone. Having been asked, in language once considered and, as far as I'm concerned, *still* unprintable, who I was and why I was "snooping around," I hurried off to find the Aborigines.

The stockman who had brought me in, an intelligent young man, had explained the purpose of my visit to his people, one or two whom I had already met at Halls Creek. A cleanly dressed native woman, looking rather embarrassed and apologetic, quickly got everyone together and helped me with the job. With the sensitivity of their race, the people had evidently summed up my situation. They no doubt saw that I could hardly stay the night at the homestead, and that if I was to make my next stop—fortunately only fifteen minutes' flying time away—before dark, there was not a minute to lose. When everyone had been dosed and the cards filled in, the stockman, who had contrived to get the boss's car going without the key, quickly got me back to the aircraft and helped me pack in my gear. I set off feeling deeply ashamed of this example of the white man's "way of life" and full of admiration for the dark people who had tried to cover and make up for their employer's shortcomings.

By contrast my next stop, which I reached just before last light, was a very normal and efficiently run establishment. I was welcomed into a happy family and slept the night in a daintily furnished room. How grateful I was to have reached this haven of peace and harmony at the end of a tough day!

Next morning, hoping that the engine trouble would miraculously improve, I flew on to Halls Creek, where I met an M.M.A. pilot whom I knew. I asked him to listen to my engine, he exclaimed: "You certainly can't move out of here on that!"

"I must. I've a tight schedule for weeks ahead, and there's nothing I can do about the engine short of going south."

153

He watched with some consternation as I refuelled and took off. I later discovered that he soon spread the word that I was last seen heading for the desert with an engine that sounded "horrible."

Actually, although it was still dropping about 250 revs and sounded very rough on one magneto, it was O.K. on "both" and seemed otherwise all right. Anyway, I managed to make it successfully from one station to another, keeping as close to the windmill roads as possible. They led to the mills which pump up water for stock, so I would at least be near water in case of a forced landing.

My fourth day out from Halls Creek took me to Billiluna station, where I found the manager laid up with a broken foot. Without equipment for such an emergency, I was not able to do much but offer my sympathies and a dose of vaccine. When coming in to this station I had noticed that fierce bushfires had burned out hundreds of miles of desert grass and scrub and as the day went on a strong south-easterly blew up, fanning the fires in the direction of the station. This reminded me that it was one of the rare occasions when I had not waited to tie the machine down, a piece of advice I had been given by every veteran flier I knew. I had just decided that I must knock off and secure the Mooney when a steady drone heralded the approach of another aircraft and before long a little red machine materialised out of the smoke haze, dipped its wings, and headed for the strip.

"We haven't had a visitor in weeks," the manager exclaimed. "Now two aircraft in one day—and me with a broken foot!"

He was the only one unable to meet the visitor at the airstrip. The pilot climbed out, cast one look at my plane and greeted me with a severe, "Haven't I told you always to tie your machine down?" It was Dr Dicks.

I felt somewhat abashed to hear how the news of my faulty engine had got to him—and also to Dad—and how between them they had found out from D.C.A. that I had last reported three days before when heading for Flora Valley. This had sounded ominous, though in fact I hadn't used my radio in the meantime because the effort of getting through had seemed hardly worthwhile. Dr Dicks had borrowed an aircraft, flown

1,400 miles north, and followed me up through about eight stations, only to be told at each that I'd been and gone. While reeling off this story he had been busy opening his tool kit. "Now run the engine," he said, "and let's see what the trouble's all about." I pressed the self-starter, whereupon the engine promptly fired and checked out smoothly and sweetly as if it had just been serviced. The resident gremlin had evidently vanished on sight of the doctor and his kit. Embarrassed for myself, I was relieved for the sake of the station manager, whose foot was soon professionally attended.

Having come so far, Doctor decided to follow me around for a while in case the engine trouble recurred. It was just as well that he did so, as quite soon the self-starter brought forth no response at all and someone had to swing the prop, "Dawn Patrol" style, for the next four days. But there was a bonus for the station folk, who received some free medical advice, including the diagnosis of acute appendicitis in a native at Mornington, who was taken to Derby for surgery in a Flying Doctor plane.

During all this travelling around I found that attitudes to my job varied considerably. Most station families were extremely helpful. They made me feel a welcome guest, included me in their week-end activities if I could stay long enough, drove me miles to outlying stock camps, and loaded my aircraft with fruit and vegetables from their gardens. A few, however, were quite unco-operative.

At one station a truckload of natives was sent to meet me with a message that "the missus" was busy. I therefore set up my clinic on the wing of the plane, and battling against flies, heat and the effect of grubby hands on the aircraft, doled out the vaccine. When the job was done and I tried to get going the Mooney simply refused to start. I thought I knew all the tricks she was capable of by this time, but she had now sprung a new one on me. I worked over her for hours in the sizzling heat while the natives sat around watching with apparent interest. Eventually, on the point of expiring from thirst, I got them to return to the homestead to fetch me a drink. They returned with a billy-can of water which, although hot from the sun, was enough to save my life. By sunset I had given up and was prepared to sit the night out in the aircraft when a message arrived from "the missus" to say that I could sleep at the homestead if I liked. I found that the lack of co-operation had not been due to pressure of work, but to the fact that the people concerned refused, for some reason, to have anything to do with "Government schemes."

It was really the first time it had occurred to me that I was working for the Government, and it upset me that people could allow their prejudices to go so far as to deny their children the chance of protection against a crippling disease.

At another station I was given a bed for the night in a squalid shed filled with the most appalling stench. I tracked it down at last to a cupboard crammed full of decaying dingo scalps, that were being hoarded for the vermin bounty. Apparently someone else was working for the Government, too.

24

FOCLI AND FOCLA

"I WAS FAIRLY SURE YOU'D BE IN IT, SO I VOLUNTEERED TO FLY one aircraft and said you'd fly the other," Dr Dicks told me. The Kimberley wet season had interrupted my Sabin programme and I was more or less at a loose end until the airstrips had dried out. The prospect outlined to me was both fascinating and frightening and I doubted my ability to carry it out.

A company called Southern Aeronautics was planning to import French aircraft, with the aim of selling them to an increasingly aviation-conscious public in Western Australia. The aircraft were "Horizons," manufactured by a branch of the Sud Aviation company. The first two machines were to be flown out on a proving and publicity flight, but being a young company it could not afford to employ ferry pilots for the job. It was on hearing this that the doctor had kindly volunteered *our* services for a mere coverage of expenses. I heard on the grapevine that the machine I was supposed to fly had started out from Paris for Australia with a British airline pilot at the controls. He had got only one and a half hours along the track when he returned and walked out on the job, saying that the Horizon iced up so badly that he felt he would never make it. This was hardly reassuring.

I gave the project careful thought. Flying a twin-engined aircraft over the Pacific had been one thing, but flying a low-powered single engine from Europe—alone—was quite another. The Beechcrafts had been thoroughly tested and proven and were of good repute, whereas we knew little or nothing of the Horizons or the company that turned them out. I remembered our problems with the "Pig" and its untimely end on the Athenian airfield. Frankly I didn't really want to accept this new proposition. I felt pretty sure I would never make it back, but found myself saying "yes" mainly, I suppose, because I hate to decline a challenge. On the strength of this decision I purchased a will form for ten cents, made it out with a sad heart and handed it to my bank manager, who looked at me as though he suspected I was about to commit suicide. Well, I thought, maybe I was.

My family on the whole took it fairly well. Gran was of course horrified, but it gave her a good, vigorous talking point which she always enjoys. Mum accepted it as inevitable—a part of the life which, for better or worse, I had taken on. Julie thought it was "good news" and gave me a book called *New Horizons* which she inscribed: "Hoping the New Horizons will return you safely to this old, familiar one." I didn't tell Dad until the last possible moment.

We flew off to Paris with an assortment of survival gear, a Bayside portable V.H.F. radio apiece, and a stock of maps and charts of the long route home. In addition to the visas required for entering various countries I was also armed with an important-looking letter signed by the State Premier and saying that any assistance that could be given us *en route* would be greatly appreciated. Obtaining this proved to be time well spent!

Paris was cold and wet, with the trees bare and the ponds in the Tuileries, near our hotel, frozen hard, but spellbinding just the same. We went at once to Toussous le Noble where the Horizon whose registration number was F-OCLA sat in the hangar of *Socata*; the light aircraft division of Sud Aviation, where she had been left abandoned by the British pilot. She looked to me extremely small and rather strange, especially with the dials and cockpit placarding made out in the metric system—and in French to boot. The other machine, F-OCLI, had still to have the ferry tanks installed, giving us ten days in which to get organised.

This time we spent in becoming familiar with the machines; not our own, which were being worked on, but others of a similar model. Monsieur Le Boucher, one of *Socata*'s chief pilots, took us up into the rain and fog until we suddenly broke through to a sunny sky criss-crossed with lazy jet trails; the Paris winter hidden under a white carpet of cloud. In spite of a sign saying *Manoeuvres Aerobatiques Interdit* and clearly displayed on the dashboard, the pilot looped, rolled, and spun the machine until we were satisfied that it was strong, if nothing else. We were then given French licences and another aircraft and told to look around the "environs de Paris" for ourselves.

As well as doing as he advised, we spent hours installing pieces of equipment we had brought with us. An H.F. radio (strapped to the co-pilot's seat) and trailing aerial was fixed in each aircraft, with heated pilot tubes and external aerials for the Bayside V.H.F. Additional crystals were fitted into the H.F. radios so that we could communicate with places along the route.

We tried in vain to get the French engineers to install a tap between the ferry tanks and the fuel selector, to prevent gravity forcing the ferry fuel through into the wing tanks and then overboard via the overflow tubes. They insisted that it was *"pas necessaire,"* and as a result we were to lose many gallons of valuable fuel.

We swept a big area of hangar floor and laid out our world series of operational navigation charts, drew up tracks, and wondered whether we would ever really come to negotiate this fascinating route. Bad weather over extremely mountainous areas was our main concern. We were anxious to get through India before the monsoon set in and as time was short we were eager to get away.

FOCLA (my machine), was a 160 horse power model, with a fixed pitch propeller. FOCLI had 180 horses and a constant speed prop, so was somewhat more sophisticated. Both had a large 105-gallon fuel tank that filled the entire centre cabin behind the two front seats. The co-pilot's seat had radio gear strapped to it and the floor was jammed with route maps and charts, survival gear and spare parts. The space behind the tanks was packed with the dismantled and folded back seats and there was no room for my suitcase, I had to dice it and stuff all my clothes around the fuel tank and in any remaining holes.

But it was not until the day before we planned to depart that I was able to test-fly the machine. I removed the H.F. radio from the seat and occupied it while M. Le Boucher did the flying. It was immediately obvious that the aircraft was very heavy. We staggered into the air after a long take-off run and porpoised about like a sinking ship, with the stall warning "bipping." Le Boucher's knuckles were white on the stick and perspiration was running from his brow as we gained sufficient altitude to try out the ferry tanks and the radios. This was done in the space of one of the tightest circuits I have ever flown and within a matter of minutes we hit the runway again with a heavy thump. Le Boucher, wiping his face, looked a little worried. "She is heavy," he admitted, "but she will be all right . . . I think . . . It will be better when you are by yourself."

Tuesday, 26 March 1968, in Paris dawned drizzly, overcast and cold. Hoping to make Rome on our first day we drove out early to Toussous aerodrome and prepared for departure. We had taken very much for granted the wonderful service and flight facilities of our Australian Department of Civil Aviation, and were surprised to find that filing a flight plan in Europe can cost quite a bit in both time and cash. Meanwhile the Horizons were topped up with fuel and oil, checked by customs, and loaded with all our last minute bits and pieces. The management, test pilots, engineers, radio men and newspaper reporters had gathered to wish us well and someone—Monsieur Le Boucher perhaps?—had the kind thought of securing a small posy of daisies to my instrument panel.

Handshakes and farewell speeches all round, doors shut, all clear, a final wave and I pressed the self starter. Nothing happened. The battery was dead flat. FOCLI, waiting patiently with engine ticking over, shut down while an engineer came over to hand-swing the prop. It took several men over half an hour to persuade the engine to come to life, and our farewell party, huddled in the cold, looked greatly relieved as we taxied to the runway holding point. On checking my instruments I found, to my dismay, that the altimeter setting knob was stuck. I groped around for some tools with which I loosened the knob, but could only make it wind down—not up—so that the altimeter read 2,000 feet below the ground. Convinced that such a bad start was no good omen for the trip, I gave the tower a "taxi-ing back" call and, followed by a disappointed FOCLI, had to front up again to the shivering well-wishers.

Not daring to stop the engine I moved over while an engineer fiddled with the instrument for ten minutes. Eventually it returned us to the earth's surface, and in spite of the fact that it was by now early afternoon we were nearly away.

To the accompaniment of a series of "blips" from the stall warning, which let me know that FOCLA was still very much overloaded, we got into the air. I started to tune my Polaris A.D.F. into Etampes. The instrument was a dual A.D.F./V.O.R. with both needles on the one dial. The A.D.F. needle swung around twice as if searching for the station, then stuck to the V.O.R. Together the two needles moved a few degrees, then both came firmly to rest for good and all against the glass. No amount of tapping or twiddling would budge them, and with a few well-chosen words I turned the useless thing off. Fortunately I had a back-up King A.D.F. which I promptly turned on and managed to pick up Etampes, but the vibrations of the aircraft kept shaking the needle off the station and I found that I had to devote one hand to keeping the knob steady. A screw was loose and we couldn't get the right minute-sized Allen key required to fix it, so I just had to *hold it* for the entire trip. By this time FOCLI had disappeared.

We were running into banks of thickening cloud and as the Central Alps lay ahead I decided to climb through it, hoping to come out on top to a fair, blue sky. I gave FOCLI a call and said I was going up, but the poor, overloaded little machine, already at 5,000 feet, was loath to climb. I could feel myself urging her on, trying to "sit light" and thinking anxiously of those "stuffed clouds" ahead.

A glance out the window was hardly reassuring. A glistening skin of ice was forming over the wing—a disturbing sight for me as in so many hours of flying in the comparatively warm Australian and Pacific skies I had never yet seen an iced-up wing. I was beginning to understand the feelings of the British pilot who had abandoned the aircraft when, quite suddenly, she broke through the cloud into blue skies and warm sunshine. My heart pounded with relief as I levelled out at 8,000 feet and watched the ice melting from the wings. FOCLI was still nowhere in sight, but I hummed happily on until I heard a sharp exclamation over the radio. "FOCLI-FOCLA!"

"What's the matter?" I asked.

There was no answer for a while, then Dr Dicks said: "I was winding in the trailing aerial and it caught around the elevator. Went into a pretty sharp dive but managed to get it free. It's okay now but I'll have to be careful. The hawse-pipe is in a bad place."

After that our problems seemed to be over for the time being and we flew steadily on for southern France. Approaching Avignon, where there is French Air Force activity, I had just noticed a warning on the map: "Beware of low-flying jet aircraft," when something very fast swooped upon me from behind. FOCLA rocked in the wake turbulence and picking up the mike I said clearly:"Rude man!" This was followed by some fast French which I think meant that I was over a military control area. Somewhat abashed, I shut up.

I had hoped to enjoy enthralling views of the Rhone Valley and Riviera, but cloud had given way to thick smoke haze which prevented any sightseeing. FOCLA, having burned off some gas, was now much lighter. We were getting to know each other and I suspected that in spite of all our early problems, I was beginning to fall in love with her.

It was now becoming clear that we could not make Rome in daylight, so a brief radio conference with FOCLI, somewhere on ahead, decided us to make for Pisa instead. Laying out a new course on the five by three foot sectional maps which had to be unwound in the small cockpit was an exasperating task. We left the mainland at Cannes and headed out over the Gulf of Genoa. I could see the snow-capped mountains of Corsica to starboard as we droned steadily on. Then the coast of Italy lay ahead and the lights of Pisa came pricking through the dusk.

"Good girl, Focla," I said, as we taxied in just after dark. "We've got our problems, but I know you'll bring us safely home."

25

MAPS AND
MOUNTAINS

A BARRAGE OF CAMERAS WITH TELESCOPIC LENSES WAS AIMED at us as we checked our machines and refuelled at the Pisa airfield. They were all no doubt hoping for a big scoop if we proved to be people of importance, celebrities such as pop singers, international spies, eloping film stars, or would-be record busters. They must have been sadly disappointed to find that we were just a couple of unnewsworthy Aussies, ferrying home French aircraft for the hell of it.

Italian customs duty and landing fees were enormous but so was the hospitality. We were driven to an hotel and no one seemed to understand why we would not stay.

The following morning we took off in fog having been given a special "minimum conditions" clearance by the controller, who cheerfully remarked that the lack of visibility shouldn't worry people planning to fly all the way to Australia. My battery was quite flat again, but apart from having to make a hand-swing start and getting squared away on instruments all was fine as we cruised along the coast of Italy. The traffic controller heard on approaching Rome might as well have been speaking Italian as English, as far as I was concerned, but I managed to make out the word "*Campino*", and as this was where we had planned to come down we assumed that we were cleared to proceed. I tried to tune my A.D.F. into this airfield frequency but with so many major airfields and radio beacons all in such close proximity to Rome the A.D.F. just kept swinging around the dial in confused circles. I was forced to go round in the same way, my eyes out on sticks trying to avoid dozens of huge jet aircraft approaching or taking off from the various aerodromes. Finding it impossible to get a word in, I eventually tuned to Rome radar and asked for guidance to Ciampiano.

Almost all we saw of Rome on this occasion was the airfield while we refuelled, having decided to push on and make Athens by nightfall. It was very hot, and poor overloaded FOCLA clawed desperately at the thin air as we took off. She barely cleared some high tension wires across a field beyond the strip, and if I hadn't retracted the undercarriage in time I could have caused a blackout over Rome.

Conditions improved as we departed the city area and tracked out on the Ostia radio beacon to a point twenty-six miles over the Tyrrhenian Sea. From there, due to heavy air traffic, we were cleared to fly by the beautiful islands of Ponza and Ischia to Sorrento. Cruising at an altitude of 6,000 feet between snow-covered mountain peaks, we crossed the foot of Italy.

The city of Brindisi and the Italian coast disappeared behind us, and FOCLA headed for the open sea. Luckily it was a clear day and I was getting used to flying with one hand on the controls and the other on my radio compass knob. As soon as we got out of radio range I could relax my hand and concentrate on map reading. Looking down I thought of Australian D.C.A.'s stiff regulations regarding flights over water, during which single-engined aircraft must remain within gliding distance of land, and so forth. The very wording of the instructions makes a pilot frightened to fly over water and not many do, so it felt a bit queer at first heading out over the Ionian Sea alone, entirely dependent on FOCLA's engine, and with little idea of what lay ahead. The first sight of land was the island of Corfu, which appeared after about an hour and a half, and then with a thrill of familiarity, I recognised the great white-capped mountains of Greece looming over the edge of the world.

TOP: F-OCLA over Indonesia, taken by Dr Harold Dicks from the cockpit of F-OCLI. BOTTOM: The author holding a clinic at Gibb River, near the northernmost tip of Western Australia

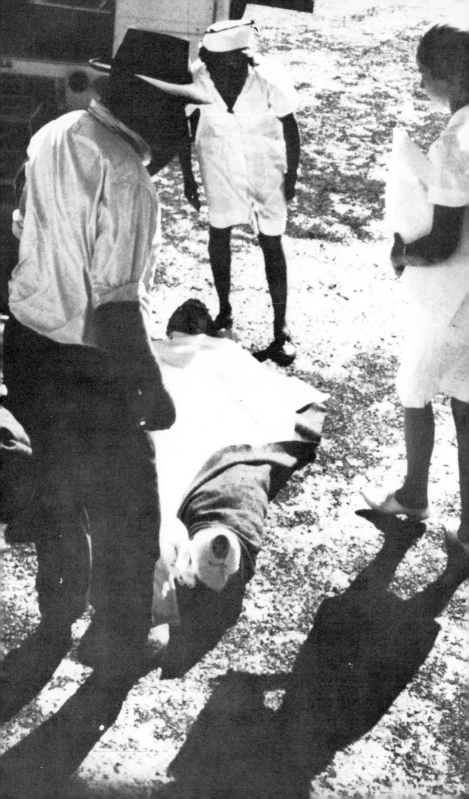

The snow was glowing with sunset against a purple sky and, after a few calculations, I realised that we were not going to reach Athens that night. In a radio chat with FOCLI it was agreed that to continue up the narrow, mountainous Gulf of Corinth in the dark, with no proper charts or navigation aids, might well prove a suicidal exercise. I suggested that we divert to Andravidha, the Air Force airfield on which we had landed the "Pig" on my previous flight in this direction.

FOCLI said he couldn't find it on the map, and suggested that I should lead the way. We turned south, flew over Araxos on the northern tip of the Peloponnesus peninsula, and descended over Andravidha airfield. FOCLI called up and asked for a clearance to land but was answered in a torrent of rapid and excited Greek. For about ten minutes there was no reply to our repeated request until suddenly a breathless voice came through in English: "FOCLI-FOCLA! Why you wish to land at MY airfield?"

FOCLI explained that we were two small French aircraft flying to Australia. As we were running out of daylight and fuel it was dangerous to continue and we wished to land. The answer came back: "But why you wish to land at MY airfield?"

I then repeated our reasons for wishing to come in by which time it was nearly dark. "But you can *not* land at MY airfield," said the tower.

"Hang it all, we're coming in anyhow," said FOCLI.

I was more or less in position for a straight in landing, so wound down the undercarriage and told the tower that I was on final approach. "Very well, you are cleared to land," said an exasperated voice.

It was almost the story of the Piaggio over again. We were met by two truckloads of uniformed men carrying enough weapons to fight off an invasion, the officers grim-faced but the soldiers inquisitive and amused. We were searched. Our aircraft were searched. Our baggage was searched. We were asked all the same questions again, and when satisfied at last, an officer shook our hands and asked what he could do for us. He arranged for the machines to be refuelled and guarded overnight, then escorted us to a primitive village on the coast, where we were served a big bowl of soup containing whole fish, and okra, goat's cheese, and resinous wine. The cafe proprietor refused any

All in a flying day's work. Preparing to load a patient with a fractured leg aboard a RFDS aircraft payment when he heard we came from Australia. He told us he had a son in "Melbon," and pointed proudly to a great modern juke box which occupied half the room, but which was useless owing to lack of electricity. "Australia plenty good," he said. "Plenty nice people. Plenty rich. My son plenty happy. You my friends."

We were returning to the barracks where there was no accommodation for females, so I was ushered into the communal male dormitory and given a spare cot, over which the airmen courteously went to endless trouble to rig up a kind of canvas tent, a comedy that caused such uproarious laughter as to attract the attention of more willing helpers. But they could not do much about the toilet facilities—a long urinal and exposed showers—into which I crept in the dead of night.

The language problem was unfortunate as our Greek friends were obviously eager to hear about our long flight in the little Horizons, which had greatly intrigued them.

We were up early next morning, with the bugle which brought the men tumbling out of bed to breakfast on Turkish coffee and buns.

We had decided to skip Athens and fly to Beirut by way of Rhodes Island, some three hours and twenty minutes over the sea on the way to Crete. Greek Air Force met. men told us that the weather was poor over the sea approaches to Rhodes and that we should plan to divert to Crete if necessary. They would be flying in the area and would give us a call if conditions deteriorated.

On a thumbs-up from the crew of a fighter squadron, we leapt into the cold morning air and headed south-east to Rhodes. We found that the flight maps issued by the Australian Department of Civil Aviation, although incomplete in many areas, were accurate. The same could not be said for the world aeronautical charts we had of Europe, which were issued by the United States.

As we headed over the incredibly rugged peninsula to Nikolas, where we left the coast for Rhodes, we were flying at 8,000 feet in an attempt to clear mountains marked on the maps as being only 6,000 feet. Never had I encountered such frightening clear air turbulence, with strong winds rushing up and down the slopes, creating fierce vertical currents that threatened to break up the overloaded aircraft. FOCLA hit one of these mountain waves, and in utter helplessness I watched the altimeter climb through nine, ten, eleven, twelve to thirteen thousand feet! I was freezing cold and shivering like a leaf but in spite of the constant "bipping" of the stall warning somehow managed to maintain the aircraft's air speed and attitude. With the nose lowered to an alarming angle we continued to rise at a rate of over 1,000 feet a minute. At the top of the "up draught" the machine acted as if in a vacuum, dropping like a brick to be returned on the "down draught" to 9,000 feet.

I picked up the mike to communicate with FOCLI that I could see as a tiny speck away behind me and below. "This is hell!" I said.

"Yeah," came the reply.

We had decided that FOCLA, being the less powerful machine, would always fly ahead, and thought that FOCLI had only to open throttle to catch up when necessary. Oddly enough, however, despite having less power, FOCLA could outdo FOCLI in getting away from any airfield and he often had quite a battle to catch up.

Out of the nightmare stretch at last we headed on over the Sea of Crete, which we found to be anything but the legendary blue waters surrounding the sunny isles of Greece. It was at that time whipped into a boiling froth by a vicious south-easterly which kept our air speed down to sixty-five knots. I had given considerable thought to the possibility of having to "splash down" while flying over water, and reckoned that I could at least make it to my dinghy. In such a cruel sea, however, I realised this would be impossible.

Instead of the expected three and a half hours, it took us considerably more to reach Rhodes, by which time it was too late to continue to Beirut. It was fortunate that we managed to arrive in daylight and reasonable weather as we were confronted, right in the circuit area, by a 800 foot hill which was not mentioned on the maps, on which the entire region was shown as being at sea level.

The sheer beauty of this island compensated for the trials experienced in reaching it. Having secured and refuelled our aircraft, we lay on the ground in the warm sun, gathering strength to explore the ruins of ancient Rhodes. We sorted out the chaos of our cockpits, reorganised the tangled mass of maps and, after a good night's rest, returned cheerfully to the airstrip to take off for Beirut.

"Oh no!" I exclaimed, on finding that FOCLA was sitting glumly in a pool of petrol. We cursed the engineer who had refused our request to install the fuel taps, and set about trying to stop a steady flow of fuel from the wing and roof overflow vents. We wasted an hour trying out various things, including blocking up the vents with spigots, but until we had removed several gallons from the bulging wing tanks, nothing worked. It appeared that pressure from the ferry tank was just too much for the fuel selector, which let the expensive gas into the wings and out the vents. Hoping that this loss would not continue in flight, we topped up and took off into a blue sky.

I was pleased to note that our map makers were now admitting, in small "caution" frames, to inaccuracies of 2,000 feet and more in relief and elevation estimates. We were flying along nicely together, about seventy miles seaward from the rugged brown Turkish coast and well south of the Gulf of Antalya, when we spotted a sleek, black jet fighter making straight towards us. We realised that we were in semi-hostile territory and had just been discussing a warning on the map that flying was "Prohibited over Cyprus and its territorial waters except airways and Nicosia control zone." We had decided to overfly Nicosia *en route* to Beirut, and as the black jet swooped down on us I heard FOCLI trying, on a fairly urgent note, to contact the former centre. There was no reply, and as the jet came in for another buzz we both grappled for our Jeppeson charts to look up "International interception signals." There we found it in black and white. We were either going to be forced to land, shot down, or cleared.

I called FOCLI: "This guy could shoot us down just for fun! No one would ever find out."

The reply was hardly reassuring: "I know. Now just keep your head and watch him closely. If he starts to shoot, I'm going to spin down. You follow."

At that moment the jet flew straight between us, passed

immediately in front of FOCLI, and dived away to the right. We were both caught in a turmoil of wake turbulence that nearly wrapped us around each other.

"Here he comes again," FOCLI advised, "Be ready to spin down."

"Not me," I replied, eyeing off the deep blue swell below. "Blow him, I'm keeping straight on."

As the jet made another close dive, inspiration struck. I pulled the ribbon from my pony tail, opened the air vents, and let my hair blow out on the wind. Within seconds the jet came past again and I caught a glimpse of the pilot's eyes above the oxygen mask. I thought they looked mean, and recalled things I had heard about the attitude to women in this part of the world. It *could* have been a bad mistake. But no. Next time past he cut me off, swooped to the right and kept going until he disappeared against the sea.

"He's cleared us," came a relieved voice from FOCLI. "Well, thank God for that, but keep your fingers crossed in case he's gone off to fetch his friends. Now let's try and get through to Nicosia. Hey there, FOCLA! You all right? You're in a steep dive!"

"Yes, I'm okay," I replied, pulling FOCLA up onto an even keel. "It's just a bit hard to steer while I'm trying to fix my hair."

Nicosia then came through with a clearance to enter the area. Cyprus looked dry, arid, extremely rugged, and far from hospitable. Moreover, the blue sky was darkening and beginning to fill with solid masses of cumulus cloud, forcing us down and down in our effort to keep below them.

After 130 miles over deep, blue waters lashed by line squalls in the fore of an oncoming front, we sighted the Lebanese mountains and soon the white city of Beirut, sprawling across the hills behind the sea. Such a place I had never seen before and was so enchanted by its beauty that I managed to dive under the seat, locate my camera and take a snap of it while lining up between heavy aircraft on a final approach to the runway.

Hovering up there over the fairytale city I had felt pretty big, but once on the ground, forced to taxi in under the wings of mighty jets, I felt very insignificant indeed. We parked under a 707 and were soon surrounded by a swarm of "trouble"—officious customs, immigration, quarantine and airport authorities.

They argued, criticised, produced innumerable forms and accounts, and generally behaved in true bureaucratic style. "Calm down," the Doctor warned me when, after about two and a half hours of this hindering process, he could see that I was approaching flash point. He was right; a feminine explosion might have relieved my feelings, but would probably have resulted only in further delay.

26

APRIL FOOL

THE SITUATION WAS SAVED BY OUR MEETING WITH A FELLOW Australian, Captain Gordon McGillivray, Operations Manager of Middle East Airlines, who steered us through a number of fiddling formalities and then whisked us off to see Beirut. This fascinating excursion concluded with a lavish Lebanese feast, served with a liberal supply of arak and enjoyed in the company of some executives of the Douglas Aircraft Corporation.

This was relaxing and we had a few hours good sleep, but our problems began again next morning when we tried to get away. An infuriating little man in the Flight Planning Department screwed up no less than five of our perfectly legible attempts to complete a flight plan over Arabia, for such trifles as a crossed out word or a badly formed letter. Eventually, with a sigh of superior exasperation, he filled it in himself.

Just as we were going out of the door we were stopped by another official. "Where are you people going?" he asked, taking our flight plans and examining them critically. We told him. "This is not right," he said. "You must do it again." We explained that it had been made out and accepted by the officer inside but he was unimpressed. "I am on duty now," he said.

After another half hour and a basket full of wasted paper he was satisfied and we were allowed to proceed, but only as far as a barrier. There, we were required to wait a further forty-five minutes for a special truck to escort us fifty yards across the tarmac to our aircraft. With nine hours' flying ahead of us we chafed anxiously at the delay, but to no avail.

During my pre-flight inspection I had noticed that FOCLA's cowl was badly cracked, and before taking off managed to prevail on a sympathetic B.E.A. engineer to drill a small hole to prevent the crack from extending any further. He helped again by swinging the propeller when, on attempting to shake the dust of Beirut airport from our wheels, FOCLA emitted only the dismal "cluck" of a flat battery. The generator had not been showing any charge and I guessed that this was the trouble. The engine came to life after a few swings and we were all set for take-off, forty-two miles over a 10,000 foot mountain range to Damascus where all aircraft flying over Syrian air space were compelled to drop in and pay landing fees. At this moment word came through that the Damascus airport was closed by fog, but, more than loath to face all the exasperating formalities again, I was prepared to give it a go. I gave FOCLI a "thumbs up" sign. He responded, so we taxied out onto the long strip and announced our intended departure to the tower. We were directed to a radio beacon on the coast where we orbited in a continual climb to 8,500 feet, at which height we could pass between the mountain peaks.

Heading east over this fascinating and historical land we noticed that fog was closing in behind us and growing thick below, and with our radio aids functioning poorly we certainly needed the help of a guardian angel to see us through. There must have been one at hand, for just when out situation looked most critical, the clouds beneath us parted sufficiently to reveal Damascus in a tiny patch of sunshine far below.

We lost sight of each other as we spiralled down through thin fog and headed for the aerodrome in minimum visibility. As FOCLA taxied in, with FOCLI not far ahead, I caught a glint of light on the brass instruments of a military band and observed a crowd of soldiers and civilians in ceremonious ranks on either side. The band struck up, and for one wild moment I thought we were being given a civic reception. Then gesticulating figures ran towards us, the band moaned into silence, and we were hurried off the tarmac just as the sound of a big aircraft began to beat down through the fog. We soon learnt that it carried Russian dignitaries on a state visit, and that our inopportune arrival had caused considerable confusion.

We had been warned that Damascus could be a difficult place to get out of, and after the run around in Beirut we expected the worst. However, on the chance of a quick get away, we arranged that I should take care of the formalities while Doctor Dicks attended to the refuelling.

At the airport office I was confronted by one of the most unusual-looking men I have ever seen. Although I had been trained never to stare at people nor to make personal comments, I just couldn't take my eyes off him and as he turned to question me I was surprised to hear myself saying: "How terribly interesting! I've never seen anyone like *you* before." It could have been disastrous, but to my enormous relief the man beamed with friendly appreciation.

"Yes, it is a phenomenon unique to my family," he said, and while busily filling in the necessary documents told me that many of his relations had the same remarkably unmatched features—one bright blue eye and one dark brown; half fair hair and half dark. "And in temperament too," he added. "Part of the East and part of the West." Still beaming he handed me the completed clearance forms. I beamed back, produced the necessary "fees," and hurried to join my travelling companion with the good news.

We flew swiftly out of Damascus in a south-easterly direction, heading across Saudi Arabia towards our next refuelling point at Bahrain on the Persian Gulf. I had a "here-we-go-again" feeling at sight of a huge wall of cumulo-nimbus hoisting itself threateningly over the desert ahead, and within a few minutes we were bucking around under violent thunderstorms. These were confined to about fifty miles and as they began to clear the already murky atmosphere turned to a dense, dirty red, and in place of showers the entire sky was filled with driving particles of dust and sand. In an attempt to get above it we climbed to 7,000 feet,—FOCLA's limit in those conditions—

but we were still in the thick of it and realised that there was no alternative other than to plough through.

My most important instrument, the artificial horizon, suddenly toppled. Fortunately I had an electric turn and bank indicator— a new "mini-sized" model which, being no bigger than a twenty cent piece, was hard to see and made flying extremely tiring and difficult. Nonetheless, it saved the day.

I decided to come down to about 100 feet above the ground, as the desert, although an average of 1,500 feet above sea level, is fairly flat and I could see straight down. There was dust on all sides, above and below, but the occasional glimpse of Bedouin tents, near a wadi among the endless sandhills, was a heartening indication of human life.

FOCLI, above and behind, was having a battle to keep me in sight as the solid black wall of a much denser sandstorm loomed ahead. "This could be pretty bad," FOCLI predicted. "We'd better stick together."

I glimpsed what appeared to be a lighter area in the frightening conditions ahead and announced that I was diverting twenty degrees right in order to fly through it.

"Don't do that," FOCLI advised. "I can see a better area over here. Follow me."

I caught a brief glimpse of FOCLI making for what looked to me like the centre of the storm, then he was gone. Continuing on my chosen route I was soon in complete, eerie darkness and being thrown about like a cork on the high seas. After fighting it for some time I decided that I might as well utter some famous last words, so picked up the mike and shouted: "FOCLA to FOCLI. Some storm! If only Gran could see me now!" There was no reply. I shouted the message again and when no sound came back I began to worry. "FOCLA to FOCLI. Where are you?" Still no reply.

After about twenty minutes the storm began to abate, and looking out along my wing I noticed that all the registration letters except LA had been sand-blasted off, and that the windscreen looked as though it had been treated with sandpaper. "Oh, la, la! What now?" I thought. I gave FOCLI yet another call, and so faintly as to be hardly audible a voice came back: "Where are you?"

"I'm over here," I shouted. "Where are you?"

"Over here. We should hit Badanah and the pipeline soon. If you get there, orbit and wait for me."

But Badanah only had a V.O.R. beacon, and as we did not possess this equipment the town was no use to us as a meeting place. In any case, I reckoned that our chances of spotting it after the storm diversions were very slim. Rafha, about 360 miles from Damascus, also on the pipeline, had a non-directional beacon, so I told FOCLI I'd meet him there.

Sand was still blowing, but the visibility had improved to about 1,000 yards. I was flying along very close to the ground, fascinated by the great Saudi desert, when I was startled to find myself ranged up beside an Arab on a horse. I caught the look of sheer terror on his face as his horse swerved to one side. He then ducked, aimed a rifle and was still blazing away as he disappeared into the dust in my wake. The reply from FOCLI when I relayed this colourful incident was made in anything but the calm manner he advocated in all circumstances. "Get up out of there immediately," I was told, "and don't be such an etc. . ." He might have spared himself the effort as I'd already taken the hint.

Actually the evidence of life—tents and groups of moving Bedouin,—in this desolate area was surprising. Heaven only knows how they survived! I arrived at Rafha—a dry, flat, treeless, end-of-the-earth looking place—and circled the town for ten minutes until FOCLI caught up. We were both relieved to have hit the pipeline at last and followed it along at 1,000 feet above ground level.

So far every minute of the flight had been so packed with incident and anxiety that, although I carried some quite tempting rations, I hadn't given a thought to either food or drink. I hadn't a free hand to deal with eating, in any case. It was the same throughout the trip. Preoccupation simply kept hunger at bay and we only realised, on landing, that we hadn't broken our fast for anything from eight to twelve hours.

After getting a ground speed between Rafha and the next small town, it was obvious that we were bucking a headwind and that we probably wouldn't make Bahrain until after dark. We had been unable to make radio contact with anyone for

175

over five hours, but had realised by this time that in spite of the insistence on detailed flight planning, no one along the route would have worried if we were never heard of again.

About an hour before sunset a faint voice from Bahrain broke through on our H.F. radios, instructing someone else to divert to Dhahran because forty-four knot winds were blowing across their airstrip. It was getting late, our fuel was running low, my artificial horizon and directional gyro were unserviceable, and there was no other light in the cabin but a torch, so we decided it would be unwise to continue into bad weather.

"Al Qaysumah is not far ahead on the pipeline and it has a radio beacon," FOCLI announced. "Let's try there."

While homing in we saw a huddle of mud-walled, mostly roofless houses, which suggested that rain falls so seldom here that roofs are not required. A rough, stony clearing, which we took to be an airstrip, lay off to one side, so we circled the "town" and came in to land. As I opened the door I was met by blowing sand and hurried to hammer my tie-down pegs into the dry earth. Doctor Dicks had landed and was doing likewise when dozens of white-robed Arab men and boys came running from all directions. They stood at a little distance, no doubt viewing our small modern type of aircraft for the first time and, I began to suspect, a smallish, modern type of woman, with some disapproval. Hammering down the pegs with one hand and trying to manage my skirt in the hot wind with the other, I was too busy to worry. I took little notice of a man who had jumped from a jeep and came running towards my machine until I realised that he was asking me something in an agitated voice. It took me some time to work out that what he was trying to say was: "Haven't you got something long?"

"Something long?" I asked. "What do you mean?"

He turned in desperation to Doctor Dicks: "Please tell the woman to cover herself!"

"But I *am* covered," I said, indicating my respectable long-sleeved blouse, skirt (admittedly mini), shoes and long socks.

"You must *cover* yourself," he repeated, looking at me as a shocked Victorian traveller might have regarded a totally naked Aboriginal.

Suddenly the penny dropped. The Arab women I had seen

in Beirut had been covered from head to foot, only their eyes visible above the yashmaks that obscured the rest of their faces. The only long clothes I had with me were an air hostess raincoat that I had borrowed from Julie and a white evening frock. I was certainly not going to put on my best evening dress (which was sleeveless anyway) in the middle of a Saudi Arabian sandstorm; so I put on the raincoat and a scarf, in which I felt utterly foolish and extremely hot. The man from the jeep, however, cooled down immediately and introduced himself as Awadh; a government officer in charge of liaison with the Arabian American Oil Company that had a pumping station at Qaysumah. He had spent a year in London and so understood "British customs" and spoke English fairly well. He seemed friendly and hospitable, but said that we would have to come with him to the "compound" or he would not guarantee our safety.

We drove with him to a fenced off and guarded area around the pumping station, where we were confronted by four Arab soldiers. Awadh acted as our interpreter and did his best to answer the questions which were fired over and over again. Where had we come from? Where were we going? Why? Who owned the aircraft? What were we carrying in the aircraft? Why had we landed here? Why didn't we get permission to land? What passports did we hold? Why was a woman flying an aircraft anyway?

We were roughly searched for weapons and hustled off to a small house, where we were told that we had violated Saudi Arabian air space and would have to wait until it was decided what was to be done with us. An armed guard was placed on the door and we were left alone.

For the time being at least there seemed nothing we could do but relax and try to figure some way out. I produced a bottle of arak, hidden in the bottom of my bag—a farewell gift from Gordon McGillivray in Beirut, but definitely taboo in this Moslem country. For a while things didn't seem too bad at all.

Awadh kept in contact with us, and next day we asked him whether we could at least get some more clothes out of the aircraft. "They are guarded by soldiers with orders to shoot anyone who comes near," he said, "but I'll see what I can do."

He obtained permission from the local Chief of Police and we were escorted to the airstrip. At the time of our arrival the guards were prostrated in the recital of one of their five daily prayers, and as we waited for them to finish Awadh explained the dilemma in which my arrival had placed the local authorities. "They have never seen a woman pilot before," he said. "They are embarrassed and do not wish any of their women to see you. That's why they have kept you shut up. You must not move from the house unescorted. It would not be safe."

"But they don't *have* to keep us at all," I told him. "We want to get on as much as they want to get rid of us." He struggled for words for a while, then shrugged and gave up.

When allowed to approach the aircraft we persuaded the Chief of Police that the Civil Aviation authorities in Bahrain would be extremely worried over our failure to turn up. We were twenty-four hours overdue and they might soon send the Air Force out looking for us, we said. We convinced the man that it would be wise to give Bahrain a call on our aircraft radio. The Arab Police Chief looked on suspiciously as Doctor climbed into FOCLI and unwound the trailing aerial while I pulled it out behind the aircraft for about 100 feet.

"Bahrain. Bahrain. This is Foxtrot Oscar Charlie Lima India. Come in, please," the Doctor called. There was no answer and I walked to and fro with the aerial, hoping to find a better position.

Then quite suddenly Bahrain replied: "Come in Lima India. This is Bahrain."

"Bahrain from Foxtrot Lima India and Lima Alpha. We are on the ground at Qaysumah. Landed in bad sandstorm. We are being held by local authorities. Please facilitate our immediate release."

We stood by while the bombshell burst in Bahrain and they contacted Dhahran. The following message soon came back: "Foxtrot Lima India and Lima Alpha, from headquarters in Dhahran. You are cleared to continue to Bahrain." Then followed a weather report and a clearance to fly at 6,000 feet.

Greatly relieved, we wound in the aerial while Awadh translated the message to the Police Chief, who did not understand English.

"I have told him what was said," Awadh told us at last, with a worried look, "but he says he does not know if what I tell him is true. Therefore he will not release you until the message comes over *his* radio in Arabic from Jeddah. This may take up to ten days. I advise you to remain calm and wait."

It was a bitter disappointment. We had been given nothing but black coffee since our arrival, so I grabbed some tins of food from our emergency rations, picked up my portable Bayside V.H.F. radio, which looked like a small case, slung a cardigan over it and returned to the waiting vehicle.

On the way back we noticed a hospital and asked whether we could have a look inside. The Police Chief agreed, so we piled out into the stone walled courtyard. I had meanwhile discarded the raincoat and put on a safari-type flying suit with a long-sleeved, belted jacket and a divided skirt. I had also covered my hair with a scarf and pinned a large pair of Flying Doctor Service wings to my collar. This get-up seemed to satisfy our "hosts" and gave me more confidence.

On entering the hospital we were surprised to meet an American, to whom we eagerly introduced ourselves. We found that his was one of three American families living at the pumping station. Hoping that he might be able to help us, we explained our predicament. "Sorry," he said, "we work for an oil company and we keep strictly out of local affairs."

"But couldn't you get a message through for us—or post a letter perhaps?" we asked, as he turned to walk away.

"Sorry," he replied. "If you want a letter posted it will cost you $15 on the black market. Goodbye now."

As Doctor Dicks was then official Medical Officer for the American Consulate in Western Australia, and had papers to prove it, we thought the wretched man might have been able to stretch a point or at least have pretended some interest in our plight.

The Arab medical staff was more friendly, but maintained a carefully neutral attitude towards our problem. It was easy to see that in that part of the world it was the men with the guns who had all the say.

But at least we had the radio, and once we were back at the house I kept an eye out for the guards and other passers-by

179

while Doctor crouched over the set. We had heard jets passing overhead from time to time and so felt reasonably hopeful of being able to raise a contact. After some hours of straining our ears we heard a promising high-pitched whine, tuned in and called at regular intervals: "Station flying over Qaysumah. Come in please."

Our hearts leapt with joy to catch at last the sound of an English voice: "Station calling aircraft over Qaysumah, go ahead."

We told our story over the microphone and awaited eagerly the reply. "What is this—a joke?" the calm, cultured voice scoffed back.

"No, not a joke. Repeat—no joke," the Doctor said, but there was no reply. By that time the aircraft was out of our radio range but we hoped that he might at least think about it and mention the suspected hoax to someone who could put him right.

We found it hard to believe that no one had made any kind of move to find out what had happened to us, and we thought glumly of all the time spent answering questions, arguing and making out flight plans in Beirut—to what end? We wondered whether Bahrain was enquiring why we hadn't continued to their city as cleared, but knowing the Arabs guessed that they would expect us if and when we turned up.

On our third night in Qaysumah, resigned to having to stay indefinitely, I decided to wash my hair. I had found some plastic curlers in a drawer in the house and never having used these devices before, decided to kill time by giving them a go. The Doctor had gone to bed and I had just succeeded in making myself look quite ridiculous when I was startled by a knock and an urgent voice at the door. It was Awadh, all aglow with the news that Bahrain had got Dhahran to contact the authorities in Jeddah. "You are now cleared to proceed," he said. "I advise you to get ready at once as by tomorrow they may have changed their minds."

It was nearly midnight, pitch dark and still blowing sand, but we packed up quickly, found torches and accompanied Awadh to the mud-walled house of the Police Chief, to whom Awadh displayed his message from Jeddah. We waited in the car while hot words were exchanged for over twenty minutes. It seemed at one stage as though there was going to be a fight, but the argument stopped abruptly and Awadh returned looking vanquished. "The message has not yet come over *his* radio. You will have to wait," he said. "Tomorrow I will see the Emir."

For once I was quite relieved, as the prospect of taking off into that dark night was off-putting to say the least. Next morning Awadh's now familiar jeep pulled up outside the house, his expressive countenance presaging further trouble.

"I have seen the Emir," he announced. "It is not good news for you."

"You mean he won't help us?"

"It is worse than that. He has heard about you and wants you for his harem."

My mouth fell open, but I quickly regained my equilibrium. "Tell him to go to hell." I said.

Awadh looked shocked. "That is impossible. It would be very dangerous."

I looked helplessly at Doctor Dicks, but met with nothing but a blank stare. Surely, I thought wildly, he's not going to accept this demand as inevitable? He must be able to do something about it. "I just won't go," I said. "It's absolutely ridiculous! He hasn't even *seen* me."

"He has heard you are blonde and has decided you would be desirable." Awadh nodded sadly towards the house. "Go and get your things! I have been ordered to drive you to the Emirate."

"Better do as he says," Dr Dicks said gloomily. "They're pretty tough, these desert Arabs. He probably won't want you after all when he gets a look at you, but if you don't go along you never know what he might do to us."

"It's not what he'll do to *us*," I exclaimed, "it's what he'll do to *me*!"

I looked frantically from one to the other. They gazed stolidly back, then Awadh's face cracked in a crazy grin.

"Do you know what is the date?"

"What's that got to do with it?" I asked.

"It is very important," he replied. "It is April the First!"

27

LANDS OF
WAITING

OUR CLEARANCE CAME THROUGH "PROPER CHANNELS" BY THE middle of our fourth day at Qaysumah, but it was five-thirty in the evening before we managed to extricate ourselves. Our story had got around and almost everyone in the village was taking a keen interest in developments. This meant that the officials, in the process of getting us away, drove around, greeted every man in sight, asked after each member of his family and then slowly unfolded all the details of our situation from beginning to end. Awadh, volubly in the thick of it, was loath to part with us. "Now you are cleared to go, you are also welcome to stay," he said. "Why don't you remain a while longer? Qaysumah is a nice place."

We were then required to sign a document made out in beautiful Arabic handwriting. As interpreted by Awadh, it appeared that this was our apology for having been so naughty as to land without a clearance and a promise never to do such a thing again. Awadh himself had composed and written it and when passed around it won gasps of approval and admiration from the white-clad Arabs. We had gathered by this time that Arabs set great store by a person's handwriting, a fact that may have accounted for the suspicion with which our flight plans—drawn up in a typical medico's scrawl—had been studied in Beirut.

It was rapidly growing dark, when after many *salam aleikum, aleikum salams* and *inshallahs,* we finally got away. As there had been no fuel available at Qaysumah, there was nothing for it but to hope we could make Bahrain, on an island in the Persian Gulf. Before long this began to seem doubtful. Fuel gauges were showing low in the light of my penlight torch and I kept my eyes glued to the tiny turn and bank indicator and the magnetic compass. The night was pitch black, even the stars being blotted out by a haze of dust and a mist of rain. I suspected that we were drifting steadily to port, but had no idea to what extent. The radio compass, suffering from "night effect," was useless, and in any case I couldn't see sufficiently to tune it in.

After about two and a half hours' flying, I thought I could glimpse the sea below but wasn't sure until I spotted a lighted ship and realised that we had hit the coast too soon and must have drifted well to the north. The situation was looking really serious when Bahrain radar station picked us up. When we corrected course I found we were laying off forty degrees of drift with a strong wind from astern. The radar guys vectored us here and there until we were back on track and heading straight for the runway.

The visibility was so poor that I did not see the runway lights until 200 feet above the water on short final for the strip. Bahrain radar did a great job and got us down as our fuel was running dangerously low.

"Well, you've made it," a British voice announced. "Come up for a cup of coffee."

"Inshallah," I replied. "We'll be right there."

What a relief it was, when we filed our flight plans next morning, to be sent on our way within minutes, with large weather charts especially prepared for us, no arguments, no fuss. We were amongst "normal" people again—but not for long.

Just before take-off I discovered that the crack in FOCLA's cowl had extended rather alarmingly, and made a temporary repair with a couple of large washers found in the sand. We set out over the Gulf of Bahrain, across the Qatar peninsula, then headed into the Persian Gulf for a 210 nautical mile flight to Sharja. It was a lot of water to cross, but reassuring to glimpse the many oil rigs standing out of the wind-whipped ocean. We hadn't reckoned on landing at Sharja—a Royal Air Force base— but the wind against us was so strong that we were forced to change our minds. Jiwani, near the Iran-Pakistan border, was an alternative, but we had been warned that fuel here was carried in buckets from the village at great cost.

The Trucial Oman coast took much longer to show up than we had expected. When we spotted it eventually in the dust haze ahead, I was advised from FOCLI to put over the request to land. "They wouldn't say no to a woman around these parts," he said.

Tuning to Sharja tower I called: "This is Foxtrot Oscar Charlie Lima Alpha."

A reply came through with prompt courtesy and in a British accent: "Good morning, Madam. What can we do for you?"

"We're flying across the Gulf *en route* to Karachi in two small French aircraft," I answered. "We're running a bit short of fuel due to headwinds and would like to come down if this is possible."

"Yes indeed," the tower replied. "We look forward to meeting you."

"Women have their uses," came the voice from FOCLI. "Permission to land here would have taken us months through the formal channels."

Sharja went about clearing traffic in the area, asking most of the jets and helicoptors if they would prefer to go to the training area or return to base. "Returning to base," they all replied.

We really got quite a welcome at Sharja. The men were all those things I'd nearly forgotten about—warm, friendly, good humoured and genuine. Cold Cokes were handed in through the door before I'd shut down the engine. The refuelling truck set about topping up the tanks and without a word two mechanics looked at my badly cracked cowl and went off for their tools.

Still in my hot safari flying suit, I was longing to shower and change, so two officers escorted me to an ablution block and stood guard until I emerged in one of my cool, north-west minis. We both felt much happier as we thanked our British friends and headed east again.

184

After a spell of shaking turbulence we climbed to clear the incredibly rugged Muscat and Oman mountains, then out across the Gulf of Oman over another 200 miles of open sea. Our charts warned us not to fly within ten miles of the Iran coast, but preferring a dusty landing to a wet one, I edged towards it as soon as the coast came into sight.

Never before had I seen such weird-looking country. Described on the map as "sand dunes, rock strata and mud volcanoes," it is a grey, waterless and uninhabitable desert broken by precipitous volcanic ranges which could well be part of the surface of the moon. After nine hours of hanging onto radio compass knobs, fighting with huge charts, and monitoring the fuel against consistent headwinds and turbulence, we approached Karachi.

At the critical moment in which clearances to fly via devious beacons to Karachi Civil Airport were coming through, my V.H.F. radio cut out. Fortunately I still had the portable emergency Bayside and hoisted this into action. I continued using this dependable little set with its makeshift aerial for the rest of the flight to Australia.

Karachi gave us a first taste of what we were to experience throughout Pakistan and India—inconvenience, inefficiency, and frustration. We landed just after sunset, but it was 11 p.m. before we got through the paper work and formalities, paid landing fees, and walked what seemed like miles between each department.

"You want dirty pictures?" a man whispered to Doctor Dicks as we headed at last for a hotel.

"Yeah," he replied, "like I need a hole in my head!"

We were relieved next morning to get away from the clamour of horns, the hawking, coughing, spitting, and filth, into the relative sanity of our cockpits. My generator was still unserviceable, so I again needed a hand to swing the engine to life. The engine itself was going fine, but with no V.H.F. radio or gyro instruments, with leaking ferry tanks and a cracked cowl, things were getting a bit tough.

We headed off north-east for Delhi and when flying over the Great Thar Desert I noticed that FOCLI had veered away to my left. I was map-reading closely and, sure that I was on track, called up to ask where he was going. An argument ensued in which we both insisted that we were on course, so as neither of us would give in, we parted company.

Having declared I was on the right track, I map-read with extra diligence and soon noticed that FOCLA's compass didn't always agree with the landmarks. Dust, smoke and occasional severe turbulence made visibility bad, and as I was unable to pick up anything on my radio compass, it seemed that very few of the radio beacons across this arid stretch were turned on.

After seven hours I arrived in the New Delhi circuit area and came down. FOCLA was immediately mobbed by beggars who swarmed onto the tarmac and kicked, poked and spat at her. FOCLI had still not arrived, so I sat tight and kept my radio turned on to listen out for him. After about fifteen minutes he called up requesting a descent clearance, but was told to maintain 8,000 feet. He reported again at ten miles from the aerodrome but received no reply. I could hear him perfectly well on my small radio and could not understand why Delhi was not answering. Eventually I spotted him in a steep descent over the aerodrome. He reported in the circuit area on base leg for the runway and again on final approach, at which Delhi tower sprang indignantly to life: "Foxtrot Lima India. Do not annoy me!"

FOCLI came in and landed, but when taxi-ing towards FOCLA the angry voice came through again: "Foxtrot Lima India! You did not get permission to land. You will report to the tower IMMEDIATELY!"

It took us exactly five hours to argue with petty officials, complete endless tedious formalities, and refuel the machines. We had hoped to change the oil after approximately fifty hours flying through so much sand and dust, but abandoned all idea of doing it in Delhi.

Exhausted more by the frustration of formalities and long delays than by our hours in the air, we decided to treat ourselves to a comfortable night in New Delhi's resplendent Ashoka Hotel. I had seen some pretty posh hotels in my travels, but never anything to compare to this extravagant palace, shut off from the shocking filth and poverty of the overcrowded city. It seemed almost immoral to turn our backs on so much abject want and misery to enter this other world of comfort and ease, but such is human psychology that we were soon able to shut it out and enjoy a good meal and a night's sleep.

Before taking off next morning we compared compasses and were amazed to find that they were thirty degrees out in opposite directions. At least we now knew what they should read and were able to work our headings out accordingly.

While we were awaiting our departure clearance a big, four-engine aircraft took off in front of us, one engine trailing black smoke and flames. We clearly heard the pilot call: "Number four out," but there was no response from the tower, which calmly cleared us for take-off. Following the progress of the troubled aircraft we heard him call: "Ditching," and saw him belly land in a paddy field about four miles from the aerodrome. We informed the tower but action of any sort was apparently not in their book of procedures, as they did not reply.

We hoped that nothing would happen to *us* in India. However, from the brief glimpse we had had of local conditions, we could hardly expect that the lives of a few foreign visitors would be seen as of the least importance in the scheme of things.

, The seven-hour flight to Calcutta was hot, hazy, and monotonous. I was beginning to feel the effects of stress and strain, and realised that if we didn't have a full day's rest pretty soon a disaster would not be due solely to the shortcomings of FOCLA.

About one and a half hours out of Calcutta, huge clouds made flying unpleasant and we had frequently to divert around heavy thunderstorms. It looked as if we were heading into the beginning of the dreaded monsoon, so we requested a radar vector to Dum Dum Airport. Instead, we were told to arrive via two radio beacons which, we discovered, had not been turned on. When our compasses did not respond we were left in doubt about exactly in which direction to fly. Visibility was very bad and we became separated. I decided to tune directly in to Dum Dum, but local storms interfered with the radio compass and there was no response. Suddenly a large 707 jet burst through a cloud just ahead, so I decided to follow it.

"Aircraft flying over Air Force aerodrome. You are in prohibited area," said a voice over the radio. I looked down to find that I was right over a large, military strip. "Foxtrot Lima

Alpha or Lima India, are you over prohibited area?" came the voice again.

"Negative," I replied, dodging military traffic. "Not me!"

Keeping the jet in sight, I made a successful arrival into Dum Dum airport, taxied to a stop and got out to stretch my legs. Half an hour went by with no sign of FOCLI. I turned on my aircraft radio and heard the Doctor asking for a radar fix as he was unsure of his position. Calcutta tower was unable to hear the calls, so I relayed them from the ground.

"They want to know where you are," I told him.

"Over paddy fields," he replied.

After talk to and fro for a further hour, FOCLI arrived, looking somewhat embarrassed. Knowing that I would "go" him for getting bushed, he got in first and blamed me for "heading in the wrong direction."

By this time our poor little Horizon machines were looking rather sad. Their registration numbers were almost gone, they were both shockingly dusty, and each was down to one oleo leg. "We sure need a friend," Doctor said, and as if in answer to a prayer an eager-faced Indian approached and introduced himself as Raza Beg, co-pilot on a Jamair DC3, who had observed our arrival. "I will help you," he volunteered.

For two days in the wretched, over-populated, filth-ridden city of Calcutta he was at our side, helping us to change the oil, pump the tyres and oleo legs, and clean the aircraft. We found that FOCLA's battery was bone dry, which no doubt explained the poor radio reception, let alone my having to prop start all the way from Paris.

With the help of "Jamair" and Mr Bagat, chief engineer for Air India in Calcutta, we investigated FOCLA's vacuum pump and discovered a broken rubber suction line which had become kinked behind the panel. Raza Beg went to no end of trouble to find a replacement in the city markets and worked with us well into the night, only to find that the tube split again every time we replaced the instrument. In the end we had to give up and leave FOCLA to continue without gyro instruments. The delay, however, had been worthwhile as it caused us to miss a violent typhoon in the Bay of Bengal.

Permission was refused to fly as planned, across the Ganges

delta to the East Pakistan coast at Chittagong and thence down the coast of Burma to Mergui. Instead, we were sent straight out over the great Bay of Bengal via reporting points "Lobster" and "Starfish," both of which were rather doubtful latitude and longitude positions.

Knowing that at least eight major—and goodness knows how many minor—cyclones had swept the Bay within the last ten years, and at a cost of over 64,000 lives, it was hardly an attractive prospect. It would have been even less so at the time of writing, when a 120 m.p.h. cyclone and twenty foot tidal wave in the same area has caused one of the greatest natural disasters in history.

Boiling cumulo-nimbus thunderheads were working up over the bay as we buffeted along wondering for just how long we could manage to avoid them. Turbulence in their vicinity was quite alarming. I began to think how foolish I was to have attempted such a flight, and how comfortable it was at home, and to wonder if I was ever to see it again. I thought, too, of Kingsford-Smith, and wondered in just what part of this bay he had come to his end.

28

HOME STRETCH

AS CONDITIONS WORSENED I BEGAN SINGING *Over the Rainbow* at the top of my voice, and now, whenever I hear that song, I think of the Bay of Bengal, where I sang it so often that its monsoon winds must know the tune by heart.

We were warned to keep ten miles from the Burma coast and so flew on, often up to eighty miles out to sea, until we headed for Sandoway, crossed the Arakan Yoma mountains and followed the brown Irrawaddy River downstream to overfly Rangoon. We felt attracted to this beautiful city and were careful to heed the warning: "Do not fly over temples or mosques."

Thence we flew out over the Gulf of Mataban, past romantic Moulmein and Tavoy. Waterspouts were visible under some of the larger storms, and as dark began to fall we appeared to be heading for an impenetrable black thunderhead. We called up Mergui, our destination for the night, and asked whether they were under a rainstorm. "Negative," came the reply. "Blue sky overhead." The unfriendly area was looming just in front when I looked out to one side and saw lights below.

"We're right *over* Mergui," I told FOCLI. "Let's get down quickly before we're drowned in this storm.

190

The reported "blue sky" had been the blue-black of the cumulus cloud and we had scarcely landed before the deluge descended, raining two inches in ten minutes.

We had a telex-type clearance from Rangoon to land at Mergui, but the local officials refused to accept it. "It will take us two days to get a message to Rangoon," they said. "Then Wednesday is a holiday, so it will be Thursday before we can confirm your clearance. We will only accept Burmese money, so that also will take time to arrange."

On our way through Mergui we saw that it was a beautiful place, though it was obvious from the faces of its basically friendly and peace-loving people that there was much unrest and unhappiness in the area. We would like to have explored further, but were ordered to confine ourselves to the upper floor of the local hotel, where we had two guards "for our protection," and for whom we were required to pay. The rooms we were given were like cells, completely bare apart from a bed and chair, and leading from a large dance floor-cum-conference room. We were proudly shown the "English toilet,"—a ludicrous arrangement sunk flush with the floor and, having no back, leaving one's bottom in full view of people eating in a restaurant below. Another guest who arrived shortly after ourselves, and was always somewhere within earshot, admitted to us the following morning that he was "security."

Drearily contemplating the long delay ahead, I remembered for the first time my letter from our State Premier. I produced it with great ceremony and insisted that it be delivered express to the local Mayor. While we were enjoying a sumptuous repast of rice, fish, chicken, pork and tea that was delivered to our rooms, this dignitary arrived in person. He courteously handed the letter back and told us that we were free to leave, but must pay forty dollars in "Fees."

We were so thankful to be cleared that we accepted this further expense without demur. We returned next morning, through thick monsoonal jungle, to the airport where hundreds of Burmese had gathered to see us refuelled and away. They seemed so nice that had it been safer—and cheaper—we would like to have stayed.

The flight from Burma, down the Malay Peninsula, Thailand

and Malaysia to Singapore, took us over the most fascinating waterways in the world. From a place called Phuket (an unfortunate name to pronounce) on an island off Thailand to Alor Star in Malaysia, we flew over islands of the weirdest shapes imaginable, emerging from the Andaman Sea in the form of pinnacles, grottos, arches and hooks, all surrounded by whirlpools and treacherous currents.

Flying above tropical jungles and often through heavy showers, we passed over Kuala Lumpur and Malacca; cities that previously had been no more than romantic-sounding places on the map. About thirty miles north of Singapore my Bayside ceased to function, and as I had not fitted my Singapore H.F. crystals I was completely out of communication. I tried desperately to let FOCLI know what had happened by flying right on his wing tip, holding up the mike and making crosses on the window. He thought I was waving, and waved cheerfully back, to my utter frustration, as coming into Singapore International Airport without a radio at "rush hour" was no joke. As we approached the city FOCLI started to orbit, so I followed, taking, in the process, a few photographs of the magnificent scene below.

Suddenly I looked up to find that FOCLI was no longer there. I made him out after a quick frantic search as a small red speck heading for the aerodrome, so pushed the throttle forward and soon found myself in the circuit with FOCLI and four jets. As it was impossible to guess when my turn to land would be announced, I decided to tuck myself behind FOCLI. We came in in good formation and landed together on the wide strip. I expected some censorious comment from the tower but nothing was said at all. Courteous and efficient service made all our Singapore transactions easy and pleasant, and I was helped to fix the radio problem, which was traced to an aerial that had been shaken from its socket.

Early the following morning we headed out for Djakarta on a 400 nautical mile hop across the Java Sea. The distance would have presented no problem had we not encountered the monsoon. We had no alternative than to plunge into the great wall of rain, sometimes so heavy that I wondered whether FOCLA was, in fact, flying under water. With forked lightning flashing dangerously close, and being thrown against the straps in turbulence, we pressed on, letting the brave little Horizons pick their own way around avoidable bad areas. When FOCLA's engine coughed and the revs dropped, I realized with near heart seizure that icing had also become a problem, but this was solved by the regular application of carburettor heat.

We became separated early in the piece, but kept in frequent radio contact with each other and also with operators in Singapore, who, knowing communications with Djakarta to be as difficult as those with India, did their best to see us through.

Things seemed to be going on in a sort of dreamy chaos at Kemajoran airport when we taxied in, having been forced to play chicken on landing with kids riding all over the airstrip on bicycles. We waited for hours, in the wet and humid heat, as one official after another turned up to discuss this rare problem of filling in forms for light aircraft.

Although Java was experiencing her worst floods in years, there was no water in our hotel except for five minutes in every hour. We found that the trick was to leave all the taps on and rush to the toilet when the water started to run. Nor was there any power before six p.m., which meant no air circulation to relieve the enervating heat.

The evening meal consisted of an interesting number of small bowls containing rice, peanut dip, chilli sauce, green beans, cucumber, omelette, spiced meat, bananas and green peppers. It was all very good except the sudden-death green peppers which anaesthetised my mouth and caused my eyes to stream for several hours. We gathered that the national drink must be hot water, as this is all that was served in the teapots. I thought they must have forgotten to put the tea in, so requested some, which was fetched from the market some time later and served in a tea bag with iced water!

At 6 a.m. on Thursday, 11 April, 1968, we found ourselves in a rickshaw heading for Kemajoran airport. On the way I was lucky enough to spot a large washer to put over a second crack in FOCLA's cowl, which by that time had several screws missing, two eight-inch cracks, and was vibrating badly.

The whole of Java seemed to be more or less under water, with only a few paddy fields visible between the many rivers and mountains with tops swathed in cloud. About an hour from Djakarta, when flying some fifteen miles out to sea, we hit more bad weather and diverted south to fly low along the coast until it cleared. We cruised along abeam mountainous islands of breathtaking beauty for six hours, until the Java coast came up and we headed around the 10,932 foot Gunung Raung Mountain into Bali Strait, bound for Denpasar. The mountain currents were so violent that during a series of crazy aerobatics I suddenly found myself looking down onto sky instead of sea.

Whether I had been less careful on this flight to limit my fluid intake or whether it was a psychological reaction because I had left my usual receptacle in the rickshaw at Djakarta, I found myself, with still five hours to go, in desperate need. The only object in the cockpit that could possibly help me out was a large tin of emergency ration peaches, and the only way of disposing of the contents without creating an unspeakable mess was to eat my way through the lot. The prospect was formidable but my situation was so dire that I groped for a pocket knife with which I had, on a previous occasion, and with considerable difficulty, made a hole in a can of drink. Getting sufficient tin out of the way for my purpose was no joke and my skyward and seaward gyrations as I hacked and battled raised anxious enquiries from FOCLI:

"What the hell's up with you?"

"Nothing."

"But you're all over the sky and a long way out to sea."

"Yes, I know."

"Well, get back over here. If anything happens you'll be in the drink."

"Don't mention that awful word, and please keep quiet. I'm busy."

"Oh!"

It took an agonising three quarters of an hour to operate on the tin and about five even more agonising minutes to consume its contents. The next problem was to make use of it without sustaining an embarrassing gash, but this too I finally achieved. It was more than worth the effort entailed.

Denpasar, a Balinese village about seven miles from the aerodrome, lies across a narrow neck of land on the south side.

The island, rising from a clear jade sea to peaks of over 10,000 feet, was even more beautiful than I had expected. Seen from the air the dense green jungle almost obscured all signs of habitation and silver-white beaches glistened in the afternoon sun. Once recovered from the shock of the high landing fees we saw that it was just as lovely at ground level; lush, fertile, and populated with beautiful people whose ancient culture is much in evidence in the stone architecture and delicate carvings that adorn every house and temple. Pigs, cows, geese and water buffalo run wild. The men appear to be cheerfully playing soldiers, strutting about in uniform with things stuck in their belts, while the women, carrying great loads on their heads, seem to do all the work.

We were mobbed by souvenir hunters, eager to pounce on any piece of rubbish, however trifling. I had planned to dispose of my peach tin discretely in the undergrowth, but all eyes followed my every move. Eventually I turfed it nonchalantly into the scrub beside the tarmac whereupon there was a wild rush and an excited scramble. The tin was grabbed, sniffed, passed from one to another, admired and finally made off with by the most enterprising collector. Advised to have our machines guarded, we readily agreed to pay for this service as it was obvious that by morning there would otherwise be little left.

These negotiations fixed, we had a few hours of glorious relaxation—a refreshing swim and a rest in the warm shade while watching the island canoes go gliding by.

An amazing world slipped past FOCLA's window on the following day. The densely vegetated islands, too rugged to support human life, were dotted with volcanoes; some with lake-filled craters, others spitting rocks, lava and steam; dramatic phenomena such as I never realised existed so close to Australia.

Once again we were very much alone, as now neither Singapore nor Djakarta answered our radio position reports. Both aircraft compasses were still considerably out, but we managed to calaculate our own deviation and compensate satisfactorily.

The most exciting moment of the whole trip was probably when, abeam Sumbawa Island in Sumba Strait at 0215 Greenwich time, we heard—clear as a bell—Broome radio calling a local M.M.A. flight somewhere in that vicinity. All of a sudden, over strange seas and volcanic islands, we seemed within reach of home.

"Broome radio. This is Foxtrot Oscar Charlie Lima Alpha," I called excitedly.

"Go ahead, Robin," Broome radio replied.

Almost too elated to get the words out, I asked them to inform Dad that we were O.K. and would see him in Broome in a few days' time.

"We'll ring him right away," Broome replied. "I can tell you he'll be mighty relieved. You can now call either Broome or Darwin with your position reports."

For the first time on the entire flight from Paris we knew that we were being looked after and that if anything went wrong someone would care. The feeling of relief was beyond words.

Passing the Flores Islands, we crossed the Savu Sea to Timor, and flew along the coast to Dili in the Portuguese section of the island. It was a placid looking place at the base of a mountain overlooking Lombar Strait whose beaches were littered with the rusting relics of war. Before landing we had to buzz a herd of goats off the short strip, which had seemed deserted as we came down, but in no time people began to emerge from the long grass. It was Good Friday and a holiday, so instead of wasting the remaining hours of daylight on the usual formalities, we took a bus 2,000 feet up to the mountain hospital. This, typical of most island "paradises," was full of cases of tropical disease. We learned something of the problems and contradictions that are everywhere part of a culture-clash situation. "Here in Portugal," the white inhabitants often say, reminding the visitor that they regard this territory as part of the mother country rather than as a colony.

However it may be for the Europeans, most of the 700,000 native inhabitants seem little removed from their tribal origins. As in Australia, there are signs of the government's growing awareness of responsibility towards the indigenous people, but despite increased grants towards their health and education the results of past neglect were everywhere in evidence. A high infant mortality rate and subsistence living standards have kept the population increase—without any attempts at birth control—at an annual 1.7 per cent, and there were no signs, as in Papua and New Guinea, whose people these so much resemble, of any urge towards independence or developing nationalism.

But generally we found Dili a delightful, easy-going place, and met some fellow Australians for almost the first time on the flight. The following morning we were visited at six a.m. by Interpol representatives, who collected the usual fees and attended to our passports. We then refuelled and headed blithely for home. What a let-down when we ran into the most ferocious of all tropical thunderstorms in the middle of the Timor Sea! We were forced to make large diversions, strange winds took us a long way off course, and great black water spouts threatened to suck us down. After four nightmare hours we hit Melville Island and tracked in to Darwin and the welcome sight of home soil.

As I was lined up on final approach, Darwin tower announced that they had two special urgent messages and put through two telegrams—one from Rosemary de Pierres, a flying friend, saying warmly and simply: "Well done." The other was from Tom Sergeant, representative of Southern Aeronautics, who had initiated our journey. He little knew how much we had been through to earn his congratulations.

After the Darwin customs had examined our machines we headed for Kildurk Station near the border between Western Australia and the Northern Territory. My Uncle Reg, Aunt Enid, and Cousin John Durack didn't know what had struck them when two dusty, slightly worse for wear French aircraft buzzed their isolated homestead and came down on the station strip. To their surprise, two weary but elated fliers alighted and announced that they intended staying the night—and for what developed into a memorable occasion of family reunion and talk.

At Broome next day we were met by Dad who, having decided that we had come somewhere to a sad end, had been preparing to lie down and die. On receiving our message off Timor he had miraculously revived and was ready with dinner in the oven and a bottle of wine in the fridge.

And so to Perth . . . and "happy hour" and all that . . .

When people asked me brightly, "How was the flight?" I hardly knew what to say. Perhaps, if they read this, they will understand why my answer was often no more than a few words and a far-away smile.

It would be satisfying to say that our experience laid the ground-work for the successful selling of Horizon aircraft in Australia. The little machines were indeed good, our troubles, minor ones at that, having been mainly connected with the temporary ferry installations, but they missed the market for light aircraft when company promotion lost its original enthusiasm.

For myself, I had fallen in love with FOCLA. She and I had proved something together. We had taken on the world and won out against every mean trick it had contrived to turn on for us. It was little wonder that, as she flew off to Sydney, I felt that I was losing someone with whom I had developed a deep relationship.

IN A FLYING DAY'S WORK

THE FINAL ROUND OF VACCINATIONS COMPLETED, I HANDED IN
my files. These consisted of thousands of record cards that I
had sorted and collated at the end of the job. The grand total
amounted to more than 37,000 doses of vaccine administered,
and about 43,000 miles of flying. Although personally satisfied
that I had covered the job as efficiently as possible, I sensed a
certain atmosphere of relief in the department at its being rid of
such an odd-woman-out. I guess I hadn't really qualified in the
essential articles of Parkinson's Law. Soon afterwards I received
formal notification that I was now off the government pay-roll.

There is always plenty of work for nurses but I was hoping
to find another job that would combine nursing and flying.
A brief trip to Sydney, in an attempt to interest various organisations in founding a Flying Doctor Service in the New Hebrides,
was unsuccessful, so I returned and accepted a job as relieving
pilot with the West Australian branch of the service.

While between jobs I was fortunate in obtaining a Commonwealth scholarship to complete my First Class Instrument
Rating, a blind flying course which enables a pilot to control
his aircraft solely by instruments in any circumstances. This

not only brings him to a much higher flying standard but keeps him up to date, as it demands six monthly D.C.A. checks for its renewal. I had now come a long way from that day when inexperience caused me to spin dizzily out of a cloud—and to lose me the confidence of my dentist passenger.

My first base was at Carnarvon, where I lived in a house built as pilot's quarters, and soon settled into work which was just routine enough to give it a pattern but with variety enough to keep it always interesting.

, The immediate reaction of the local doctors to my posting in that area was antagonistic. They wrote a joint letter to the Flying Doctor operations manager saying that they refused to fly with a woman pilot. Headquarters assured them of my qualifications and added that any tragedy resulting from their refusal to fly with me would be their responsibility. The strained atmosphere continued for some time but I was happy enough flying off alone to bring patients in to the base hospital.

On the first routine clinic flight I picked up a doctor at Exmouth and flew him to Onslow. He had no complaints, but Carnarvon doctors still refused to fly with me. When requested to perform a post-mortem at Onslow on two children who had perished in tragic circumstances near a station east of that centre, they asked the Exmouth doctor to do the job, although it was not one of his duties. They received no sympathy from this quarter and were simply told that if they wouldn't fly with me they could "damn well drive."

They did damn well drive, but they must have decided in the process that North Australia—heat, dust, desolation, women in men's jobs—was not for them. They shortly afterwards found a cosier niche with the Immigration Department in Italy, and were replaced by doctors with less sex discrimination.

A typical day would begin at seven a.m., with the opening of the medical session on the Flying Doctor radio network. Often on a basis of the symptoms described, the doctor could prescribe treatment or medicines from the standard chest with which all outposts are equipped. In other cases he would decide to go himself, or to send a nurse, and within fifteen minutes the aircraft would be on the way.

Patients usually travel extremely well and rarely require

200

sedation. The majority can be treated either on the spot or at the nearest hospital, but in cases of grave illness or accidents they are flown direct to Perth.

Superseding the Fox Moths with which the Service was initiated are six twin-engine Beechcraft Barons and two Cessna 180s, all fitted out for ambulance work. The Beechcrafts can carry six passengers, including a doctor and nurse, or two stretcher cases plus the medical attendants. Oxygen equipment and a Bird Resuscitator machine, which can "breathe" for the patient, are also carried.

But, of course, every response to a call does not represent a "winged errand of mercy." Much time is spent in routine clinic flights, which eliminate the necessity for many emergency flights, with a doctor prepared to face a line-up of patients suffering from anything from piles to pyorrhoea. And, as already told, there are the inevitable false alarms, often from callers in pathetically isolated situations. Such people put on a dramatic act over the radio, but turn out to be suffering from nothing so much as the need to contact another human being. Nevertheless this need may be as great as that of any physical sufferer.

In this category are a number of calls that come at night, when things always seem so much worse. Night flights to stations are undertaken only in extreme emergencies and at considerable risk to pilot and aircraft. With no visible landmarks to aid navigation, a small cluster of lights is extremely hard to find. If the station homestead happens to be situated amongst hills, the "blind" approach is especially dicey. All too often people requesting such "mercy" flights do not appreciate the difficulties and dangers involved, including obstructions such as trees, windmills, and wires, that may not be seen until too late.

Typical enough was a recent case in which I was awakened at night to be told that someone on a station over 200 miles north-west of Meekatharra was in a very bad way. It appeared that he had got his hand caught and partly severed in the blades of a windmill, the reason for the call not having been made until hours after the accident being that it was only discovered when the victim failed to return to the homestead after dark. The station was in a part of the Barlee Range with which I was not familiar, and there was a thirty knot wind howling outside. The doctor, however, was anxious to get to the case, and although I warned him that our chances of finding the place were pretty slim, he thought we should do our best.

I asked the station people over the radio to position their three cars facing into wind at an angle of forty-five degrees; two where I could touch down and one where I must stop. Also I asked them to light as many fires as possible along the sides of the strip. I warned them not to turn on their car lights or light the fires until they actually heard the aircraft as their batteries might become flat and the fires die long before our arrival.

We took off, and flew for an hour without spotting a single light or landmark below. My map indicated a high, fairly isolated mountain not far from the homestead site, so I came down to 300 feet above its estimated height and searched anxiously in the dim moonlight for a sign of its looming mass. With relieved surprise I sighted it off to one side, flew over it and tracked away in the supposed direction of the strip. After ten minutes a light showed up, then another and another. Not knowing the actual elevation of this strip I came down cautiously to 2,000 feet, which I thought to be a safe height for the circuit, put down the wheels and prepared to land. Suddenly a ridge loomed up directly ahead and with pounding heart and lightning reflexes I managed to pull up over it in the nick of time; then, wary of encountering more such obstacles, made a steep descent and landed before the people below had finished lighting their fires. (The strip elevation turned out to be 1,750 feet!)

"We saw you pull up sharp over Suicide Ridge," someone announced cheerfully as we emerged from the Baron rather shaky at the knees. "Another aircraft packed up on that jolly thing last year."

Thankful for this timely information, the doctor and I were driven to the homestead, where we found the patient, surrounded by a sympathetic audience, with his hand neatly bandaged and looking quite fit. The doctor administered a pain killer while I took his blood pressure, from which it was obvious that he could easily have waited until morning.

I pointed out that it was very risky coming out at night and that most things *could* wait until daylight. "But we thought everything was automatic these days," someone exclaimed. I refrained from replying that modern aeronautical instruments, although a vast improvement on the old, are not yet endowed with extra-sensory perception.

On take-off with the patient I was somewhat put out when the aircraft did a series of kangaroo hops—not, as I remarked to the doctor, my usual style. But we cleared Suicide Ridge, made Meekatharra without further incident, and soon had the patient's badly crushed fingers professionally sewn up.

A few days later I was asked about the condition of the station airstrip.

"Fairly O.K.," I replied.

"Last time I went in there," the enquirer told me, "there were three creeks running across the north end."

"Now you come to mention it," I said, remembering those kangaroo hops . . .

The logs of the Flying Doctor Service are full of stories covering aspects of life from tragedy to comedy, drama to monotony. One finds bawdiness side by side with heroism, madness with sanity, helplessness and stupidity with amazing intelligence and initiative, callous indifference or thoughtlessness with touching consideration and selfless co-operation. All members of the Service can recount stories very similar to mine — happy-ending incidents of the saving of life and limb; sad cases of attempts that did not succeed.

Inevitably it is the tragic episodes that leave the deepest mark on one's memory; cases like that of the year-old baby with meningitis who, during the flight to hospital, sat up and smiled at us with outstretched arms and starry eyes as if suddenly cured, and then collapsed abruptly into death.

Then there was the little girl found floating, unconscious, in the dam on her parents' farm. I took off with another nurse and an anaesthetist to find the child only just alive. Using the aircraft as an operating theatre, and with the grief-stricken parents standing by, we soon had the child breathing satisfactorily and on her way to the intensive care ward in Perth. D.C.A. organised direct clearances and held up other aircraft as we came in. The Police were standing by to escort the ambulance, but the little one died soon after reaching hospital. It was difficult to feel that this was not for the best as, had she lived, she would inevitably have suffered brain damage from the prolonged lack of oxygen.

Once, while stationed in Carnarvon, I received a call from a station about 100 miles inland. The patient was a thin, bare-footed little Aboriginal girl of about eight, whose face lit up in recognition when she sighted me. "I know you, Sister," she said. "You sugar lady. Remember—I helped you in the school?"

I realised that the child was one named Linda, a bright, healthy kid who had been the first to offer herself for vaccination and eye examination and had insisted on holding my bowls while I treated the other children. She had told me she planned to be a nurse herself when she grew up.

I learned from the child's mother that she had been coughing blood and had a pain in her chest. "She's a good little girl," the woman said. "Helps missus in the house and that and she's saved up two dollars in her purse. She wants to buy a pair of shoes."

Linda was seized with paroxysms of coughing while in the air and I was anxious to get her to hospital without delay, but on landing she held up her purse as a reminder of the shoes. I told her the shops were shut and that we'd get them next day, but I was then called off on another job and didn't see her for over a week. In the meantime her trouble had been diagnosed as rheumatic fever and I was required to fly her to Perth.

She was waiting, purse in hand, and still concerned about her shoes. We stopped at a store on the way to the airfield and asked the storekeeper to bring out all the children's shoes he had. "Those," Linda said, pointing to a blue pair ornamented with coloured beads. They cost more than two dollars, but it was worth the difference to see the joy on her face as she sat, clutching them tightly, all the way to Perth.

Before leaving Perth next morning I called to see her at the hospital. In the duty room just outside her ward I noticed the blue shoes and little kangaroo skin purse placed neatly on the sister's desk. I knew the answer, but asked: "How's Linda?"

"She died early this morning."

There was nothing more to say. I picked up the shoes and the purse and returned them to her mother.

A story with a happier ending was that of an eight year-old boy who had developed tetanus after treading on a nail. In an effort to overcome violent spasms that would have resulted in death, he was treated in the Geraldton Hospital with carefully controlled doses of curare—a poison used on the arrows of South American Indians—which causes complete paralysis. As he was unable to breathe for himself, a tracheotomy had been performed and he was connected to an artificial respirator before being placed in the R.F.D.S. aircraft for a 250-mile flight to Perth. As luck would have it, it was a smooth trip and he survived it without further ill effects. An ambulance, with police escort, was awaiting our arrival to convey the patient to the Princess Margaret Hospital. The airport authorities had done everything in their power to assist, including the delay of two mid-day jet flights for thirty minutes and switching off all loud speaker systems to keep the area as quiet as possible. Their efforts proved well worthwhile.

We accompanied the patient in the ambulance, which, with the police car in the lead, crawled at a minimum pace, often on the wrong side of the road to avoid bumps. Every intersection had been manned by police who stopped the traffic to let us through without delay. Motorists had been asked to shut down their engines and everyone to be as quiet as possible, with the result that one could almost have heard a pin drop as we passed down the city's main street.

Thousands of people had been held up, many without knowing why, but there appeared to be no complaints, no impatient drivers trying to barge through. I would like to have thanked every one of them for the part he had played in saving this child's life—for, although his condition remained critical for some time, saved he was, and returned to his parents.

30

"WHERE'S THE PILOT?"

•

"WHERE'S THE PILOT?" THE DOCTOR ASKED, WITH A GLANCE past the stretcher patient and the surrounding relatives to the waiting aircraft.

"It's Robin Miller," someone volunteered.

The doctor took his bag from the car and scanned the rain-washed landing strip. "Well, where is he?"

"Right here," I said, and proceeded to check the oil.

From the corner of one eye I observed the expected reactions— the quick look of dubious surprise, the hesitant half-turn. There was a sudden flash of forked lightning and a deafening thunder clap, after which the doctor completed his turn and put the bag back in his car.

"It's all right," my spokesman assured him. "She's had plenty of experience."

"Aren't you taking your bag?" enquired one of the anxious family.

There was a pause of obviously agonised indecision before the doctor managed to pull himself together, resolutely take out his bag again, and help get the stretcher on the plane.

The patient had suffered a severe coronary and there was

no time to be lost waiting for the weather to clear up. We took off into lowering thunder clouds, but apart from a certain amount of turbulence and one blinding flash of lightning that seemed to miss the aircraft by the merest fraction, it was a routine enough trip.

The behaviour of my uninitiated male passengers often follows this pattern. First comes the apprehensive *look,* then, as the door is closed, the clearing of throats and loosening of ties, presumably anticipating air-sickness. As we begin to move they sit grimly clutching the seat, legs braced for the crash take-off, but once safely in the air and over the initial "woman pilot" shock they usually relax and confess to having enjoyed the flight.

For apprehensive passengers my prize must surely go to a Japanese student from Tokyo who had hitch-hiked his way to Leopold Downs station in the Kimberleys. He had turned up there just before heavy rain closed the roads and put the airstrip out of commission for several weeks.

In order to earn his keep he had volunteered to help in the kitchen, but after serving one "Japanese-style" dinner of meat and eggs, arranged with consummate artistry but completely raw, his services were tactfully declined. He spoke very little English and found it hard to understand, as the days and weeks went by with his visa running out, why no one turned up to take him on. He suggested that he should walk, but was convinced, with reference to the map, that this would amount to suicide.

My aircraft was the first to brave the sodden strip, and I was met by a hardy station vehicle that somehow managed to get me seven miles to the homestead through fast-flowing creeks. The good news of impending release was then conveyed to the Japanese "guest," whose visa was due to expire the following day and who, within minutes, was ready with his knapsack on the front steps.

On our way to the strip we visited a stock camp where I immunised everyone present, including some mules that were wistfully eyeing off the sugar lumps. It was no use anyone trying to explain the purpose of this curious process to the bewildered boy, who stood by meanwhile looking utterly nonplussed. He appeared quite vexed when the truck, instead of continuing along the road as he had evidently expected, stopped at the airstrip and everyone piled out. Someone threw his knapsack into the Mooney along with two bags of mail and a water melon, pushed him into the passenger's seat and secured the door. Never have I seen such terror and confusion on the face of a passenger as he displayed when I climbed into the pilot's seat.

"You'll be right, mate," I told him, with a reassuring smile, as we zoomed into the air, made a farewell pass over the homestead and climbed over the rugged Leopold Ranges in the turbulent summer heat.

After some time my passenger summoned sufficient strength to form a sentence: "Where to . . . you . . . take me?"

"Hall's Creek," I replied.

"Hall's Creek . . . near Sydney is?"

I tried to explain that it was, in fact, several thousand miles from that city but that it was on a main highway where he could get a lift to Darwin or Perth before long. How much of this he understood I don't know. He just sat, shaking his head, fingering his visa and checking the expiry date.

"Relax," I told him. "The worst they can do is send you back to Japan."

But communication was almost impossible, so I decided, as we flew on over that rough and desolate land, to introduce the boy to the Shire Clerk in Hall's Creek, explain his predicament, and see what could be done for him. If he hadn't the money for an air fare to Sydney, via Darwin, he could be put on a truck to Derby and thence on his way to Perth, where the Japanese Consul, a helpful man, as I knew, would no doubt arrange to have his visa renewed.

As soon as the aircraft touched down the boy turned and formally shook me by the hand. I accepted this as an apology for his lack of faith in me, but as we came to a stop he opened the door, removed his pack and within a few seconds was a speck on the shimmering horizon. Yelling at the top of my lungs I set off after him, but he had vanished at a rate that could well have got him to Sydney before his visa expired.

I reported his disappearance to the police, who presumably caught up with him, but how the story ended I never heard.

I often wonder just how he described his north Australian adventures to the folks at home.

On one of my weekly clinic rounds of the Carnarvon area I was required to return an Aborigine to Onslow, landing at Exmouth en route to pick up the doctor for a clinic at the Onslow hospital.

"Come on, Jacky—we're going home!" I told the patient brightly. He made no reply but fixed me with a peculiar stare. He was a well-built Aborigine, dressed in a bright yellow hospital dressing-gown and clutching a large paper bag.

"He's been receiving mental treatment," the Sister at Carnarvon had told me, and added cheerfully, "He's usually pretty well-behaved, but they sent him down because he hit a woman over the head with a piece of wood. He hardly ever talks, but I don't think he'll give you any trouble."

My passenger seemed most unwilling to accompany me. I led him firmly into the car and when we reached the airfield I said, "Stay here, Jacky," but received no answer. When I returned from filling in my flight plan and checking on the weather he was gone, so I drove over to the creek-bed to which "bush natives" naturally seem to gravitate. I saw a flash of yellow in the scrub, and braced myself for an argument. He got calmly back into the car, but when the time came to get out he jibbed again. I had to pull, persuade and bully him into the plane, while he stared at me with the same strange, vague expression, not uttering a word. I couldn't decide whether he was frightened of the aircraft or of me, but finally managed to get him into a seat diagonally behind me, where I could keep an eye on him and he couldn't reach the door handle or controls. As we took off I glanced round to see whether he was settling down and noticed that he had shoved the big paper bag under his dressing-gown. He was playing with something inside it under cover of its bright yellow folds. I heard a jiggling, metallic noise that I could not identify. A razor, perhaps? From his shaving gear? Surely they wouldn't let him carry a *razor* around? Not a *mental patient* . . . ?

I tried to concentrate on flying, and to put the mysterious clinking noise out of my mind, but was just coming in over Exmouth Gulf to pick up the doctor when I felt a clammy hand on my bare shoulder. I nearly jumped out of my skin, and hardly daring to look round asked: "What's the matter, Jacky?"

For the first time, I heard him speak. "Might be we lost," he said, his deep voice quite rational and clear.

"No, we're not," I assured him. "I know this country."

"Onslow thataway," he said, and pointed across the Gulf.

He watched me carefully as I explained that we were stopping at Exmouth first. He then gave a nod of satisfaction and settled back in his seat. He was delivered at Onslow without any more problems.

Months later I asked the nursing staff at this port how he was getting on. "Oh, he's fine," I was told. "But guess what? He's stone deaf!"

It only then dawned on me that his peculiar, intent stare had meant that he was lip reading. I was cross with myself for having failed to tumble to it earlier, especially as I knew the prevalence of ear trouble in the north. No doubt the poor fellow was quite sane and had merely hit a woman over the head in exasperation at her inability to understand his problem. Since then I have checked carefully for deafness in any Aborigines believed to be "backward," or "unreasonable."

But of course many of the worst Aboriginal problems are the result of drink. How to handle this question is one of the most complex Australia has to face and that I, as a nurse and flying doctor pilot, have to deal with. When granted their citizen rights, Aborigines could no longer logically be withheld the right to drink. For the majority, this was more important than the right to vote. In any case, drink could hardly have been a greater problem that it already was. Unscrupulous whites had for decades worked a fruitful black market in supplying Aborigines with inferior grog at inflated prices, while the natives in many areas had become adept at concocting dangerous alcoholic drinks based on methylated spirits. The granting of "rights" was not, as some are inclined to think, the cause of the problem. It was the instrument which brought it out into the open.

One is on controversial ground in declaring that Aborigines "just can't take alcohol," for there are some who can enjoy a few drinks without ill effect, just as there are a good many Europeans who can't. On the whole, however, as the more responsible Aborigines themselves admit, alcoholism has become the ruin of far too many. The reason for this may be found in a combination of factors; sociological, psychological, physical and spiritual. I have heard it aptly described as a "device of discontent . . . a means of enduring the mind-blowing tension of absolutely opposed outlooks." Whatever the cause, it is a major factor in retarding Aboriginal living standards and chances of regular employment, and the reason why so many are dependent on the soul-destroying system of Government handouts.

An example of the chaos that drink so often causes in Aboriginal families occurred when I was summoned recently to a north-west station. The R.F.D.S. message had sounded ominous; someone had been stabbed, another shot. There was blood everywhere—people screaming, children crying. In short: "Get here quick."

When I arrived at the station just before dark with a doctor and a police constable, we were told that the trouble had been started by a part Aboriginal employee "on the grog" who had taken to his missus with a knife. She had received severe stab wounds in her arm and side, and her screams had resulted in a general pandemonium during which a white employee had produced a gun and shot the belligerent husband in the arm. By the time we got to the scene everyone had more or less pulled around except the wounded woman, who greeted us with the hysterical announcement that her husband had "bloody murdered" her. Besides the injured couple, we were asked to take along their two wide-eyed, shivering children, who sat crouched together on a wired-up tucker box containing all their possessions. We got them on board all right, but were no sooner in the air than the woman began throwing herself about and telling us that she was "dying of pain and bleeding to death." In fact the wound in her arm was bleeding quite smartly, but an injection had no effect than to make her vomit all over the air-craft. Neither the doctor nor the constable could exercise much restraining effect on her, but when her husband put his hand on her shoulder and said, "You'll be okay, Mum," she quietened down immediately.

We delivered the patients and their children to the hospital. When I called back, some time later, I found the two children huddled on a bench outside the casualty ward where their parents were being treated. The hospital was short staffed and no one had had time to give the kids a thought. I dug some woollies out of their tin box, then sneaked into the kitchen and found a couple of apples and oranges. I never saw children eat so hungrily. When the charge sister realised their plight she gave them a meal and a bed for the night. But what was the end of an incident for me was no doubt only the beginning of another round in a tough battle for those poor, bewildered waifs, with their father in jail and their mother back on social services handouts.

Some of the most difficult patients I have had to handle in the north have been Southern Europeans. There is something about this country, with its sheer, awful emptiness and lack of normal community life, that can drive them to frenzy. Especially is this so in the intense heat of the summer months that tries to breaking point the endurance of any but the most dogged, phlegmatic, and inured.

Flying Doctor pilot Rob Rowson had one nearly fatal experience with a mentally disturbed Italian who was being accompanied to Carnarvon from Exmouth by a policeman and a nurse. Although sedated he became so violently restless during the flight that the policeman reached for some handcuffs he had hidden under the seat. Unfortunately the patient spotted them first, grabbed them and started bashing them against the perspex window. In trying to restrain him the constable received a severe bite on the wrist that severed his radial artery. The frenzied patient then got down on the floor, braced his head and shoulders against one door and kicked out at the other with the result that both doors sprang open. This time, when the struggling policeman tried to pull him up again, the Italian kicked out at the front seat. The pilot was pushed forward against the instrument panel, causing the aircraft to enter a steep dive, both doors swinging open the while. Somehow he regained control of the machine, and the policeman of the patient, and a safe landing was eventually made at Carnarvon. His spate of violence by this time spent, the Italian, when about to step quietly into the waiting ambulance, turned and smiled back charmingly: "I hope I have not been the cause of any trouble." In fact the policeman never regained the full use of his thumb, and, as he had been officially off-duty at the time, could not claim any compensation. Since that incident the R.F.D.S. has insisted that mentally deranged patients must be confined to strait-jackets and be escorted by a policeman—*on duty*.

It would be ungracious, however, not to mention that I have received the most touching appreciation from my "New Australian" patients. Somehow or another an article about my activities in the outback got into an Italian periodical, after which I not only received a flood of Italian fan mail, including proposals of marriage (photographs enclosed!) but was honoured with a Certificate of Merit from the International Council of Nurses in Mantova, which was formally presented by the Italian Consul in Perth.

Some of my most trying passengers have been not deranged but abysmally stupid. I was called out once to Wittenoom, in the iron ore country on the edge of the Hamersley Ranges, to pick up the victim of a mining accident. The patient had suffered a head injury and after several days of unconsciousness in hospital had "come to" sufficiently to obey simple commands. An ambulance had brought him to meet the aircraft accompanied by his wife, a young woman with a high-pitched, whining voice who regarded me open-mouthed.

"Do you fly-i-ee?" she asked.

"There's nothing to it," I replied. "I just sit there. The instruments do the job."

"Oh," she said, "would you have to have any special training for that?"

I ignored this question and helped get the stretcher case on board.

"I want to sit next to him," the woman whined on, "not that he recognises me or anything, but after all I *am* his wife."

The patient gave me a wink that indicated he was well aware of everything that was going on.

The arrangement suited me very well, as it meant that my friend and fellow flier Anne Hatfield, who had come along to assist, could sit in the co-pilot's seat and chat on the four-hour flight south. We had not been long aloft and were cruising along comfortably when I became aware of a shuffling in the back of the aircraft.

"Excuse me," announced our lady passenger, "I want to go to the toilet."

"Can't you wait until we get to Meekatharra? It's only about fifty minutes."

"Oh no, it's *urgent*," she wailed. "Couldn't you land somewhere down there? It looks fairly flat in places."

Leaving Anne in charge of the controls I scrambled over the seats and dug out a bedpan from the emergency equipment. After a good deal of fumbling around the woman had just got herself settled on this object, when we struck turbulence. As the machine began to bounce we expected the worst, but were reassured by the information that she couldn't "*do-o-o* anything," and that anyway it wasn't "so urgent any more."

The pan was disposed of and we brought out a thermos of coffee and some chicken sandwiches which our friend declined to share as she was feeling sick. "No, I don't want a bag," she said. "It's not that sort of sick. You know, sick in the head. It's all the worry and everything."

Anne and I were just about to enjoy our little repast when the voice from the back seat bleated out again: "I think my husband has disgraced himself."

Normally in these circumstances one pretends not to notice, but in this case it was well nigh impossible. I grappled for the air vent and the sandwiches were quietly put away.

At Meekatharra we fixed the patient up, took a breath of fresh air and got aloft again. On entering the Perth control area we had run into instrument flying conditions that required my full attention when there was a nervous tap on my shoulder.

"I can't see the ground."

"Sit down," I replied. "Neither can I."

"Well, how do you know where you're going if you can't see? Why don't you come down out of the clouds?"

Anne explained that I was flying on instruments at an assigned altitude to avoid collisions with other aircraft.

"O-o-o-o!" she said. "If I'd known it was so dangerous I wouldn't have come."

The ambulance, punctual as usual, was awaiting our arrival at the Perth Airport and the bracing winter atmosphere brought the patient "to."

"Did you enjoy the flight, darling?" his wife enquired.

"No!" replied the patient firmly, and lapsed back into unconsciousness.

Every day, even in the process of scribbling these scattered notes, further incidents keep cropping up. Recently, there was that day which began at the Marble Bar hospital. I was waiting for the doctor to finish a routine clinic, and talking to one of the local Aboriginal celebrities; an achondroplastic dwarf who has spent much of her life (when not in gaol on charges of drunkenness) touring the country in side-shows.

"You know, Sister," she told me with an infectious grin, "those men down at the camp call me 'the low loader.' They reckon I give 'em V.D. Well, serves 'em right for loadin' me with a name like that."

"Port Hedland for Flying Doctor pilot," a nurse called. A message had come through to pick up a native woman from Jigalong mission, about 170 miles south-east of Marble Bar on the fringe of the Great Sandy Desert, and the centre for over 300 Aborigines.

There were no further details, so, leaving the doctor to complete his clinic, I headed out into the hot afternoon. Jigalong is always difficult to find, as the area map is unreliable, and the mission is well camouflaged among gibber plains and scrubby hills. I managed, however, to pick up the native camp, the usual running figures, and the truck hurrying towards the strip.

The patient was a thirteen year-old girl who had been in labour for sixteen hours and was having painful, four-minute contractions. Looking at her tired, distressed little face, I wished I had brought an escort. Not long before an R.F.D.S. pilot named Bob Neille had warned me never to take off alone with a woman well advanced in pregnancy. He had had two experiences of babies being born in his aircraft. One was a thirteen-stone woman he had been called to bring into Meekatharra in a Cessna aircraft. She had come into labour in mid-air, and, with each contraction, had pushed the front seat forward with her powerful knees, forcing the pilot against the control column and sending the plane into a steep dive. The baby was delivered unaided, and to prevent its rolling around the cabin, Bob held it in one hand and flew on to Meekatharra with the other.

215

"You don't think she'll have the baby on the way?" I asked the mission sister.

"Most unlikely," I was assured. "She has a pelvic deformity I think. She'll probably have to have a caesar."

After about twenty minutes of turbulent flying over the desert hills I was alerted by a shrill scream from the back seat. Setting the Baron up on auto pilot, I left the controls and went aft to investigate. Sure enough, the baby's head was already on view and the patient well into the second stage of labour. I grabbed linen and other emergency equipment from the hat-rack, laid the seat back, spread plastic sheets and got the girl into position for delivery.

"Foxtrot Delta Papa. Foxtrot Delta Papa. This is Hedland," the radio boomed. I realised I had over-shot a position report but had to let the call go on for several minutes. I then dived back to the cockpit, grabbed the mike and yelled: "Foxtrot Delta Papa. Operations normal. Stand by."

With little help from the mother, who was quite exhausted, a healthy six and a half pound boy soon made his appearance and the cabin was filled with his lusty wails. I wiped his tiny face, wrapped him in a pillow slip, and laid him on the pilot's seat while I attended to the mother. The operation completed and the girl happily holding her little one, I then resumed navigation.

"Port Hedland—Foxtrot Delta Papa," I called, "Was abeam Hillside Mine, one six, six five zero zero feet, Hedland four seven. Sorry for the delay. Persons on board now increased to three."

There was a short silence, then came the reply. "Congratulations, Foxtrot Delta Papa! Boy or girl?"

"Boy," I replied. "Name of Skipper. Must be the youngest pilot on record."

"How was the flight?" the doctor asked on my return to Marble Bar.

"Fine," I replied, "got in some midwifery practice on the way."

Since, as my writing mother tells me, this story is more like a letter than a book, I suppose it would not be complete without the women's inevitable postscript. So here goes . . .

Just as I was completing the manuscript for this book, Doctor

Dicks asked me to accompany him on a fourth Pacific flight for the R.F.D.S. This time I joined him in Wichita, Kansas, the heart of the American aircraft industry, where Beech, Cessna, Lear and Boeing all have their factories. What a thrill it was to see the birthplace of all these lovely aircraft and to meet Olive Ann, widow of the late Walter Herchal Beech, founder of the company. Olive Ann, an astute business woman, remains Chairman of the Board of Directors of the Beechcraft Corporation.

We set out in a December snowstorm in the Beech Baron purchased by the Royal Flying Doctor Service and headed south to Mexico, hoping to strike better weather. Not far out of El Paso we were intercepted and closely inspected by something that looked like a huge flying saucer, but which we knew to be a radar patrol plane on the alert for drug haulers crossing the Mexican border.

Flying the complex network of visual omni range "victor" routes was a novelty to us as navigation aids in Australia are comparatively few and far between. Weather details obtained at Yuma were not encouraging and we were advised by a local pilot that our only chance of getting away within a foreseeable time lay in climbing to 16,000 feet above the mountains ahead. We took his advice and despite extreme discomfort from lack of oxygen and the icing of propellers and wings, made it safely to San Jose. Here we found perfect conditions for continuing the flight and in spite of desperate weariness, refuelled and set out into a black night on the long fifteen hour haul to Honolulu.

For a change good weather favoured us all the way, our only trouble being a complete lack of H.F. communication, due to a badly located aerial. However, a woman's voice in the cold and lonely night brought ready 'relay' assistance on V.H.F. especially from Air Force MAC jets ranging the skies *en route* to Vietnam. Inviting me to change to a discreet frequency, they launched, one by one, into charmingly uninhibited descriptions of their places of birth, the occupations of their parents, their educational backgrounds, air-force training, and family life. My contribution was an occasional exclamation of encouraging interest, as these homely confidences were curiously welcome in the circumstances and served to keep us awake. We sought and were granted special permission to land at Johnson Island to take on fuel. This allowed us to proceed with a lighter load so that in the event of one engine failing we could possibly stay aloft on the other.

Johnson, a military base, is strictly male territory and its officials had not bargained on one of the intruding pilots being a woman. By the time they heard my voice making our hundred mile position report it was too late to call the deal off. Some mighty quick thought and action must have gone into preparing for my arrival, otherwise why the brand new flowered towels, scented soap, and prevailing fragrance of the Colonel's bathroom?

Although it was just after dawn on Christmas Eve when we arrived, the entire garrison of 2,000 men had been hurried through breakfast in order to leave the mess hall clear for us. We more than made up for the frustrated hopes of breakfasting at Johnson on our previous flights by choosing from the rich variety of items a meal of pineapple juice, paw-paw, ham and eggs, curried sausages, cheese toast and coffee! Official photographs taken—no doubt for security reasons—will serve to remind the station of a woman with an incredible appetite who dropped in one morning for breakfast.

Owing to a particularly bad tropical cyclone in the New Hebrides we decided on a different route, this being from Tarawa Atoll to Guaudalcanal and thence to Townsville, Queensland. On Christmas morning 1970, having opened some gifts that our Beech factory friends thoughtfully stowed aboard, we headed for Honiara on Guadalcanal.

At the point of no return between Tarawa atoll and Honiara, a hop of about 1,100 miles, we had burnt off half the fuel in the wing tanks and switched to our cabin ferry fuel. A few minutes later the engines lost power and threatened to give out from fuel starvation until we managed to get them going on the wing tanks again. Suspecting either water in the ferry fuel or a blocked line I investigated, with the aid of my compact mirror, under the glass filter on the cockpit floor. This ruled out the water theory. We then used a nail file to undo some screws which secured the system of cocks and lines going from tanks to engines. This masterful strategy also failed to reveal any obvious

218

blockage. After several further unsuccessful attempts to get onto the ferry fuel we decided to refrain from further meddling so far from land, in case the problem extended to the main fuel lines. Instead we reduced power and went wallowing along at maximum range—forty-five per cent power.

Calculating and recalculating, we figured that at this rate we would splash down somewhere about fifty miles north east of Honiara. It was a tremendous effort of will not to watch the fuel gauges going down and down over that seemingly endless ocean stretch. I pulled the inflatable dinghy to a position near the door and cleared the cockpit of unnecessary gear. Honiara, on being informed of our plight, came through with the good news that there was an airstrip on the island of Malaita; the first of the Solomons chain on our track and close to where we calculated that our fuel might run out. Owing to reduced power we were over an hour late reaching this objective, only to find it guarded by a fierce tropical thunderstorm. Although our fuel gauges read less than one-eighth above empty we were forced to divert, and at last spotted the airstrip on the far side of the island. This was situated on a narrow headland with a hill in the middle, and we realised with bitter disappointment, that our overloaded aircraft could never pull up in time to avoid disaster. So it offered no safer alternative to splashing down in the sea.

"This is it," Doctor Dicks said, as he handed over the controls to me. "Circle the beach while I have a last attempt to get this ferry fuel flowing."

He began to loosen one of the fuel caps on a tank behind our seats. There was a sudden near explosion from the release of tremendous pressure and we were both douched with petrol. Almost simultaneously the starboard engine began to lose power and, resigned to the outcome, I announced that the right engine was out of juice. Doctor Dicks hurriedly turned on cocks and boost pumps. For a few minutes the motors surged and died, then, with a welcome roar, sprang to life again. We later discovered that a large air lock had developed due to a faulty fuel cock detent sucking air into the system from an empty nose tank. The fault had been overcome when we released the pressure build-up in the main ferry tanks.

Happily we headed low over the sea towards Honiara and Christmas dinner. After all we were able to count it as a successful day, for we had encountered a trap which we would not fall into again. It is by such dire means that pilots develop their cunning, and come to realize the truth of the adage that: "There are old pilots and there are bold pilots, but there are no old bold pilots."

So, all in all, I guess there is more to be said on the credit than the debit side, and I know that in having found a job that is also my hobby and my recreation I must count myself among the truly fortunate. I take each day's adventure as it comes and don't believe in looking too far into the future, but there is one ambition to which I must confess. That is to complete my own circumnavigation of this fascinating planet Earth. After all, I have only one little old ocean left to fly, and have already mapped the route—from Goose Bay on the eastern coast of Newfoundland to Narssarssyaq on the southern tip of Greenland, a mere hop across to the Icelandic port of Reykjavik and a final pull to Prestwick airport, near Glasgow, on the west coast of Scotland.

I can already see that grey Atlantic swell and hear her cold winds calling . . . .

60°

PARIS

PISA
ROME

ANDRAVIDHA
RHODES IS.

DAMASCUS
BEIRUT

30°

QAYSUMAH

BAHRAIN

DELHI

SHARJAH

KARACHI

CALCUTTA

MERGUI

0°   EQUATOR   SINGAPORE

DJAKARTA   DILI
DEN PASAR   DARWIN

BROOME

30°

PERTH

HORIZON FLIGHT — PARIS TO PERTH